SUPERVISING
NEW PROFESSIONALS
IN STUDENT AFFAIRS

SUPERVISING
NEW PROFESSIONALS
IN STUDENT AFFAIRS

A Guide for Practitioners

Steven M. Janosik
Don G. Creamer
Joan B. Hirt
Roger B. Winston, Jr.
Sue A. Saunders
Diane L. Cooper

BRUNNER-ROUTLEDGE
NEW YORK AND HOVE

Published in 2003 by
Brunner-Routledge
29 West 35th Street
New York, NY 10001
www.brunner-routledge.com

Published in Great Britain by
Brunner-Routledge
27 Church Road
Hove, East Sussex, BN3 2FA
www.brunner-routledge.co.uk

Brunner-Routledge is an imprint of the Taylor & Francis Group.
Printed in the United States of America on acid-free paper.

10 9 8 7 6 5 4 3 2 1

Library of Congress Cataloging-in-Publication Data
Supervising new professionals in student affairs : a guide for practitioners / Steven M.
Janosik . . . [et al.]
      p. cm.
    Includes bibliographical references and index.
    ISBN 1–56032–880–0 (pbk. : alk. paper)
    1. Student affairs services—Administration. 2. College student personnel
    administrators—In-service training. 3. Student counselors—In-service training . I.
    Janosik, Steven M. (Steven Michael)

    LB2342.9 .S86 2003
    378.1'98–dc21   2002010839

CONTENTS

CONTRIBUTORS

Steven M. Janosik is a Senior Policy Analyst and Associate Professor in the Department of Educational Leadership and Policy Studies at Virginia Polytechnic Institute and State University (Virginia Tech). In addition, he serves as the Co-Director for Educational Policy Institute of Virginia Tech. He received his bachelor of science degree (1973) in business administration from Virginia Tech, his master's degree (1975) in Higher Education and Student Personnel Services from the University of Georgia, and Ed.D. degree (1987) in educational administration from Virginia Tech. Prior to assuming his faculty position, he served as Deputy Director of Education for the commonwealth of Virginia where he worked closely with the State Council of Higher Education for Virginia, the Virginia Community College System, the Council for Information Management, and the State Department of Education. Janosik also has over 20 years of experience in college administration. He has served on the media board of the American College Personnel Association (ACPA), as editor of the *Journal of College and University Student Housing*, and a member of the executive committee of the Association for Student Judicial Affairs (ASJA). He is currently a reviewer for the *Journal of College Student Retention* and the *Journal of Counseling and Development*. He has written over 20 articles on topics of campus crime, law in higher education, liability and risk management, residence life, and student development. Janosik received the Outstanding Research Award from Commission III of the ACPA and the D. Parker Young Award for outstanding scholarship and research in the areas of higher education law and judicial affairs from ASJA.

Don G. Creamer is Professor of Higher Education and Student Affairs and Director of the Educational Policy Institute of Virginia Tech in the Educational Leadership and Policy Studies Department at Virginia Polytechnic Institute and State University. He received a bachelor's degree (1960) in American History, an M.Ed. degree (1961) in Counseling and Guidance from

Texas A & M University at Commerce, and an Ed.D. degree (1965) in Higher Education from Indiana University. Prior to assuming teaching duties, he was Dean of Students at El Centro College of the Dallas County Community College District and previously served in several student affairs administrative roles at Texas A & M University at Commerce. He is past president of the American College Personnel Association (ACPA) and president of the Council for the Advancement of Standards in Higher Education (CAS). He is a member of the Editorial Board of the *Journal of College Student Retention*. He is author or editor of four books including *The Professional Student Affairs Administrator: Educator, Leader, and Manager* (with R.B. Winston and T.K. Miller, 2001) and *Improving Staffing Practices in Student Affairs* (with R.B. Winston, 1997). Creamer is an ACPA Senior Scholar Diplomate and holder of the association's two highest awards, the Contribution to Knowledge Award and the Ester Lloyd-Jones Distinguished Service Award. He also received the Robert H. Shaffer Award for Academic Excellence as a Graduate Faculty Member from the National Association of Student Personnel Administrators and the Robert H. Shaffer Distinguished Alumnus Award from the Indiana University Department of Higher Education and Student Affairs. He has supervised students in internships for over 20 years.

Joan B. Hirt is an Associate Professor in the Higher Education and Student Affairs graduate program in the Department of Educational Leadership and Policy Studies at Virginia Tech. She earned her bachelor's degree (1972) in Russian Studies from Bucknell University, her M.A.Ed. in counseling and Personnel Services from the University of Maryland, College Park (1979), and her doctorate in Higher Education Administration and Policy Studies from the University of Arizona (1992). She spent 17 years as a student affairs administrator in housing and dining services in California and in the Dean of Students office at the University of Arizona. A past president of the Western Association of College and University of Housing Officers, she is a reviewer for the *Journal of College Student Retention*. She has authored or co-authored 15 articles in refereed journals and 14 chapters in books and monographs. She has presented over 35 sessions at regional and national conferences. She received the Annuit Coeptis Award from the American College Personnel Association (1997). Her current research interests focus on professionalization issues and administrative culture in higher education. She has served as a faculty member since 1994.

Roger B. Winston, Jr., Ph.D., is Professor Emeritus of College Student Affairs Administration in the Department of Counseling and Human Development Services at the University of Georgia in Athens. He received a bachelor's degree (1965) in History from Auburn University, a master's degree (1970) in

Philosophy, and a doctorate (1973) in Counseling and Student Personnel Services from the University of Georgia. Prior to assuming teaching duties at the University of Georgia in 1978, he was the Dean of Men at Georgia Southwestern State University. He has served on the American College Personnel Association's Executive Council and the Council for the Advancement of Standard's and the National Academic Advising Association's Board of Directors, been editor of the *ACPA Developments*, and is currently on the editorial board of the *Journal of College Student Development* and is a reviewer for the *Journal of College Student Retention*. He is author of 11 books and over 100 journal articles and book chapters. His most recent books are *The Professional Student Affairs Administrator: Educator, Leader, and Manager* (2001 with Don G. Creamer and Theodore K. Miller), *Improving Staffing Practices in Student Affairs* (1997 with Don G. Creamer), and *Student Housing and Residential Life: A Handbook for Professionals Committed to Student Development Goals* (1993 with Scott Anchors). Winston is an American College Personnel Association (ACPA) Senior Scholar Diplomate, holder of the Southern Association for Student Affairs Melvene Hardee Award for Contributions to Student Affairs, and the recipient of the ACPA Contribution to Knowledge Award and the National Academic Advising Association's Outstanding Researcher Award. He has been a faculty supervisor of master's and doctoral level interns in Student Affairs Administration for over 25 years.

Sue A. Saunders currently serves as Dean of Student Affairs at Lycoming College in Pennsylvania. Her career includes service as a faculty member in the College Student Affairs Administration Program at the University of Georgia, Dean of Students at Longwood College in Virginia, and other administrative positions in Georgia and West Virginia. She has served the American College Personnel Association on the Executive Council, as chair of the Core Council for Dissemination and Generation of Knowledge, and as president of the Virginia state division of ACPA. She is also author of more than 30 publications and regularly presents at national conventions and regional workshops. Her research interests include staff supervision, patterns of professional development, and developmental interventions. Her contributions to the profession have been recognized through her selection for ACPA Annuit Coeptis, Leadership Foundation Diamond Honoree program, and Senior Scholars.

Diane L. Cooper is an Associate Professor of College Student Affairs Administration in the Department of Counseling and Human Development Services at the University of Georgia. She received a bachelor's degree in Marketing Management from Miami University, Oxford, OH (1978), an M.Ed. from the University of Missouri-St. Louis in Counseling (1979), and a doctorate from the University of Iowa in Counselor Education (1985), with a concentration in postsecondary education and vocational development. She served for eight years as a Student Affairs Practitioner at the University of North Carolina at Greensboro before joining the Student Development faculty at Appalachian State University from 1992 to 1995. Dr. Cooper served for six years as the Editor for the *College Student Affairs Journal* and on the editorial board for the *Journal of College Student Development* and the *Georgia Journal of College Student Affairs*. She is the coauthor of a New Direction Series monograph (*Beyond Law and Policy: Reaffirming the Role of Student Affairs*, 1997, with James Lancaster), the *Student Developmental Task and Lifestyle Assessment* (1999, with Theodore K. Miller and Roger B. Winston, Jr.), five book chapters, and numerous journal articles. She is currently serving as a SACSA Scholar and has served on the Professional Development Core Council for the American College Personnel Association. Recently, Dr. Cooper received the Melvene Draheim Hardee Award from the Southern Association of College Student Affairs for outstanding research, scholarship and leadership in student personnel work. In addition, she has received the Annuit Coeptis Award from the American College Personnel Association in 2000 and the D. Parker Young Award for outstanding scholarship and research in the areas of higher education law and judicial affairs from the Association for Judicial Student Affairs in 2001. Her research interests are in program design and assessment, legal and ethical issues in student affairs practice, and in professional issues related to underrepresented groups in higher education.

PREFACE

Higher education, and student affairs in particular, is a labor-intensive enterprise. The vast majority of services and programs provided by the typical division of student affairs are delivered by a variety of staff with various levels of expertise. These staff members may be undergraduate students who are volunteers or work for wages. They may be college graduates with little or no experience in working with students on college campuses. They may be professional with newly minted diplomas from student affairs professional preparation programs or they may be experienced professionals who have switched careers. Winston and Miller (1991) suggest that 75% to 85% of the total budget of most institutions of higher education is generally devoted to personnel costs. Effective supervision of these individuals is critical to meeting the goals of the organization, the successful delivery of the programs and services connected to these goals, and the development of students through the out-of-class experience. Yet, Winston and Creamer (1997) found in their study that only about half of the student affairs professionals in the respondent group indicated that they had received any formal training in providing supervision to those in their charge. One reason that so many professionals fail to receive training in this area may be that the professional literature in higher education and student affairs does not address the issue of supervision in a comprehensive and systematic way. This book addresses this most important issue.

PURPOSE AND GOALS

The purpose and goal of this book is to fill that void in the literature by defining a comprehensive model for effective supervision and by providing the reader with practical suggestions on how a good supervisor provides the necessary guidance to increase the likelihood of success of new staff members.

By attending to the staffing practices that make up the model, the authors believe that new staff members will be able to make larger and more positive contributions to the organization more quickly and that the newly hired professionals will be more effective and more satisfied in their positions.

OVERVIEW OF THE CONTENTS

This book is organized in seven chapters. In chapter 1, the reader is introduced to the refined and expanded model of staffing practices developed by Winston and Creamer (1997). The rationale for the model is also presented.

Saunders and Cooper discuss the importance of good staff orientation in chapter 2. The special concerns of the new professional are addressed and an orientation checklist is also reviewed. Each major topic in the orientation process is followed by an "action plan" designed to help supervisors follow through on what they have learned.

Chapter 3 is devoted to the principle issue of supervision. Winston and Hirt make special note of the process we call "synergistic supervision." Readers are urged to view supervision as a cumulative process, not an event. This notion of synergistic supervision is broader in scope than the more traditional view of supervision in that it explicitly focuses both on promoting the interest of the institution and the staff member's present and future welfare. We believe that this distinction is critically important and is a linchpin of the model presented in these chapters.

Hirt and Winston address the process of professional staff development in chapter 4. Several case studies are used to illustrate how different professional staff development plans must be created to meet the needs of various members of the same staff. They define a conceptual model for professional development and link this process with performance appraisal.

Creamer and Janosik review performance appraisal in chapter 5. They suggest that performance appraisal is an ongoing process just like supervision. Both the new professional and supervisor must be actively engaged if the evaluation is to have real impact. A variety of appraisal methods and strategies are illustrated. Readers are encouraged to pay careful attention to the suggestions made in this chapter since appraisal is the most often-neglected human resource function.

Chapter 6 is devoted to the process of employee separation. This topic is particularly important in the field of student affairs. Turnover rates are particularly high and most new professionals will seek promotions by relocating to other institutions. Voluntary and involuntary separations are discussed in detail. The connection between separation and other stages of the model are also made for the reader.

The last chapter is devoted to how student affairs professional and other higher education administrators might adopt the principles and suggestions offered in this book when working with students who are engaged in independent studies, internships, externships, or practica.

SUGGESTIONS ABOUT HOW TO USE THIS BOOK

The tasks connected with supervising new student affairs professional are represented in separate chapters and the Model for Staffing Practices presented in chapter 1 appear to be somewhat linear despite the overlapping of the major staffing functions and their spherical representation. The content of each chapter stands on its own and may be read independently of the others based on the perceived skill level of the reader. But the integrated nature of effective supervision and the model presented here cannot be overemphasized. Although some may view the orientation process (chapter 2) as a task completed early on in the tenure of a new staff member, the entire process may take months to complete and does not occur in isolation of other major functions such as supervision (chapter 3). Developing a sound professional development plan for a staff member (chapter 4), for example, cannot be constructed without attending to skills necessary to conduct an appropriate performance appraisal (chapter 5). Good performance appraisal cannot be completed without knowing how to supervise effectively and provide feedback on a regular basis (chapter 3). Carefully developed professional development plans (chapter 4) and effective performance appraisal (chapter 5) should help a staff member make the eventual transition to a new career opportunity (chapter 6). In this sense, the process of supervision presented in this book must be understood as a whole—a complete skill set.

To help with that understanding, chapter 1 describes the model and its philosophical underpinning. These are critical foundations and set the stage for what is presented in the chapters that follow. In this sense chapter 1 should be considered a "must read."

AUDIENCE

As the title implies, this book is written specifically for middle and upper level managers who hire and supervise entry-level student affairs professionals. It may also be of interest to those who teach administration courses in graduate professional preparation programs as they respond to requests of practitioners who want to hire staff members who are better prepared to supervise staff at every level of their organization. Entry-level staff may also find this book helpful. New professionals can use many of the suggestions found in these chapters as they supervise paraprofessionals, work-study students, and student volunteers. Finally, student affairs professionals and other higher education administrators who direct independent studies, internships, externships, and practica for graduate students may wish to add this book to their reading list. Chapter 7 summarizes the principles contained in the book in the context of this special educational experience.

While this book is written with student affairs organizations in mind, the model of staffing practices and the principles expressed here are applicable to other disciplines and other administrative areas in higher education.

ACKNOWLEDGMENTS

As with any large project, delays are inevitable, and we are especially grateful to Emily Epstein and the editorial staff at Taylor & Francis for their support and patience.

> Steven M. Janosik
> Don G. Creamer
> Joan B. Hirt
> Roger B. Winston, Jr.
> Sue A. Saunders
> Diane L. Cooper

Chapter 1

INTRODUCTION
A Comprehensive Model

Steven M. Janosik
Don G. Creamer

Getting things done well and being successful depends on the effectiveness of the people in those organizations—not the organizations themselves (Upcraft, 1988). An organization's greatest assets include the people who work within it. It is the people who achieve the purposes of an organization such as a college or university. Previous educational leaders will have established the purposes and the structure of most colleges and universities, but these purposes and structures are entrusted to current leaders to succeed or fail depending on the work of the people of the organization. The policies and procedures, especially what are called staffing practices (Winston & Creamer, 1997), of institutions of higher learning reveal how the people are nurtured and may provide a predictive lens concerning their success in achieving their purposes.

Supervision of people always is important to an organization, and is a key ingredient in any staffing plan, but supervision of new professionals may be among the most critical supervision tasks or responsibilities of a college or university. New members of institutions, or even old members with new jobs, need guidance from supervisors to enable them to work effectively from the beginning of new assignments. The range of these needs is sweeping, but at their heart is understanding expectations of performance, institutional culture, goals and objectives of the assignment, skills required, institutional values, essential relationships, and vital constituencies. Proper supervision of new professionals will attend to these and other needs of new or newly assigned staff members and enable them to be productive from the first days on the new job. Failure to attend to these crucial needs of new professionals will at least hamper their early productivity and may contribute their dissatisfaction and possible departure from the job.

This book addresses in detail approaches to the supervision of new professionals that are grounded in the comprehensive staffing model proposed by Winston and Creamer in 1997. The elements of this staffing model, along with some recent additions to it, provide the conceptual framework for the book, but also deeply delve into the significance for new professionals of each element. The purpose of this chapter is to demonstrate the importance of quality supervision for new professionals and to provide a preview of the remainder of the book.

Professionals are attracted to the field known as student affairs for a variety of reasons. Some are drawn to the collegiate and intellectual environment. Some find the quality of life, the pace, and the vast array of cultural and recreational opportunities offered on college campuses enjoyable. Others are committed to the values to which higher education aspires and the opportunity to teach and to help others. As for most professions, no one profile or career path for the new professionals can be defined. Many will be energized and view student affairs as their chosen profession. Some will be following a spouse and be taking the job to earn a paycheck. A few may even be looking for a place to rest as they wait for retirement. To be sure, their knowledge base and work experiences will be as varied. Although many new student affairs professionals come to their first job in student affairs with undergraduate academic credentials in the social sciences, experience in the helping professions, and graduate diplomas from student affairs preparation programs, this is not always the case. As student affairs organizations become more complex, professionals from business, computer science, information technology, and the liberal arts also will be well represented in the student affairs organization. As our workforce becomes more diverse and the complexity of the positions increase, the selection, development, and retention of staff will become more and more difficult, yet all the more critical (Taylor & von Destinon, 2000). Unlike the nursing, accounting, or legal professions, however, the student affairs profession has no entrance examination and no test for certification of basic skills. Unfortunately, how new professionals become acclimated to and productive in the student affairs enterprise is sometimes much less structured and much less constructive than one would hope. Most professional conferences offer a few programs dealing with a few specific supervisory techniques, such as performance appraisal, and most professional preparation programs offer a course or two on administration where discussion about effective supervision occurs (Saunders, Cooper, Winston, & Chernow, 2000). In recognition of the need, most professional associations also offer to specially targeted managers special institutes that focus on effective supervision, but all of these activities seem woefully inadequate given the time student affairs professionals spend managing their human resources. As the title implies, the purpose of this book is to address these issues directly by defining a model of supervision and the activities that when well practiced by supervisors will result in higher levels of staff productivity and satisfaction.

SUPERVISION DEFINED

Supervision is not a topic written about with any great frequency in the student affairs literature (Carpenter, Torres, & Winston, 2001; Saunders et al., 2000; Winston & Creamer, 1998). Research on the topic also is scarce (Cooper, Saunders, Howell, & Bates, 2001). One reason for this may be that many student affairs professionals are recognized and rewarded for other activities related to their positions within the organization. Many professionals and their supervisors, for example, view the primary role of a department as providing services to students. Not surprisingly, conference programs, trade magazines, and professional journals devote a great deal of time and space to describing new programs, their delivery, and their impact on students. Focusing on how one develops the skills necessary to accomplish the program, or how to organize and motivate staff to complete the tasks, receives less attention. Yet, proper supervision is the key to this productivity.

Dalton (1996) defines supervision as "talent development." This definition focuses on the individual. He lists the assessment of employee skills and knowledge, the design of performance goals, measuring outcomes, and staff training as the important components of this type of supervision.

Mills (2000) defines supervision as the accomplishing of goals by working through others. The emphasis in this definition is on the institution and the accomplishment of organizational priorities. Essential skills of the supervisor acting on this definition are (a) the ability to communicate the tasks to be accomplished, and (b) the ability to motivate and inspire individuals and groups.

Schuh and Carlisle (1991) use a different focus in their definition. They define supervision as the process of one staff member providing opportunities, structure, and support to another. Schuh and Carlisle emphasize relationships in their view of this process.

Winston and Creamer (1998) go beyond these perspectives and define supervision in higher education as a management function intended to promote the achievement of institutional goals and to enhance the personal and professional capabilities of staff. This definition, unlike the previous three, combines two priorities. Their focus is clearly two-dimensional. They focus on institutional goals and the goals of the individual.

Writers outside student affairs and higher education share this perspective. Bunker and Wijnberg (1988) define supervision in their work on health service organizations by emphasizing (a) facilitating successful performance of the work by increasing the capabilities among the unit's professional staff, (b) linking the unit harmoniously with other parts of the organization, (c) quality relationships, and (d) the conscious use of persuasion. They suggest that these supervisor-created conditions will encourage levels and qualities of performance that are simultaneously responsive to the patient's needs, satisfying to the worker, and in harmony with organizational goals. They identify several key functions in their model. These include:

1. Articulating mission and purpose.
2. Monitoring and managing organizational climate.
3. Fostering worker development.
4. Developing a team.
5. Participating in agency planning.
6. Representing the unit to other constituents.
7. Coordinating work activities.
8. Clarifying goals and tasks.
9. Promoting active problem solving.
10. Managing daily operations.

These functions emphasize the supervisor's role in advancing the position of the department and several that focus on the individual employee—a good example of this dual focus of supervision as advocated by Winston and Creamer (1997).

Arminio and Creamer (2001) go even further by defining "quality supervision" as an educational endeavor that focuses on the essential functions of the institution: promoting learning and personal development of students. They suggest that quality supervision requires (a) synergistic relationships between supervisors and staff members, (b) ubiquitous involvement with and constant nurturing of staff members, (c) dual focus on institutional and individual needs, and (d) a stable and supportive institutional environment to be effective. This definition not only places the focus on the individual and the institution but also directly addresses the nature of the relationship that the authors believe leads to higher productivity and higher morale. It is this philosophy that provides the foundation for the comprehensive model of supervision outlined in this book.

THE SUPERVISION MODEL

Steps for effective supervision have been outlined before. Upcraft (1988), for example, identifies four steps for managing people effectively and suggests that managers should: recruit and select the right people, orient and train the right people, supervise for productivity and morale, and evaluate performance for results and morale. His model focuses primarily on the needs of the organization and emphasizes a top-down perspective, however, where the supervisor assumes primary responsibility for outcomes.

Other authors have written about other supervisory functions. For example, staff development has been addressed by Cox and Ivy (1984) and Bryan and Schwartz (1998). Performance appraisal has been addressed by Marion (1985), Holmes (1998), and Creamer and Winston (1999). But these works do not address supervision in a comprehensive way.

Instead of dealing with these important supervisory functions in a piece-meal fashion, the authors of this book rely heavily on the definition of supervision and the staffing model outlined by Winston and Creamer (1998). First, these authors argue that supervision should not be viewed as something done to an employee when an error has been made. Instead, they propose that "supervision should be viewed essentially as a helping process provided by the institution to benefit or support staff rather than as a mechanism for punishment inflicted on practitioners for unsatisfactory performance" (Winston & Creamer, 1998, p. 30). They call this *synergistic supervision* and suggest that characteristics of such supervision include "dual focus; joint effort; two-way communication; focus on competence; goals; systematic, ongoing processes; and growth orientation" (Winston & Creamer, 1998, p. 30).

The original staffing model by Winston and Creamer (1998) identified five interlinked and overlapping functions: (a) recruitment and selection, (b) orientation, (c) supervision, (d) staff development, and (e) performance appraisal. This staffing model reflects the strong values that have historically undergirded the profession of student affairs, especially values of human dignity, including freedom, altruism, and truth; equality, including individuals and groups; and community, including justice. It effectively asserts that the people of the organization deserve the same treatment as students and that these values should guide our intentional actions toward them.

In the original staffing model, recruitment and selection were viewed as resting on two commandments: first, hire the right person, and second, do it the right way. Recruiting and selecting the right person include assessing the need and establishing the purpose of the position, conducting a position analysis and preparing a position description, creating and implementing comprehensive recruiting processes, and selecting people according to specified need.

Orienting staff to new positions was seen in the Winston and Creamer (1997) model as an explicit and thorough process that can be accomplished formally or informally. This process includes inculcating new professionals with the educational and operation philosophy and the culture of the institution and the student affairs division. Expectations for professional and personal performance and relationships between faculty, staff, and students are included in these orientation proceses. These processes cannot be taken for granted; they must be executed in some manner to ensure proper grounding of professionals to their assignments.

Supervision was seen by Winston and Creamer (1997) as a linchpin of the staffing model and was conceptualized to function synergistically. This synergism included a dual focus on the individual and the institution, joint effort between the supervisor and staff member, two-way communication, and orientation toward growth in the individual and the institution, proactivity, goal-based, systematic and ongoing, and holistic in its views of people. The process is dynamic and requires active participation by staff member and supervisor.

Staff development was seen as attending to individual staff and organization development simultaneously. The process included using a developmental plan for staff members, keeping in mind the importance of both process and product, anchoring the processes in day-to-day work, recognizing the multifaceted, ever-changing nature of work environments and people within them, and recognizing maturation and growth in both individuals and institutions. Intentionality is a key to this aspect of the Winston and Creamer (1997) model.

Performance appraisal was seen in the Winston and Creamer (1997) model as having a dual purpose of evaluating individuals and developing them simultaneously. Likewise, the processes were seen to focus on organizational productivity and rewards for performance. The use of contextual standards and participatory and interactive evaluation was highlighted, as well as certain performance appraisal system attributes including clarity, openness, and fairness. Winston and Creamer also recommend ongoing reviews of positions and performance of people holding the positions. They recognize in their model the role of leadership in the appraiser and acknowledge the formats for appraisal must be workable and must avoid systematic biases.

In their model, Winston and Creamer (1997) acknowledge that these functions take place in an organizational culture particular to an institution and that institutional culture is driven in part by its external environment. They also suggest that these functions should be viewed as processes that must be attended to over time in a systematic way rather than episodic, unrelated events. Viewing the management of human resources as a process is particularly appropriate given the nature of the organization we call higher education (Balderston, 1995).

As practitioners and students used the staffing model and the accompanying recommendations for best practice in their jobs and in their classes to better understand how effective organizations work, a refined model for supervising staff emerged. Initially the model consisted of five processes: recruitment and selections, orientation to position, supervision, staff development, and performance appraisal. In time, Conley (2001) suggested that a sixth process, separation, be added to the model after observing that some employees eventually leave their positions for promotions, for other personal reasons, or for poor performance. For our purposes, we have added the process of *separation* as an integral part of the supervisor's responsibility and critical part of *synergistic supervision*. This six-part model is illustrated in Figure 1.1. Since the purpose of this book is to address supervision of new professionals, the authors have assumed that recruitment and selection, shown at the far left of the model, have already occurred. Each of the remaining functions shown in the model is addressed comprehensively in its own chapter.

Orientation to Position

Orientation is not just the activities scheduled for the first morning of the new staff member's first day at work. It is a much more complex and much more labor-intensive process. Actually, orientation begins when the vacant position is advertised and the application materials are developed. Once individuals apply, employers should respond in a timely fashion and provide sufficient information for an applicant to get at least a superficial understanding of the institution's nature, mission, and goals; its culture; and how the department and division of student affairs fit into those aspects of the institution. If an interview is arranged at a conference or a career fair away from campus, applicants should have the opportunity ask questions they may have about the institution and the job. If an on-campus interview is scheduled, applicants should be given an opportunity to meet a variety of individuals in the department and the division, met with some students, and receive a campus tour. If the successful applicant will live off campus, a brief tour of the areas surrounding the campus also should be offered.

Once new employees are hired, the orientation process should continue in a systematic and comprehensive manner. If it will be some time before new staff members actually arrive on campus, then supervisors should contact their new staff on a regular basis to share information and answer questions. Once new employees arrive on campus, the orientation process should continue over several days and even several weeks until these individuals are fully integrated into the organization.

Staff members who are promoted within the institution, division, or even the department also should receive an appropriate orientation. Although they may have a good understanding of the institution, they may not always be familiar with all of the policies and procedures that affect their new positions. Similarly, they may have new colleagues to whom they should be introduced. As Winston and Creamer (1998) suggest, do not assume that

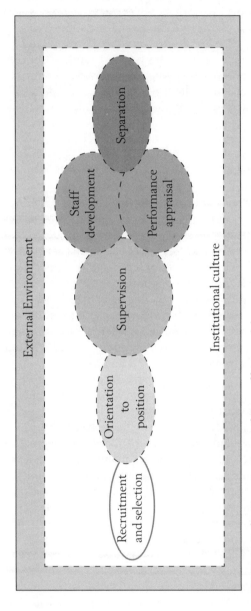

FIGURE 1.1. Refined components of the staffing model.

successful internal candidates have a full grasp of things outside the scope of their previous position. The importance of the orientation process and suggestions for effective orientation are reviewed in chapter 2.

Synergistic Supervision

Although each component in the model is crucial to increasing performance and enhancing growth, supervision is the key. Again we remind the reader that the approach outlined is this book represents what we believe to be a departure from the way other authors have discussed supervision. Synergistic supervision has a dual focus. This type of supervision recognizes the need to obtain the goals of the organization but it also recognizes the developmental needs of the staff member. Accordingly, both the supervisor and the employee must learn how to devote greater energies toward joint efforts, two-way communication, a focus on competence and goals, and an orientation toward personal and professional growth. Developing the skills necessary for this type of supervision is addressed in chapter 3.

Staff Development

Staff development has two primary purposes. First, staff development should focus on helping individual employees meet the requirements of their jobs. Ensuring that staff members have the necessary knowledge and skills to do their jobs is crucial to the effectiveness of the organization. Second, staff development should focus on the personal and professional growth of the individual. Attending to the needs of the individual helps improve morale and can aid in decreasing unwanted staff turnover.

Effective staff development is much more than encouraging individuals to attend workshops and conferences. If staff development is to be purposeful, it must be inextricably linked to the supervision and performance appraisal processes. Supervisors who observe an individual's strengths and weaknesses on the job are in a much better position to help a new professional identify staff development activities that may aid in better performance. Similarly, performance appraisal, when conducted in the manner suggested in this book, can help both supervisors and new professionals identify personal and professional goals that may be met through staff development activities.

Finally, remember that staff development may be best accomplished in the department or on the campus by using internal resources to address identified needs. Specific concentrated training also may be a much more effective method for enhancing skills and knowledge when compared to regional or national conferences that address the training need in only a superficial way. These concepts are explored fully in chapter 4.

Performance Appraisal

As this model suggests, performance appraisal is linked to supervision and staff development. For purposes of this book, performance appraisal must be thought of as a systematic process for determining staff accomplishments for the purpose of improving their effectiveness. Although this seems rather simple, performance appraisal that actually results in improved performance is not an easy task and is one that is rarely viewed as positive.

For performance appraisal to be effective, it must be integrated with other supervisory functions—supervising and staff development. For performance appraisal to be effective, an open relationship where mutual respect and two-way communication have been developed and are well practiced must exist. The role of performance appraisal for new professionals is developed substantially in chapter 5.

Transitioning

Conley (2001) identifies five situations where staff leave their positions: (a) professional reasons, (b) personal reasons, (c) retirement, (d) involuntary separation, and (e) incapacitation, illness, or death. In student affairs, in particular, new professionals often leave one position for another to advance their careers. Helping staff members make these decisions regarding their careers is part of a supervisor's responsibilities given the model that we propose here. When an individual leaves an organization regardless of the reason, those left behind and the organization itself are affected. Shifts in work assignments may be necessary. The search process may be initiated. Depending on the circumstances surrounding the staff member's leaving, supervisors may have to address the emotional loss felt by those staff members who remain. These activities may take a significant amount of energy and time if the supervisor is to maintain the productivity of the organization. Chapter 6 is used to explore this aspect of supervision of new professionals.

SUPERVISING THE NEW PROFESSIONAL

As previously mentioned, new professionals in student affairs come from a wide variety of backgrounds and experiences. Many have already been socialized in the profession; others may not have been. Many will have experience in higher education and will come to their new jobs with appropriate professional preparation but others may not. Regardless of their skills and backgrounds, we know that workers who are attracted to the human development fields have high expectations for a caring nurturing supervisor. They have concerns about their quality of life and their personal and professional development (Woodard & Komives, 1990).

Another way to think about crucial attributes of new professionals is to imagine their developmental status and the role that this may play in their success on the job. Admittedly, developmental status may be very important to the establishment of working relationships, and supervisors should employ appropriate strategies to determine this status and act accordingly. Obviously, a mid-life, mid-career professional will bring developmental background to the new job markedly different from that of the inexperienced new professional directly from graduate school. Both types of new professionals need and deserve careful and appropriate supervision, and approaches to their work oversight may vary because of these differences. In this book, however, we mainly address supervision tactics applicable to all new professionals, whether new to the profession or new to the assigned duties, without explicit attention given to variations in developmental status of staff members. We encourage supervisors to study these important human attributes in the people whom they supervise, but because of the extremely complex nature of this phenomenon in all types of student affairs professionals, we have provided little guidance in this book on the role of developmental status of staff members to success in their supervision.

Employers who hire those who were born between 1966 and 1975, popularly referred to as Gen Xers, will face specific expectations from this group (Losyk, 1997). Those 20- to 30-somethings are individualists, have less loyalty, communicate differently from their Baby Boomer counterparts, crave attention, ask questions, and seek flexibility in all that they do. They expect to be given responsibility, to be treated fairly, to be taught skills that they can carry with them to other jobs, and to have meaning in their jobs created for them (McMakin, 1998). Those even younger individuals born between 1976 and 1995, known as Generation Y, may have an even stronger influence on the workplace than Gen Xers (Wallace, 2001). Wallace suggests that the early signs are that these workers will bring with them a remarkable set of technical skills, a strong entrepreneurial outlook, a deep-seated social consciousness, and a healthy dose of questioning and change. Despite time spent alone in front of computers screens, they will have a strong need for personal interaction with their supervisors.

These differences are more likely to be recognized, accommodated, and nurtured in a positive and productive manner when supervisors use the tenets of synergistic supervision: dual focus, joint effort, two-way communication, focus on competence, goals, systematic, ongoing process, and growth orientation (Winston & Creamer, 1997).

Dual Focus.   As Winston and Creamer (1997) suggest, synergistic supervision focuses both on accomplishing the institution's goals and unit's goals and on promoting the personal and professional development of staff members. The institution, through its supervisors, creates a legitimate set of expectations and rightfully anticipates that those it employs are dedicated to promoting accomplishment of its mission. Individual professionals also have a legitimate expectation that the institution will show concern for their welfare and provide the support needed for a nurturing work environment and career advancement.

Joint Effort.   The synergistic approach to supervision requires cooperative and joint effort between the supervisor and the person being supervised. Responsibilities for initiating and maintaining the process fall on the shoulders of both, although supervisors generally should be expected to assume a larger share of the responsibility, because of their experience in the field, familiarity with the institution, and by virtue of their positions in the institutional hierarchy. If the supervisory relationship is to be successful, it is essential that both the supervisor and each staff member invest time and energy in the relationship. Neither party acting alone can make the supervisory process work effectively.

Two-Way Communication.   Open and honest communication is necessary to implement the synergistic approach. It is critical that a genuine respectful, personal relationship be developed between the supervisor and each individual staff member. Absent this relationship, the supervisory process may become meaningless or a disincentive for staff development. There can be no substitute for clarity and candor.

Focus on Competence.   Synergistic supervision focuses on four areas of competence: knowledge, work-related skills, personal and professional skills, and attitudes (Winston & Creamer, 1997). Each of these areas requires ongoing, although not necessarily equal, attention.

All staff members need to know certain things to carry out their assigned duties. In all areas, staff members need to know about legal constraints to practice, the history of the institution, the organization's mission, and professional ethics standards. Functional areas require specialized knowledge. Staff are expected to possess much of this knowledge when they assume their positions, but changing societal conditions and institutional needs require staff to remain current with contemporary events and the current thinking on what constitutes best practice in the field. Sometimes it will be necessary to broaden one's area of expertise.

Depending on the specific demands of the position, staff members need a variety of skills such as interpersonal communication, leadership, confrontation, and clerical and research capabilities. Generally, possession of necessary skills is identified in the selection process, but even if a new professional is proficient when first employed, it remains necessary to stay abreast of changes and new information.

Another category of professional skills needed by student affairs staff may be classified as "personal and professional." Examples of these skills include writing, time management, stress management, and public speaking. This category of skills blurs the distinctions between personal and professional, but most scholars and seasoned practitioners agree that deficits in these areas result in impaired student affairs practitioners (Winston & Creamer, 1997).

Attitude is the final category that should be addressed through synergistic supervision process and is, perhaps, the most difficult to influence. The attitudes a staff member displays when undertaking a responsibility are often as important as, or in some instances even more important than, the actual behavior. Enthusiasm, cynicism, negativism, bitterness, excitement, boredom, cooperation, support, and resistance are attitudes that can have significant effects on staff performance (Winston & Creamer, 1997). Because attitudes affect performance, they are legitimate concerns of supervisors. Aiding individuals to test their attitudes against some standard of professionalism, and to become better aware of how their attitudes influence their thoughts and behavior, is an important part of the personnel management process. There will generally be less resistance to addressing these areas if positive attitudes are regularly commended, in addition to problematic attitudes being addressed when they occur.

Goals. Supervision requires a degree of mutually agreed-on structure for the process to be effective. This structure can be built around a series of short and long-term goals that are systematically reviewed and evaluated. By carefully establishing goals, each party in the supervisory process can come to an agreement about expectations of each other. To be successful here, the concepts of joint effort and two-way communication must be fully embraced by both parties.

Systematic, Ongoing Process. For the synergistic supervision process to be effective, it must be approached in a methodical manner. Each supervisor and those who are supervised should have regularly scheduled one-on-one sessions for the sole purpose of examining progress in meeting goals, discussing emerging issues or priorities, exchanging views about current activities, identifying potential "hot spots," and revising agreed-on goals (Winston & Creamer, 1997). This is also a time for the staff member to solicit advice and guidance from the supervisor about possible ways to attack problems. The timing of these sessions should be based upon the experience and competence of the person supervised and the quality of his or her work performance. New staff members—especially at entry level—generally require more frequent sessions than experienced professionals who are performing at an exemplary level.

Growth Orientation.   The final characteristic of synergistic supervision is its focus on enhancing the personal and professional growth of staff members. The supervisory process should be deemed a failure if the staff involved do not become better or more proficient in carrying out their responsibilities and have a sense of accomplishment and personal satisfaction in their positions. It is necessary to help each staff member assess his or her current level of abilities, skills, and knowledge and to explore with each staff member his or her career aspirations, current stage of development, and expectations of work.

We believe this orientation, when integrated into the supervisory functions of orientation, supervision, staff development, performance appraisal, and transitioning, will result in more effective supervision and greater organizational and personal success.

SUMMARY

Arminio and Creamer (2001) found that high-quality supervisors engage in commonsense, ordinary supervision activities such as listening, role modeling, setting the cultural context, motivating, teaching, giving direction, and caring. Further, they suggest that what seems to distinguish these supervisors most from less successful supervisors is their persistent and direct approaches. This book provides readers with a wealth of excellent resources that will improve their ability to be direct and to persist. Most importantly, it provides an integrated context for the process we define as synergistic supervision.

REFERENCES

Arminio, J., & Creamer, D. G. (2001). What supervisors say about quality supervision. *College Student Affairs Journal, 21*(1), 35–44.

Balderston, F. E. (1995). *Managing today's university* (2nd ed.). San Francisco: Jossey-Bass.

Bryan, W. A. & Schwartz, R. A. (1998). *Strategies for staff development: Personal and professional education in the 21st century.* New Directions for Student Services No. 41. San Francisco: Jossey-Bass.

Bunker, D. R., & Wijnberg, M. H. (1988). *Supervision and performance: Managing professional work in human service organizations.* San Francisco: Jossey-Bass.

Carpenter, D. S., Torres, V., & Winston, R. B., Jr. (2001). Staffing the student affairs division: Theory, practice, and issues. *College Student Affairs Journal, 21*(1), 2–6.

Cooper, D. L., Saunders, S. A., Howell, M. T., & Bates, J. M. (2001). Published research about supervision in student affairs: A review of the literature 1969–1999. *College Student Affairs Journal, 20*(2), 82–92.

Conley, V. M. (2001) Separation: An integral aspect of the staffing process. *College Student Affairs Journal, 21*(1), 57–63.

Cox, D. W., & Ivy, W. A. (1984). Staff development needs of student affairs professionals. *NASPA Journal, 22*(1), 26–33.

Creamer, D. G., & Winston, R. B., Jr. (1999). Performance appraisal paradox: An essential but neglected student affairs staffing function, *NASPA Journal, 36*(4), 248–63.

Dalton, J. C. (1996). Managing human resources. In S. R. Komives, D. B. Woodard, Jr., & Associates (Eds.), *Student services: A handbook for the profession* (3rd ed., pp. 494–511). San Francisco: Jossey-Bass.

Homes, T. A. (1998). Performance-based approaches to human resources development. In W. A. Bryan & R. A. Schwartz (Eds.), *Strategies for staff development: Personal and professional education in the 21st century* (pp. 29-42). New Directions for Student Services No. 84. San Francisco: Jossey-Bass.

Losyk, B. (1997). Generation X: What they think and what they plan to do. *Public Management, 79,* 4–9.

Marion, P. B. (1985). Use of performance appraisal and staff training with student affairs staff. *Journal of College Student Personnel, 26*(2), 175–176.

McMakin, T. (1998). Jazzed: Turning on generation X. *Franchising World, 30*(5), 13–14.

Mills, D. B. (2000). The role of the middle manager. In M. J. Barr, M. K. Desler, & Associates (Eds.), *The handbook of student affairs administration* (2nd ed., pp. 135–153). San Francisco: Jossey-Bass.

Saunders, S. A., Cooper, D. L., Winston, R. B., Jr., & Chernow, E. (2000). Supervising staff in student affairs: Exploration of the synergistic approach. *Journal of College Student Development, 41*(2), 181–191.

Schuh, J. H., & Carlisle, W. (1991). Supervision and evaluation: Selected topics for emerging professionals. In *Administration and leadership in student affairs: Actualizing student development in higher education* (2nd ed., pp. 495–532). Muncie, IN: Accelerated Development.

Taylor, S. L., & von Destinon, M. (2000). Selecting, training, supervising, and evaluating staff. In M. J. Barr, M. K. Desler, & Associates (Eds.), *The handbook of student affairs administration* (2nd ed., pp. 154–177). San Francisco: Jossey-Bass.

Upcraft, M. L. (1988). Managing staff. In M. L. Upcraft & M. J. Barr (Eds.), *Managing student affairs effectively* (pp. 39–50). New Directions for Student Services No. 41. San Francisco: Jossey-Bass.

Wallace, J. (2001). After X comes Y: Millenials enter the workforce. *HRMagazine, 46*(4), 192.

Winston, R. B., Jr., & Creamer, D. G. (1997). *Improving staffing practices in student affairs.* San Francisco: Jossey-Bass.

Winston, R. B., Jr., & Creamer, D. G. (1998). Staff supervision and staff development: An integrated approach. In W. A. Bryan & R. A. Schwartz (Eds.), *Strategies for staff development: Personal and professional education in the 21st Century* (pp. 29–42). New Directions for Student Services No. 84. San Francisco: Jossey-Bass.

Woodard, D. B., Jr., & Komives, S. R. (1990). Emerging staff competence. In M. J. Barr & M. L. Upcraft (Eds.), *New futures in student affairs* (pp. 217–238). San Francisco: Jossey-Bass.

Chapter 2

ORIENTATION
Building the Foundations
for Success

Sue A. Saunders
Diane L. Cooper

For most new professionals (NPs) in student affairs, entry to their first full-time professional positions is filled with excitement, enthusiasm, and trepidation. The reasons for trepidation and confusion are numerous. NPs are making both professional and personal transitions. Most often these professionals are entering their first jobs directly from a graduate student role, where support and structure from faculty and assistantship supervisors is often quite intense. For those who enter the field without benefit of professional preparation, the trepidation is even greater, or at least should be, because they generally have very little (other than personal experiences as a student leader or paraprofessional and perhaps as a teacher, minister, or coach) to fall back on when presented with issues and problems of practice.

Most graduate preparation programs are housed at major research universities, with large enrollments, extensive resources, and often a traditional-aged student population. Few NPs have prior fulltime work experience in professional positions. Many new professionals start their first professional positions in locations distant from their home or graduate school communities. At smaller institutions, there may be only a couple of new student affairs professionals entering the institution in any given year. At community colleges, NPs from major research universities may have limited understanding of the institutional culture and mission, particularly if they have no direct experience at this type of institution.

When discussing the transition between preparation programs and practice, Komives (1997) noted, "there is no doubt that the first few years of entry into professional work are times of intense continued learning and socialization. While practitioners are eager to hire a new graduate student who can hit-the-ground-running, it is more imperative than ever before to provide intentional continued learning experiences" (p. 193). The way one is oriented to the first professional position influences whether new professionals can effectively manage the many personal and professional transitions they experience, whether they will engage in continuous professional education and development, whether they will achieve high levels of productivity, and even whether they choose to continue in the student affairs profession.

Even though it has been argued that new employee orientation is a crucial determinant of staff members' productivity and success, very little literature exists related to orienting new employees to student affairs or higher education administrative positions (Winston & Creamer, 1997). The business literature about employee orientation (Arthur, 1991; Cadwell, 1988) does provide some transferable information on the topic which, when combined with knowledge of environmental differences, can provide useful ideas about optimal orientation efforts. Even with the difference in environmental pressures from private industry to an educational setting, some of the orientation principles easily apply to both settings. For example, Estrin (1997) described the first day on the new job for legal assistants as being reminiscent of the first day of school:

> What should I wear? (I want to be liked by the other kids.) Will the new boss (teacher) like me? Will I like my new colleagues (classmates)? The new recruit fantasizes about "how it's going to be" at the new job. . . . Upon arrival, however, the balloon pops. Many recruits are handed off to the first available person and given the I-don't-have-time-for-this-mini-tour. Dashing through the firm, the I-don't-really-have-time important person begins gesturing. "Here's the bathroom, the kitchen, the office services center." The tour guide picks up speed and switches into high gear: "Here's your office, your key, employee manual, that's Joan. Say hi, Joan!" Now we're rounding the corner, the finish line is in sight: "PleasefillouttheW4andreturntopersonnel. Areyoufreeforlunch? Callyoulater-welcomeaboard!" (p. 70)

No matter where a new professional is going to work, this scenario probably occurs all too frequently and cannot lead to a productive orientation to the new job. Zemke (1989) noted that as cocktail conversation this is a funny situation to pass along, but to the organization the costs in reduced effectiveness and initial dissatisfaction are much too high.

Cooke (1998) suggests that those in the employing organization need to consider their goals and objectives for orienting new employees long before that person arrives on site. Besides making the new employee feel at home, they also want to increase the likelihood that people go home after the first day on the job feeling that they did not make a mistake in deciding to work there. Dworak and Glogowski (1982) also point out that "an effective orientation program reduces the adjustment problems of new employees by creating a sense of belonging and by building up confidence of employees in the early stages of employment" (p. 30). According to Reinhardt (1988), new employee orientation also reduces turnover and absenteeism, prevents performance problems, instills positive attitudes about the organization, and paves the way for better communication between the supervisor and the new employee. Loraine (1997) goes even further to say that "when an institution hires new employees, it has a responsibility to assist them to adapt to the new situation and feel comfortable as soon as possible" (p. 35).

Brechlin and Rossett (1991) outlined the following reoccurring and common errors associated with orientation:

1. No information—Often supervisors provide a good bit of social support but not enough *how-to-do the tasks of the job* information.
2. Too much information—A day of sitting through a string of people talking about different topics can provide all the information a new employee may ever need. However, if it is not information that is useful for *beginning* the new job, it is a waste of time to talk about it now. Employees can only take in so much information at a time. Supervisors need to make sure that the information provided during orientation does not lead to information overload.
3. Conflicting information—Few things are worse than sitting though days of orientation meetings and speeches, reading policy manuals, and then getting to the work site and having fellow employees telling you that "none of that is really how we do it."

Supervisors of new student affairs professionals need to be especially conscientious in avoiding the problems just listed. New professionals, because they frequently lack prior professional experience, need orientation that is intentional, explicit, and practical. It is important that orientation be structured enough to reduce ambiguity and to ensure confidence rather than confusion. It is most important to recognize that, for orientation to be sufficiently comprehensive, it must continue for several weeks or months and should not cease at the end of a new staff member's first few days.

The remainder of this chapter is devoted to components of effective new professional orientation programs. We describe a comprehensive orientation curriculum that begins at the time of recruitment and selection and continues throughout the first year. In addition, concerns cited by a selection of new student affairs employees are outlined and addressed. Finally, the authors share a checklist that identifies practical issues that need to be discussed during orientation.

AN ORIENTATION CURRICULUM

Because orientation is such a crucial educational process for new professionals, it is a good idea to develop a "curriculum" consisting of learning outcomes and activities as well as a "pedagogy" that outlines the methods and strategies used to achieve the learning outcomes. The prospect of developing an "orientation curriculum" may sound daunting to busy professionals charged with supervising entry-level staff. Yet this prior preparation for an intentional orientation helps to ensure that "every new member of the [institutional] community is accorded full opportunity to contribute to the achievement of institutional, departmental, and personal goals" (Winston & Creamer, 1997, p. 161). The sections that follow outline the fundamental elements of an effective orientation curriculum. At the end of each section, the authors provide a list of suggested tasks that lead to an optimal orientation curriculum.

ASSESSMENT OF ORIENTATION EFFECTIVENESS: VOICES FROM THE FIELD

The first step to building a successful orientation is to understand perceptions of recent NPs about the adequacy of their orientations to their first positions. Before planning a new employee orientation, it is wise to consult with recently employed new professionals about their reactions to their first few days or weeks in their positions. Asking these individuals to share stories about their experiences and what could make the transition easier provides a foundation for building an effective orientation. Although asking current employees about experiences at their current institution provides the rich information, often new professionals may be reluctant to share information that could be perceived as a negative comment about their current supervisor. Asking for anonymous comments or asking new employees at other institutions to comment about orientation may be a way to obtain forthright responses. One must also evaluate these responses in light of whether the new professionals can adequately conceptualize what a *good* orientation looks like.

As a way to share general information about the efficacy of typical orientation programs, the authors asked recent master's and doctoral graduates, currently enrolled doctoral students, and new professional staff at a large research university in the Southeast about the orientations they received to their first professional positions. Some of these stories reflect purposeful and well-planned orientation programs that truly assisted the new professional during this transition process, whereas some stories revealed a very different outcome.

The most helpful aspects of orientation shared by these professionals included:

- Before arriving on the new campus, staff received letters from other colleagues at the institution along with resources about the town, such as maps, newspapers, and real estate information.
- Supervisors who spent one-on-one time orienting new staff to their style and beliefs about success.
- Supervisors who treated new staff like they were important and had things to offer beyond fulfilling job descriptions.
- Autonomy to do new and innovative things. Feeling free to get to know the students and surroundings, without being micromanaged.
- Supervisors who introduced new staff to the "right" people and, in essence, empowered them by saying to others, "contact our new staff member, she or he is doing that job now."
- Supervisors who organized welcome events such as a small breakfast the first day so that new staff could meet the other administrators in the unit.
- Supervisors who made it clear that there was freedom to innovate and no pressure to continue all of a predecessor's programs.
- Opportunities to shadow the supervisor and to learn about the daily operation of the work site.
- Supervisors who encouraged and supported the new professional to attend a professional conference that was focused on some of the job's new responsibilities.
- Welcoming banners and a schedule of orientation activities and appointments that were presented to new employees when they arrived on campus that first morning.
- Being informed about the culture and climate of the university—specifically, having the supervisor sit down and explain roles and responsibilities of various staff members and the best ways to get cooperation from individual colleagues.
- Being assigned a colleague as an orientation host who helped with introducing the new employee to the job and institution.
- Supervisors who scheduled 30- to 45-minute interviews for the new professional with each other staff member during the first week. This provided an opportunity to get to know each staff member.

On the other hand, most respondents also shared some concerns about their orientation process:

- Feeling as if many of the aspects of the position were learned about "over lunch and in passing."
- Never having a clear idea of what was expected in the new position.
- Not being forewarned that new employees did not receive their first paychecks until the end of the first complete pay period, which was six or seven weeks after starting the position.
- Being told by the supervisor to "spend time getting the office arranged, and not to worry about appointments with students for a few weeks." This resulted in feeling marginalized.
- Supervisor who promised many things that did not come to fruition in the job for the new professional: for example, "learning that my position, a new one, that I had been led to believe was confirmed, was in fact not confirmed. Here I was starting a new marriage, new life and might have been coming back from my honeymoon without a job."
- Supervisors who did not protect the new staff from political controversies during the first few weeks or months.
- Inability of the supervisors to give up the job they had been doing to let the new staff members do it once they arrived.
- Supervisor who "didn't train me, didn't have any type of orientation, and said that I could start by going through all the files in the office and start cleaning things out."
- Supervisor who provided no real explanation of what the office is supposed to do for the organization and how office staff were expected to relate to others with the institution and the outside world.

These examples are likely representative of those repeated by new professionals all over the country. The themes that emerged indicate that it is critical for new professionals to gain a comprehensive picture of what is expected of them. Not only do NPs want to know how their job description and supervisor expectations will be accomplished, but they also need to know about the context of the institution—its history, mission, behavioral norms, political realities, and current institutional priorities. Furthermore, respondents to this query about effective orientation wanted to feel that their potential contributions were important and that they had sufficient autonomy to be innovative.

ASSESSING PAST ORIENTATION EFFORTS: ACTION STEPS

One way to improve future orientation efforts is to look to recent history and to complete comprehensive evaluations of each element of the orientation program. The following points outline specific strategies that can be used to assess the effectiveness of an orientation effort.

- Evaluate elements of the orientation program shortly after they occur. Include such elements as (a) feedback forms for all candidates interviewed for a position that assesses the adequacy of information shared prior to and during the interview, and (b) if possible, an anonymous survey that evaluates the postselection and arrival orientation activities.
- Assuming there are sufficient numbers to protect anonymity, administer an anonymous survey to new employees six months into their tenure, asking for positive and negative comments about orientation and encouraging respondents to share ideas for the improvement of future orientation activities.
- At the time when the new professional's performance appraisal is discussed, offer the staff member the opportunity to identify ways in which orientation was or was not helpful in fostering success during the first months of employment.
- If resources are available, conduct a focus group of current new professionals to examine the effectiveness of orientation activities. It is important that these focus groups be facilitated by a staff member who has no supervisory responsibility or direct working relationship with the new professionals who participate.

ORIENTING POTENTIAL NEW EMPLOYEES DURING RECRUITMENT AND SELECTION

Some would argue that effective orientation programs begin during the initial job interview and before arriving for the first day at work (Patterson, 1997). The potential new employee develops a sense of what it would be like to work at the new institution. This is a good time to begin the orientation process, much as institutions do with information and processes designed to recruit new students.

The position announcement is the first contact that most potential new employees have with the expectations of the institution, division, and supervisor. It should contain an explicit statement of job responsibilities, necessary qualifications, and characteristics of the institution and/or workplace. Often, through written communication or screening interviews at professional association placement activities, supervisors have opportunities to share additional information with the most promising candidates before campus interviews. This supplemental information can be a wonderful opportunity to share expectations and a picture of the institutional culture. All serious candidates should receive a copy of the complete position description, including title of the supervisor, goals of the position, work activities, procedures of the position, and minimum requirements (Winston & Miller, 1991). Potential employees can benefit from receiving copies of currently existing publications, such as:

- The admissions viewbook and institution fact book.
- An outline of brief facts about the institution (e.g., enrollment, retention, overall budget).
- An outline of benefits and remuneration issues (e.g., when first paycheck is received, amount of annual and sick leaves, provision for overtime pay or compensatory time, if any).
- A statement of institutional vision, mission, values, and strategic directions.
- A statement of division and department missions.
- A copy, for the unit that has the vacancy, of the annual report from the previous year.

Furthermore, supervisors would be well advised to write to each candidate invited for an interview a letter describing the ways in which the position contributes to the institution or division mission, the professional development support that is available, the performance appraisal procedures, the type of supervision that can be expected, and a description of other staff units that work closely with the new position. In addition, the letter from supervisors could include an indication of specific knowledge and skills (such as understanding of the Americans with Disabilities Act [ADA] or Family Educational Rights and Privacy Act [FERPA]) that may be addressed during on-campus orientation activities. If the division endorses a particular statement of ethical standards, it is also wise to advise potential new employees of that fact.

Once candidates arrive on campus for interviews, there is another opportunity to set the stage for successful and productive employment. Typically, new professionals are interviewed by a variety of people, including students, staff, and faculty, in addition to the search committee. The individuals who interview a candidate provide an impression of the institutional and division culture, the social environment, and the nature of the position that gives powerful messages to a potential new staff member. Those who interview candidates should receive a briefing about their roles as guides to the division and institution.

It is important that the potential new employee receive the benefit of honest and forthright perceptions of the institution from search committee members and others who interview candidates. Failing to share important information, such as the anticipated retirement of a chief student affairs officer or continuing tension between the student affairs division and faculty, can give the new employee a false impression that can later cause the new professional who is hired to question the credibility and personal integrity of institutional officials. Interviewers, however, especially those on the search committee, need to take care to differentiate among personal opinions, reports about commonly held perceptions, and factual information. On-campus interviews also provide an opportunity for prospective employees to become more familiar with the campus and community through tours, visits to student programs, and casual conversations with a variety of community members. An interview that is jam-packed with formal interviews and presentations does not allow the candidate to gain a comprehensive picture of the institution or community.

The ways in which recruitment and selection are handled also give candidates an impression of how the division or unit conducts its business. Poorly organized searches give candidates and potential employees the impression that the division does not take its work seriously or that the current staff is incompetent. Lack of attention to such details as inappropriate questions or failing to inform candidates in a timely fashion about their status gives the impression of an unprofessional or even unethical operation. Winston and Creamer (1997) state, "The ethics of the profession should be behind every action taken to recruit and select staff. A premier value and ethical principle of the profession is respect for the individuals involved in the process" (p. 157).

ORIENTATION DURING RECRUITMENT AND SELECTION: ACTION STEPS

- Create a comprehensive plan to distribute information other than the position announcement to interested candidates. Determine which types of information should be sent to applicants in the early and later stages of the process.
- Devise a letter from the direct supervisor to be sent to interested candidates that outlines such items as the ways in which the position contributes to the mission, the professional development opportunities available, the ways in which supervision is conducted, and performance appraisal procedures.
- Brief those who will interview candidates about ethical and legal implications of the interview process, as well as the importance of giving an unbiased yet forthright picture of the institution and division.
- Create an interview schedule with adequate time for the candidate to explore the campus and community and to ask questions of the supervisor and other potential colleagues.

ORIENTING THE NEW PROFESSIONAL PRIOR TO ARRIVAL

Once a candidate has been offered the position and has accepted, there are typically several months in which the supervisor can provide important information about the position, division, institution, and community. (See page 37 for additional information about orienting new professionals to the community.)

As a supervisor, it is important to set aside time for telephone conversations or e-mail exchanges with the new employee. The agenda for these conversations might include answering questions that the new employee might have, discussing current events within the division, and communicating a general welcome to the division or unit. Written information is also very helpful to send during this period between accepting employment and starting work.

Supervisors should consider sending:

1. Information about events on campus to help new staff identify with the institution.
2. Information specific to the new job that would be helpful to review prior to arrival.
3. Information about the institution, employee benefit programs, or other specific reports (that have not been sent earlier).
4. Instructions for arriving on the first day of work, including maps of the campus, parking passes, and dress code.
5. If the institution has been designated as a "drug-free workplace," make sure the new employees know that they may be required to undergo drug testing at some point in the orientation process.

It is also recommended that supervisors identify a current employee who can also act as a contact person to the new employee. As a general rule, it may be most comfortable if this contact holds a position similar to that being assumed by the new staff member and has had only a few years of professional work experience.

In the work setting, supervisors can also make preparation for the arrival of the NP. Arrival dates should be agreed on during the hiring process so that supervisors are able to set up the orientation. At large institutions in units that generally have several new staff members each year, such as housing, it may be useful to have an intermediate level staff member who is responsible for organizing and managing NP orientation each year. Supervisors, however, need to have a significant role in the orientation process, including multiple times for individual meetings. Supervisors may also want to check with the human resources office to see if and when a general orientation program to the institution, an explanation of employee benefits, or safety training will be offered. If none are offered, then supervisors should set up a time to visit the human resources office on the first day of employment to complete any necessary paperwork. Parking passes, office keys, computer access, and e-mail address should be arranged prior to the new employee's arrival, if at all possible.

For many people, the language of staff benefits, such as insurance options and retirement plan alternatives, is difficult to comprehend, and this sometimes seems remote to younger staff members. If the human resources unit does not provide an ordinary-language explanation of these things and advice on request, then the supervisor, or a knowledgeable designated person, should assist the new staff member in making these important decisions that can have long-term financial implications. Cadwell (1988) suggests other items that should be considered in the prearrival planning. These include:

1. *Publicity about the new employee*—Supervisors should check with the public information office on campus to see about having the new employee's hiring publicized to the campus, local community, professional resources (such as regional professional association newsletters or statewide listservs), and other sources. Some institutions even send announcements of the new position to the new employee's hometown newspaper.
2. *Initial office set up*—Although decorating the space should be left to the new employee, the office space he or she will be moving into should be cleaned and readied for the first day of work. It is not enjoyable to come into the new office and find it dirty or filled with posters, pens, or personal items left by the previous occupant. Supervisors should ready the office area by stocking general office supplies, and making sure resources such as telephone directories, staff manuals, computer and software manuals, and operating procedures handbooks are available. If there is some flexibility about computer operating systems available, check with the new employee about preferences. Make sure that any other equipment necessary to do the job is placed in the office ready for the new employee's arrival.
3. *Set up initial meetings*—In some cases, supervisors will want to go ahead and make appointments for the new employee's first week. There may be some individuals who will be working closely with the new professional (NP) who will need to meet with him or her right away. Supervisors may also want the new employee to meet some staff he or she did not meet when on campus for an interview. If time is needed at human resources or other administrative sites (e.g., payroll and computer services) schedule those appointments as well. It is also important to have some arrangements made for lunchtime during the first day at work. It can be very lonely to eat by oneself when a person is not familiar with eating alternatives.
4. *Arrange for a welcome get-together*—Depending on the customs and traditions in the organization, supervisors may want to arrange some type of welcome gathering that will allow for informal interactions during the first few days at work.

Making these preparations prior to the first day at work can help ease the transition and help create a welcoming environment. The supervisor's goal should be for the NP to leave after the first day on the job pleased with his or her employment decision. It may be very difficult to overcome initial negative evaluations.

ORIENTING BEFORE ARRIVAL: ACTION STEPS

- Create a plan to send pertinent information to the new employee at various points during the period between selection and the first day at work.
- Allot time for several telephone calls or e-mail conversations during this period.
- Construct a first-week orientation schedule for the new employee, including meetings with the human resources department, participation in any institutional orientation activities, meetings with colleagues and representatives from offices that work closely with the position, and attending any division or departmental welcome activities.
- Publicize the NP's selection through the campus information office and other appropriate media.
- Make sure that the office is ready for the first day and that the new employee knows the specific details for arriving on campus.

GETTING STARTED: INITIAL ORIENTATION

What information does the NP have to have on the first day at work and what can be part of the ongoing orientation process (Federico, 1991)? For purposes of this discussion, it is assumed that the initial orientation will focus on the logistics of getting started, such as understanding benefits, participating in institution-wide orientation activities, and becoming acquainted with colleagues and the work site. Other elements of the orientation curriculum, such as becoming familiar with job tasks, understanding the community, working within the organizational culture, and helping the employee set performance goals for the first few months in the position, are included in the ongoing orientation section.

As stated previously, the human resource (HR) office requirements regarding new employees may help dictate the answer to the question of what part of orientation should be accomplished initially and what can wait. It may be necessary prior to beginning the orientation process in the office to take the new employee to HR to complete paperwork associated with employment. They may also need to attend special orientation programs (e.g.,

OSHA, legal and ethical issues, specific policies) prior to being in the office. Work in the prearrival stage will let a supervisor know exactly what needs to happen to get this process off to a good start. Lindo (1995) suggests that supervisors consider a number of issues as they prepare for the arrival of a NP in a department. These items, modified to fit a higher educational setting might include:

- Personnel policies and practices—a clear understanding of the position description, probationary period, payroll, retirement, insurance, leave policies, professional development.
- Work life at our college/university—work time-keeping policies, break times, use of the telephone, travel, computer use, and "unwritten rules" that are important to being successful in that setting.
- Issuance of institutional property—these might include keys, parking passes, uniforms, handbooks.
- Discussion of institutional philosophy—concerns about relationships with students, faculty, external constituents, and other departments.
- Where and why things happen here—orientation tours, introduction to other staff, meeting key staff in other departments or programs.

The supervisor needs to make sure that between the HR office orientation and the department orientation each of these items is explained and discussed with the new employee to prevent misunderstandings later on.

Several of the items just listed deserve special attention. First, NPs do not fully understand the long-term ramifications of selecting a retirement plan. At many institutions, that is an irrevocable decision that is made, often on the spur of the moment, without much discussion of the possible outcomes of the decision. Supervisors to new professionals need to caution them to get adequate input into that decision before committing to something they might later regret. Often new professionals do not understand the differences in various retirement policies and may, for example, choose a fixed-benefit retirement option that requires 10-years of employment to become vested even though the employee plans to stay at the institution only 3 to 5 years. Next, many professional positions in student affairs do not require keeping a time sheet and do not pay for time worked over 40 hours a week. It is also common for student affairs professionals to work more than 40 hours per week. Supervisors should explain their expectations about peak work periods and "comp" time policies if they exist. Also, it is not uncommon for two employees who are colleagues in the same department to fall under two different personnel policies based on the classification of their positions. In such cases, supervisors may have one employee who does complete time sheets and is paid overtime and another employee who is not required to record work time but is also not paid overtime. Supervisors must be very specific with NPs about any pay/work policy differentials that exist in the work site up front, rather than having them guess or rely on rumors for their information.

BECOMING FAMILIAR WITH THE WORK SITE

Arthur (1991) suggests that as soon as supervisors know the day the NP will begin work, they should make every effort to free their time as much as possible. Although supervisors do not want to overwhelm the new employee by never leaving him or her alone, supervisors should be available to answer questions and make introductions. If the new professional has time when supervisors cannot be available, another member of the unit should be there to help with the orientation process. Loraine (1997) cautions that supervisors will want to give serious consideration to who they select to assist the NP during this introductory time. "If at all possible, new employees should not be paired with an incompetent, negative person or one who will not demonstrate high standards. Supervisors should make sure the person doing the orientation has thorough knowledge, is patient, and a good teacher" (p. 35). On the other hand, it is generally good policy to utilize recent arrivals to the institution in the orientation process because they have fresh memories of their own arrival and understand the needs and interests of NPs. Also, the organization always looks different from the bottom than it does from the top.

When supervisors begin to orient the new employees to their office space, any policies regarding office decor should be explained. Policies about pictures on the walls, repainting, plants, or other personal touches should be reviewed. Policies about food and drinks in the office work areas should be explained. Other questions to answer at this point in the orientation might include:

1. Are there scheduled break times? Lunch hours? Do employees generally go out for lunch together? Bring lunch and eat together? Each go his or her own way?
2. Where are office supplies located? Are these materials provided for employees or do they need to purchase some of them? How does one get supplies? Just take? Fill out request form? Ask support staff for what is needed?
3. How does one operate the office equipment? What does one do if the equipment malfunctions? How does the fax work? Are there restrictions on receiving/sending personal fax messages?

4. How does the phone system work? How are long-distance calls made? How are personal phone calls handled?
5. What are the regulations about e-mail? Being on the Internet?
6. Where are the office files housed? How are they maintained? What are the distinctions between personal files and institutional files? What is and is not entered into students' "educational records"? Are there educational records for which the NP is the "official custodian"?
7. What are the confidentiality regulations? How does the institution implement FERPA?
8. Where are the restrooms? Water fountains? Vending areas?
9. Are there customs in the office that need explanation (e.g., coffee pool, birthday celebrations, who goes to lunch at what time)?

Patterson (1997) also points out the importance of providing training on any computer program specific to the office operations, explaining the location and use of safety equipment in the office, and reviewing safety procedures. In addition, if employees have access to recreation facilities, a credit union, or other employee benefits, have sign-up information available in the office for the new employee. These may seem like insignificant questions and suggestions, but knowing this type of information early on will help facilitate a smoother transition to the workspace.

BECOMING FAMILIAR WITH COLLEAGUES

An important part of the initial orientation is to become familiar with colleagues. The initial orientation period should include some opportunities to meet with colleagues who have direct interaction with the NP. Supervisors would be well advised to brief those colleagues who will be meeting with the NP about what topics need to be covered. Typically, these topics include discussion of the joint or shared initiatives that the new professional and colleague will work on, details about the colleague's position and responsibilities, introduction to support staff who may interact with the NP, and discussion of the ways individuals in the two positions communicate and work together. The colleague and NP should certainly feel free to discuss other topics, but without an agenda, these initial meetings can become rambling discussions without any focus on goals or productivity. It is tempting to "overbook" an NP's initial orientation with numerous meetings involving individuals that are not central to the position responsibilities. Without time for the new employees to reflect on what they are learning, the outcome is likely to be confusion. Supervisors play an essential role in helping new professionals "make meaning" of what they are hearing from a variety of sources. Supervisors should set aside some time during the first few days after the new employee arrives to have private conversations. It is common for even the most experienced employee to experience some anxiety when starting a new job (Zemke, 1989). This meeting can go a long way toward reducing anxiety and helping NPs understand why they were hired and how they fit into the mission of the department. This is a time for supervisors to be very specific about their expectations for work performance and for setting up the method of supervision that will be employed (see the chapter on supervision for further information on this topic). At the least, the new employee should leave this meeting having had time for a reality check about expectations.

INITIAL ORIENTATION: ACTION STEPS

- Create a plan that outlines which orientation items need to be covered initially and which can be covered later. Consult with the human resources (HR) unit to determine which initial orientation topics are covered. (See Figure 2.1 for list of topics that should be covered initially.)
- Make sure that the new professional is familiar enough with the work site to be comfortable. Information about such details as key policies, copying procedures, technical assistance, office supplies, and rules regarding telephones and computers should be addressed (see the familiarization with the work site section for further information).
- Brief those colleagues who will be meeting with the NP about topics that should be covered. Possible topics include discussion of joint initiatives, introduction to the colleague's position and responsibilities, and ways the two positions operate collaboratively.
- Set aside time with the NP to discuss expectations, performance appraisal systems, the department's mission, and how the position contributes to it.

ONGOING ORIENTATION: UNDERSTANDING THE POSITION AND THE CONTEXT

Ongoing orientation will really take place for several weeks, preferably several months. In fact, often not until NPs have gone through an entire operation cycle (semester, year) will they feel comfortable and knowledgeable. A sense of history, or what Federico (1991) refers to, as "when 'they' become 'we'" (p. 69), is often the point at which formal orientation processes can come to an end. However, as roles and expectations change, job-related orientation will need to continue. If supervisors are to equip new professionals with adequate information and understanding to be successful, it is not sufficient to tell them what is required. Orientation to job tasks needs to include detailed instruction and support about what procedures should be followed and what should be accomplished. As noted in chapter 3, NPs need to be told what is given and done in a prescribed way and what is open to innovation and experimentation. If everything is a given, then the supervisor is micromanaging. If everything is open, then the NP may not be able to handle the ambiguity and multiple occurring tasks.

In addition, for many positions such as those in registration or financial aid, supervisors may need to instruct new professionals about institutional interpretations of FERPA, or Title IX, or the ADA. Supervisors will also need to provide an organizational context for the position, including the informal decision-making structure and institutional politics. Since NPs are members of a community beyond the campus, it is important to help them understand how to make a life outside of work for themselves and their friends or families. Figure 2.1 provides a detailed list of topics to be covered in ongoing orientation.

ORIENTING TO THE NEW JOB TASKS

At the same time that the employee is getting acquainted with coworkers, departmental customs, and personnel policies, orientation to the tasks of the job needs to begin. Tilton-Ginzberg (1990) noted that supervisors must make sure that, as they orient the new employee to the job and organization, they do not forget to also make it clear who is being served and what needs must be met. Professionals cannot just focus on the skills needed for the new job without also paying attention to how the new job fits into the overall mission of the organization.

Individuals are hired to a position because of the particular skills, strengths, or experiences that they bring to the organization. Yet supervisors need to spend time during the orientation period assessing what additional training may be necessary for the NP to be successful in the job. For most NPs there will be ongoing professional development that can be useful in expanding required skills. However, supervisors, or their designees, may need to provide some additional training right away. Much of the new job orientation will be to a new system or method of doing the work: new formats, computer programs, methods for working with students or other users of the services, and programs to develop. If a new employee lacks adequate professional education, the supervisor must also devise a plan to assist him or her to acquire the background knowledge and skills professionals need to work with students. (See Creamer et al. [1997] for discussion of the institution's responsibility in educating staff without professional credentials.)

Job-Related Responsibilities
__ Review staff handbook and university policies
__ Review job responsibilities and expectations
__ Provide overview of the departmental history and organizational chart
__ Explain union issues (if applicable) and provide pertinent sections of the collective bargaining agreement
__ Explain pertinent institutional policies for EEO (Equal Employment Opportunity), AA (Affirmative Action), ADA (Americans with Disabilities Act), sexual harassment
__ Explain specific departmental policies (e.g., relationships with students or consumption of alcohol when students are present)
__ Explain the performance appraisal process
__ Set up time for goal setting and ongoing supervision

Technical Skills
__ Explain about technological support and training
__ Discuss on-going professional development and develop a plan
__ Explain telephone and telecommunication systems
__ Explain mail system (both e-mail and surface mail)

Campus Culture
__ Explain institutional and departmental identity
__ Define environmental effects
__ Identify the role of such institutional units such as athletics
__ Provide political slants
__ Discuss town–gown issues
__ Explain student involvement and campus climate
__ Explain faculty interaction patterns
__ Provide profile of faculty
__ Provide profile of students
__ Explain parent involvement on campus
__ Explain institutional governance structure(s)

Departmental Culture
__ Interdepartment communication—weekly meetings, e-mail, departmental "lingo"
__ Explain how much individual autonomy staff members tend to have in making decisions about particular issues
__ Work styles and dress expectations
__ Decision-making policies—official and unofficial
__ Role modeling and mentoring opportunities
__ Describe how staff are (or are not) collegial outside the office
__ Community service opportunities
__ Describe opportunities and support for affiliation with professional organizations
__ Explain what type of behavior and involvement students expect from staff
__ Performance review and salary adjustment
__ Development (fund-raising) expectations/activities

Individual Wellness
__ Personal interests—inquire about hobbies
__ Tour of the community
__ Life issues (housing, banking, driver's license, and day care)
__ Stress management

FIGURE 2.1. Orienting new employees to the job-related responsibilities. Based on and adapted to fit higher education from Dowling & Eaker (1996).

One of the final steps in ongoing orientation to job tasks is for the new professional to begin to set goals and objectives for accomplishment over the next semester, quarter, or other near-term time interval (see chapters 3 and 4 of this volume). This step allows NPs to begin to synthesize what they have learned about the position and organization. For this step to be successful, the supervisor must function as a consultant to this process: giving opinions, recommending changes, and offering encouragement. Such help is particularly useful in helping the new professional develop realistic, attainable, and meaningful goals. Ideally, these goals and objectives form the basis for a short-term performance appraisal (see chapter 5).

Winston and Creamer (1997) provide a listing of minimum content requirements for orienting entry-level staff to a new position. Even though most of these requirements have been addressed elsewhere, several of the requirements they outline warrant further consideration.

1. *Discussion about the unit, division, and institutional reward system*—New employees need to clearly understand what reward structures the supervisor, the Chief Student Affairs Officer (CSAO), and the institution use. Each of these may differ somewhat, so the differences need to be explained in detail. To be successful, new employees need to understand how supervisors will define success and what rewards can be expected for exceeding minimal expectations.
2. *Identification of past problems or issues, interpersonal conflicts encountered by previous position holder*—It is difficult coming into a position where the previous employee was either a star and loved by all or had performance problems and left on bad terms with the institution. Supervisors have an obligation to explain the issues related to the previous problems and to alert the new employee to any potential negative concerns that may remain on campus related to those events.
3. *Discussion of ethical standards that staff are expected to observe*—It is reasonable to expect that NPs coming out of student affairs/higher education preparation programs have been exposed to ethical standards from professional organizations such as American College Personnel Association

(ACPA) or National Association of Student Personnel Administrators (NASPA). The application of these ethical principles to the work site requires the supervisor's guidance and support. In addition, there are often ethical standards that have been written and endorsed by the work unit or division. These should have been provided to the new employee before he or she accepted the position. A discussion of the supervisor's expectation related to the ethical standards should take place shortly after the NP begins the new position so that no misunderstandings occur.

ORIENTING TO THE DIVISION AND ORGANIZATIONAL CULTURE AND POLITICS

Providing NPs with information about the politics and personalities of a division and organization is often a challenge. Supervisors do not want to provide only their opinions or bias information provided to new employees, but also want to provide enough of an overview so that they can listen, watch, and form an opinion on their own. Supervisors should be particularly careful not to express negative opinion about people in the work site who have reputations for being difficult. Instead, supervisors should suggest the best ways to approach particular colleagues or representatives of other departments and offer them in as unbiased fashion as possible. According to Arthur (1991), "new employees should be permitted to form their own opinions. Any statement that is subjective or judgmental should be avoided. Instead, focus on being descriptive" (p. 249). Perhaps the best approach is to clearly explain to NPs the importance of spending the early part of their tenure at the institution listening, taking in information, and then making informed decisions about people, policies, and other aspects of the workplace.

Often new professionals are justifiably concerned about getting caught in a negative political web without a clear understanding of the underlying dynamics at play. It is important to convey to new staff that "political behavior is inevitable in every organizational setting, is found at every level in the hierarchy, and intensifies as the decision making possibilities are greater and more important" (Appleton, 1991, p. 5). So, how then do supervisors prepare NPs for the political dynamics without biasing their opinions about particular individuals? Providing a new employee with opportunities to understand the cultural elements of the institution, division, and department is a necessary strategy. Understanding the culture of a department, a division, or an institution is a long-term learning proposition, and teaching about these cultures should be more comprehensive than simply conveying opinions about personalities.

According to Schein (1985), organizational culture is the pattern of basic assumptions that determine what people think, feel, and value and how they spend their time. A full understanding of an organizational culture is difficult, because the basic assumptions are often unstated and are frequently revealed in subtle and symbolic ways through an organization's stories, heroes, heroines, traditions, and language (Kuh, 1991).

For example, the small residential institution may resemble a family where small, informal groups make decisions over the lunch table and where students, faculty, and staff expect a minimum of bureaucracy. For instance, this institution's new student activities advisor, who was educated at large research universities, is likely to face significant difficulties when she wants her programming board to set up an elaborate approval mechanisms for allocation of funds. The student programming board, which had previously made decisions in a more casual way, is likely to see the new advisor as trying to change the fundamental character of their organization. As a result, the NP has forfeited some of her "political capital" and will find it difficult to collaborate with the board to make needed changes in policies or procedures.

It is vital to encourage NPs to be careful not to always compare the new workplace with the former workplaces. Nor should an NP try to change structures or programs too quickly. One oft-cited piece of advice has relevance here—during the first year in a new job, "don't change anything but your underwear." Although this maxim should not be taken literally, NPs should make sure that they understand all the dynamics in situations before proposing new structures or approaches. NPs should have permission to check out their perceptions and diagnoses with their supervisors before launching major actions.

Supervisors also have an obligation to discuss the importance of valuing diversity issues during the orientation period. Freeman, Nuss, and Barr (1993) point out that "an effective orientation of new staff members will reinforce the expectations and values of diversity and multiculturalism within the institution, division, and functional area" (p. 463). They also suggest that new employees visit various offices on campus during orientation, including offices that serve students of color or other underrepresented groups. This will help new employees understand the importance placed on serving all members of the institution's community.

ORIENTING NEW EMPLOYEES TO THEIR NEW COMMUNITY

Most people have experienced how it feels to move into in a new environment. New employees who are preparing to come to new institutions are no doubt experiencing very mixed emotions: excited about all the possibilities the new job, institution, and town have to offer, but scared about leaving the familiar. There are a number of things supervisors should consider and plan for in advance to help make the transition to the new community as comfortable as possible. It is also important that the supervisor be sensitive to the NP's desire to have privacy or appropriate boundaries for a personal life. Therefore the supervisor needs to work closely with the NP in planning transition arrangements to avoid having "supervisory helpfulness" being perceived as meddling.

Housing Needs.   If the NP is not going to be living on campus or provided with housing by the institution, finding appropriate housing will be one of the most critical needs to address. Either when candidates visit the campus for their interview or as soon as a job offer is accepted, supervisors need to provide information about the local housing market. This information is often easy to access through local realtors, newspapers, apartment guides, or chamber of commerce. Information about availability is certainly important, but in and of itself is rarely sufficient to help new employees make housing choices. Other recently hired staff might be encouraged to assist in this process. Often when people have lived in a town for some time their perceptions about "good location" do not always match what NPs might be looking for to meet their housing needs. Some things that may be issues for NPs selecting housing might include traffic patterns; availability of public transportation; access to recreation, churches, synagogues, and schools; ability to walk/bike to work; neighborhood safety; and parking near the work site.

Health Care.   Even though the HR department will usually provide health insurance information, it typically does not provide information about the local health care systems, especially in regards to managed care providers. The local chamber of commerce and local health organizations or medical associations may be able to supply additional information. This information might include which physicians are taking new patients, special needs, and applicable clinics in the area. If there is a health maintenance organization (HMO) associated with the institution, specifics of things like preexisting conditions will be useful information. Employees should be encouraged to bring medical records with them.

Educational System and Child Care.   NPs with children or those planning to have children may be concerned about the local educational system. Information from the local board of education will be useful but perhaps not as useful as talking with other employees of the institution who have children in the school system. NPs may also want a contact in the institution's college or school of education if applicable. In addition, supervisors will want to be able to provide new employees with information about available day care in the area.

Role of the Family for New Employees. Although usually negotiated in the hiring process, work opportunities for spouses and partners are often an important consideration in the NP transition period. Arthur (1991) points out that today's employees bring a better focus on balancing family and work. Employers need to consider not just the employee they just hired but also that NPs may be part of a large unit that is all moving into a new environment. Because of this, some institutions consider hiring spouses or partners to get the employees they want for specific positions. Even though this is not the norm, it is important for supervisors of new employees to be very aware of the needs of the entire family unit. To do this effectively may mean helping with the networking necessary to assist a spouse or partner also find employment in the area.

Contacts for Utilities. It would be advisable to create a listing of area utilities, including telephone numbers, addresses, and e-mail addresses. It is often necessary to make some of these arrangements before moving into the area. For example, electric, cable TV, and telephone service often need to be scheduled at the new residence before the actual move. In addition, other useful information might include procedures for getting a driver's license, banking or credit union information, and contact information from area religious organizations.

In general, most supervisors and their staffs are excellent resources to help in the transition to a new community. With adequate discussion and prior planning, supervisors can work with staff to create a transition plan that is both detailed and comprehensive. Even though we have advocated that supervisors take initiative in informing new staff about opportunities in the community, it is important to refrain from saying or doing anything that would lead the employee to believe that the supervisor is recommending particular choices about what is, in essence, the NPs personal life. Nothing said should suggest, for example, that a new employee should live in a certain neighborhood, go to a particular religious institution, patronize a specific bank, or use a particular dentist. Being helpful while respecting the autonomy of the new employee is the goal of providing a good transition to the community.

ONGOING ORIENTATION: ACTION STEPS

- Using Figure 2.1 as a guide, develop a "syllabus" for ongoing orientation. Even if orientation is to be conducted informally, it is important not to forget important content areas that need attention.

- Work with staff to make sure that all recognize the importance of explaining the culture while not biasing the new staff members about the politics and personalities in the department, division, or institution.
- Create a detailed plan to help with the transition to the community. Encourage staff to share information about housing, banking, health care, etc. On the other hand, recognize the importance of letting the new professional exercise his or her judgment about these personal matters.

CONCLUSION

Most supervisors and staff in student affairs see orienting new professionals to their first positions as an important function. According to Winston and Creamer (1997), even though this function is seen as important to successful performance on the job, appropriate orientation to positions is not received by many new staff members. In the Winston and Creamer study of more than 300 professionals, 60% of staff reported receiving some type of orientation, and a large number of respondents received some orientation but were not given information about such important topics as position expectations and performance appraisal.

Because student affairs professionals tend to be experts at organizing learning tasks for students and other constituencies, these results seem incongruous. Perhaps orienting staff seems less central to our function of promoting student learning and development. Yet when we design educational programs for students, we create learning goals and pay careful attention to both the content to be covered and our methods for delivering that content. The elements of an effective staff orientation curriculum outlined in this chapter provide a content outline and methodology that could be easily adapted to particular organizational circumstances.

REFERENCES

Appleton, J. R. (1991). The context. In P. L. Morre (Ed.), *Managing the political dimensions of student affairs* (pp. 5–16). New Directions for Student Services No. 55. San Francisco: Jossey-Bass.

Arthur, D. (1991). *Recruiting, interviewing, selecting, & orienting new employees.* New York: American Management Association.

Brechlin, J., & Rossett, A. (1991). Orienting new employees. *Training, 28*(4), 45–51.

Cadwell, C. M. (1988). *New employee orientation.* Los Altos, CA: Crisp.

Cooke, R. (1998). Welcome aboard. *Credit Union Management, 21,* 46–47.

Creamer, D. G., Winston, R. B., Jr., Schuh, J. H., Gehring, D. D., McEwen, M. K., Forney, D. S., Carpenter, D. S., & Woodard, D. B., Jr. (1997). Quality assurance in college student affairs. In R. B. Winston, Jr., & D. G. Creamer (Eds.), *Improving staffing practices in student affairs* (pp. 352–367). San Francisco: Jossey-Bass.

Dowling, E. J., & Eaker, M. A. (1996, March). *New directions for new professionals.* Paper presented at the Annual Convention of the American College Personnel Association, Baltimore, MD.

Dworak, L. L., & Glogowski, M. R. (1982). Orientation for new non-faculty members. *Journal of the College and University Personnel Association, 33,* 30–35.

Estrin, C. B. (1997). Orientation: The best kept secret for preventing turnover. *Legal Assistant Today, 14*(3), 70–72.

Federico, R. F. (1991). Six ways to solve the orientation blues. *Human Resources Magazine, 36,* 69–70.

Freeman, M. A., Nuss, E. M., & Barr M. J. (1993). Meeting the needs of staff diversity. In M. J. Barr (Ed.), *The handbook of student affairs administration* (pp. 455–467). San Francisco: Jossey-Bass.

Komives, S. R. (1997). Linking preparation with practice. In N. J. Evans & C. E. Phelps Tobin (Eds.), *The state of the art of preparation and practice in student affairs: Another look* (pp. 177–200). Lanham, MD: American College Personnel Association.

Kuh, G. P. (1991). Characteristics of involving colleges. In G. P. Kuh & J. M. Schuh (Eds.), *The role and contribution of student affairs in involving colleges* (pp. 11–29). Washington, DC: National Association of Student Personnel Administrators.

Lindo, D. K. (1995). Employee orientation: Not a self-study course. *Training, 31*(11), 16.

Loraine, K. (1997). Orientation is as simple as 1–2–3. *Nursing Management, 28*(1), 35–36.

Miller, T. K., & Winston, R. B., Jr. (1991). *Administration and leadership in student affairs: Actualizing student development in higher education* (2nd ed., pp. 449–494). Muncie, IN: Accelerated Development.

Patterson, V. (1997). The employers' guide: Successful intern/co-op programs. *Journal of Career Planning & Employment, 57*(2), 30–34, 55–56, 59.

Reinhardt, C. (1988). Training supervisors in first-day orientation techniques. *Personnel, 65*(24), 26, 28.

Schein, E. H. (1985). *Organizational culture and leadership: A dynamic view.* San Francisco: Jossey Bass.

Tilton-Ginzberg, S. (1990). Orienting new employees in intraorganizational service. *Journal of Supervisory Management, 35*(6), 9.

Winston, R. B., Jr., & Creamer, D. G. (1997). *Improving staffing practices in student affairs.* San Francisco: Jossey-Bass.

Zemke, R. (1989). Employee orientation: A process, not a program. *Training, 26,* 33–35, 37–38.

Chapter 3
ACTIVATING SYNERGISTIC SUPERVISION APPROACHES
Practical Suggestions

Roger B. Winston, Jr.
Joan B. Hirt

Supervision is a cumulative process, not an event. Good supervision must be measured by the additive effect of numerous interventions, which include instruction, psychological support, directives, and sometimes crisis management. To be effective, one must provide supervision on a regular reoccurring basis. If supervision is only provided when there is a problem or the new professional has made a mistake or error in judgment, then supervision likely will be viewed as punitive—no matter the supervisor's intentions. If supervision becomes linked in the new professional's mind only with negative feedback, she or he is likely to deploy strategies that will limit or avoid interaction with the supervisor and to attempt to conceal problems as long as possible (Winston & Creamer, 1997). Synergistic supervision explicitly focuses both on promoting the interests of the institution and the staff member's present and future welfare. It is the totality of the interactions with the new professional that ultimately determines the supervisor's effectiveness and worth (Winston & Creamer, 1997). (See chapter 1 for a detailed description of the theoretical underpinnings and constructs that define synergistic supervision.)

This chapter deals with some of the issues that supervisors of new professionals (NPs) face on a regular, if not daily, basis and suggests approaches supervisors can consider when devising their supervision schema. For most problems there are no easy, formulaic answers. What we offer are some perspectives to frame issues and suggestions that supervisors might try as they work with new professionals. As in all human relationships, one must take into account many variables, including personality characteristics, the situation, level of knowledge and experience, background, and the institutional and societal context, when supervising both new and seasoned professionals.

This chapter begins by discussing the hectic pace most student affairs professionals maintain in their positions and the difficulties of making supervision of new professionals an ongoing high priority. That is followed by some of the unique challenges supervisors of NPs face and a discussion of what NPs say they want from their supervisors. Next, there is an extensive treatment of the role of power in supervision. This leads to a discussion of micromanagement by supervisors. Finally, strategies for improving supervision of NPs are explored.

NATURE OF WORK IN STUDENT AFFAIRS

The responsibilities and duties of student affairs administrators typically include regular interactions with students that are intended to enrich or enhance their educational and developmental lives. As a result, the work of professionals shares a number of characteristics.

The pace of work is hectic and unrelenting. Most student affairs practitioners involved in the kinds of activities described above work long hours, frequently are on campus well after 5 PM interacting with students, and take work home. During the day they receive numerous requests for information and assistance; they are required to make scores of decisions that are directly and indirectly related to their primary responsibilities.

Work is varied and fragmented. Many activities are very short in duration, such as answering telephone calls and e-mail messages and giving instructions or approving requests made by professional and support staff, student paraprofessionals, and students. Interruptions occur frequently; conversations are disjointed; decisions range from urgent and strategic to routine and trivial.

It is within this context that staff supervision must take place. Staff members (supervisors and supervisees both) on most campuses and in most student affairs units move at a frenetic pace. There are generally far more demands for attention and reaction than one could reasonably expect to address in thoughtful, ratiocinative ways. In such an environment, it is often easier to neglect supervision and simply allow staff to fulfill their duties as best they can. To do so, however, can exact a stiff price. Staff supervision should be one of the highest priorities, if not the highest priority for those assigned that responsibility. Careful, close attention to supervision can produce a manyfold return on the investment. Few other activities have the potential of producing such rich rewards for the individuals involved and the organization.

CHALLENGES OF SUPERVISING NEW PROFESSIONALS

In an attempt to gauge the frequency and scope of issues that practitioners experience in supervising new professionals in student affairs, Winston (2001b) conducted an informal poll of supervisors of new professionals by posting questions to two listservs known to have a large number of mid-level practitioners as subscribers. They were asked to identify the principal challenges of supervising new professionals; 25 usable responses were received. Several themes emerged from their responses: (a) institutional culture and politics, (b) patience, (c) big picture, (d) change in the work ethic, (e) time, and (f) dealing with errors. Much of what we learned in the informal poll was corroborated by Arminio and Creamer (2001) in their structured qualitative study of superior staff supervision. We found the experiences described in the poll to correspond closely to what we have heard in the past several years from new professionals who graduated from our preparation programs and from professional colleagues on our campuses and across the country.

Institutional Culture and Politics   *Culture + politics*

The most frequently mentioned challenge of supervising new professionals related to helping NPs gain an understanding of the institutional culture and attendant politics. The respondents commented that some new professionals "assume that their new institution is just like where they went to graduate school." Another supervisor said: "They don't understand that not all problems can be solved the way they were at their undergraduate/graduate institution. Or that some problems cannot be solved in the short term."

In a similar vein, several supervisors indicated that new professionals often do not have a good sense of which "battles" to undertake and which ones are "unwinnable." As a consequence, NPs sometimes create unnecessary and debilitating controversies in which the unit ends up looking inept or foolish. Supervisors noted that learning to pick one's battles is difficult, and even "seasoned professionals make mistakes in this area." There also is another danger here: New professionals sometimes "loose a few internecine skirmishes and then just give up. They forget why they entered the field." Because they lack a long-term view, they assume that today's defeat means a total surrender. One supervisor commented, "Politics is profoundly challenging for both the new professional[s] and for the person supervising them."

For many seasoned student affairs professionals, politics are the sauce that adds flavor and makes the work interesting and challenging. For NPs, politics may seem pointless, demeaning, and frustrating and may cause some to abandon the field because they lack the skills and experience (or perhaps temperament) needed to be successful in this arena.

Arminio and Creamer (2001) found that quality supervision included interpreting the institutional culture and having a vision of where the institution is going.

Patience

Related to picking one's battles, the supervisors commented that frequently new professionals lack patience. One supervisor noted that "not everything can happen how and when the NP thinks it ideal." Partially because of their personal immaturity, professional inexperience, and "greater emphasis on immediate self-gratification of the 1980s and 1990s," they expect immediate results. Sometimes, when supervisors urge caution or suggest approaching an issue at a slower pace, they are misunderstood as being an uncaring professional or an "old stick in the mud who has sold his soul" or someone who is too invested in the status quo. Also, some NPs fail to fully appreciate the importance of addressing the needs and interests of the whole staff. For instance, NPs new to an organization do not know how much other staff members, who have been at the institution longer than they, have contributed. Supervisors need to address the wants and needs of the whole staff, which may mean that NPs "will have to wait their turn. It seems that today many [NPs] are unwilling to demonstrate their value to the institution first before expecting lots of 'goodies' to come their way."

Big Picture

Numerous supervisors commented on the difficulty of helping NPs see the "big picture." NPs often have difficulty seeing how their work fits into the larger scheme of higher education or their particular institution. They also need to understand that what they do is not (and perhaps never will be) considered the most important aspect of the institution. As one supervisor said, new professionals "need to learn that sometimes personal sacrifices must be made for the good of the department, division, or university." Another supervisor commented that many NPs have difficulty comprehending that "their goals and personal objectives may not always be the best route for the organization at the time. Maybe later." Yet another noted, "Supervisors need to help new professionals to put their jobs in the context of the big picture.

They come in with a limited scope of experience so their work world is IT."

Another supervisor offered a different slant on the need for NPs to see the "big picture." This person emphasized the importance of sharing with the NP the institution's dream or vision of what it is trying to do with students. "Only if the new professional understands where the college is trying to go can he/she be reasonably expected to make a contribution. Supervisors must be the conveyer of that vision to new staff." They also need to continuously point out how what the NP is asked to do is connected with the "big picture."

Change in the Work Ethic

Informal conversations with supervisors of NPs suggest they believe that there has been a change in the work ethic among those newly entering the student affairs field. As one supervisor stated, "Today's new professionals seem unwilling to go the extra mile." Or as another supervisor put it, NPs "are more savvy in their wants—benefits, fewer hours, more technology—but are less loyal and committed to the institution and the profession." Another example of a change in the work ethic was offered: "Once . . . [NPs] are recognized as good at what they do, they are almost always looking for the next step up." Few NPs seem to feel that they have some "obligation to give back to the institution once they have acquired some experience and are fully capable of making really important contributions." Some supervisors of NPs appear frustrated in that they seem always to be working with brand new staff and do not get to see the fruit of their labors to help NPs make successful transitions into the profession.

Time

A frequent comment from supervisors is that working with new professionals is time-consuming. One commented that "there are no short-cuts in supervising new professionals and there is no substitute for lots of one-on-one interaction." Multiple respondents to Winston's (2001b) questions reported that NPs require lots of feedback about their performance and expect supervisors to be available nearly immediately when a problem arises, which requires a considerable amount of the supervisor's time.

Arminio and Creamer (2001), in their study of "high quality" supervision, concluded that "time is an important commodity in our work. . . . Spending time supervising in principled ways through setting the context, motivating, teaching, listening, observing, giving direction, role modeling, and caring responses reaps definite benefits" (p. 43).

Dealing with Errors

New professionals should be expected to make mistakes or to engage in imprudent or ill-conceived activities from time to time. If NPs do not make mistakes, they probably are not taking many risks (or perhaps are simply doing very little of anything) and, consequently, are having little or no impact on students' lives. As a result, supervisors of new professionals must be adept at correcting mistakes and errors in judgment in ways that are not personally demeaning but are perceived as constructive. As one supervisor of NPs stated "They [NPs] want someone to challenge them to grow by giving them appropriate responsibilities, yet be supportive whenever they may struggle to become their best." Because NPs crave autonomy, their supervisors walk a fine line between allowing them to make preventable mistakes and learning from those mistakes and protecting NPs from making mistakes that can be catastrophic. This balancing act must be performed in ways that do not dampen NPs' enthusiasm, creativity, and self-confidence.

SUPERVISION: THE NEW PROFESSIONAL'S PERSPECTIVE

To get a perspective on how new professionals view and experience supervision, an informal survey was conducted by posting three open-ended questions to two listservs known to be frequented by substantial numbers of new professionals (Winston, 2001a). New professionals were asked what they wanted or wished for from their supervisors and what had proved helpful in supervision. Nine themes emerged from their responses. In no particular order of importance, new professionals reported wanting the following from their supervisors: (a) structure, (b) autonomy, (c) frequent feedback, (d) recognition of limitations, (e) support, (f) effective communication, (g) consistency, (h) role modeling, and (i) sponsorship.

Structure

New professionals want supervisors who are organized and can teach them how they can organize and manage their responsibilities efficiently and effectively. One NP stated, "Don't make me pay for my supervisor's inability to organize his responsibilities and to tell me what is required of me in enough time (so) I can do a good job." Similarly, another NP said: "I don't want to have to guess what my supervisor wants; tell me! If you want things done a certain way, explain what you want and when you want it. If there's a deadline, tell me in time to allow me to get done what is required. I don't enjoy working in crisis mode all the time. If I have discretion, don't second guess me; if I don't, tell me directly." Several NPs wanted supervisors who assisted in the formulation of goals and objectives for each term and who followed through to see if those objectives were met. On the other hand, one NP stated that she wanted a supervisor who was "intentional in setting up boundaries, rules, guidelines, and expectations at the very beginning." This suggests that this NP is looking for a supervisor who is intentional in her or his approach to supervision and who includes the NP in the structuring process.

Autonomy

Many of the NPs mentioned a desire for autonomy in performing their responsibilities. One NP stated: "Trust that I can do the job for which I was hired. . . . Allow me to try something new and venture into new areas. . . . [I want to be] able to use my creativity and to think outside the box." Many NPs seem proud of their newly acquired professional skills and knowledge and want opportunities to try them out. As an NP stated, "I want autonomy to develop my own style and leadership, but I welcome feedback too." Numerous NPs criticized supervisors who were perceived to be micromanagers. One NP captured the spirit of the comments about such supervisors—"My [first] supervisor was a micromanager, which I perceived as mistrust in my professional ability. This practice took away confidence I had in myself to do my job and turned me into a very bitter professional. Why hire me if you don't trust me to do my job to your satisfaction?"

Frequent Feedback

Many of the NPs who responded to the open-ended questions mentioned that they wanted frequent feedback from their supervisors. One NP declared, "[I want] someone who will tell me when I am messing up and help me figure out how to fix it." Numerous NPs expressed a desire for frequent one-to-one supervision sessions with their supervisors. Many expressed irritation at supervisors who allowed other things to get in the way of regular supervisory sessions. Several first-year NPs expressed a desire for formal (or at least semiformal) evaluations of performance and progress each term. Because many NPs are still unsure of their skills and competence, they want reassurance and confirmation from the supervisor or, if there are problems, to be assisted in overcoming those problems. Many NPs expressed the sentiment of one NP: "[I want] feedback, correction when necessary, and a pat on the back when doing a good job." "[I want] constructive feedback that will help me advance to the next level professionally," said another NP. Other NPs expressed a need for frequent recognition of good work and praise.

Recognition of Limitations

New professionals repeatedly expressed a desire for their supervisors to recognize their limitations, especially their lack of time available to take on new assignments. Several NPs opined that their supervisors did not appreciate how much time and effort was required to fulfill the "usual" job responsibilities. A few NPs stated that their supervisors took such a "hands-off" approach that the NPs lacked sufficient information about the institution and its culture to function effectively. Due to an inadequate orientation, the NPs were in constant fear of inadvertently stepping into a minefield. In terms of limitations, several NPs admonished supervisors not to act on untested assumptions about NPs' backgrounds and experience. As one NP noted, her supervisor "thought I knew all about advising Greek organizations because I was a member of several honoraries as an undergraduate. In fact I knew nothing about advising social sororities. If my supervisor had asked, I would have readily admitted my ignorance. Instead, I was in over my head from day one." Finally, one NP summed up the need to recognize limitations this way: "Supervisors need to remember that as a new professional I may not be as efficient at doing some things as they are. I'm still learning. But all of us have only 24 hours in the day."

Support

Many of the NPs described a need for support, frequently expressed. As one NP stated: "I want to feel that there is always someone covering my backside, someone who wants me to be successful, and is willing to help me if I find myself in trouble." Another NP expressed the need for support this way: "[I want my supervisor to] challenge me to handle things on my own, but in such a way that I never feel abandoned." One stated that he wanted his supervisor to "provide support and appropriate training, as well as a safe and comfortable working atmosphere." Another NP said that she wanted a supervisor who would "turn mistakes and difficulties into learning moments."

Effective Communication

Most of the NPs mentioned the vital importance of open, frequent communication between the supervisor and new professional. Of particular importance is for supervisors to:

- *Pass along information from those higher in the administrative chain and from other segments of the campus.* One NP stated: "A supervisor needs to let me know what is happening in the department, division, and university. That communication makes me more effective and better able to do my job." Another NP put it succinctly—"lack of information makes one appear incompetent and in higher education ignorance is not bliss."

- *Act as a sounding board.* New professionals often want a chance to bounce ideas off their supervisors before they act on them. Because they may be somewhat unsure about themselves or lack an in-depth understanding of the institutional culture, they want someone to listen, ask lots of questions, provide relevant background and history, but limit judgments. Asking a supervisor to be a sounding board, however, is not the same as asking the supervisor to make a decision or to tell the NP what to do. Supervisors need to be cautious in responding to NPs; it is important for supervisors to respect the NPs' scope of delegated authority. One NP requested: "Ask me lots of questions about why I made the decisions I did. This will help me develop my personal foundation and mission in student affairs." Another NP requested that her supervisor "take time out of the week to sit down with me one-on-one and talk to me about what is happening. . . . I need someone who has been there to talk about [my experiences] with and to offer me guidance."

- *Be honest and straightforward.* Several NPs decried supervisors who were unwilling to confront unsatisfactory behavior directly. As one NP stated, "*Don't* send messages to me through other staff. Deal with me face to face. Also, don't talk to me about other staff members' problems. Deal with them face to face." Another NP expressed a slightly different slant: "I want someone [as a supervisor] who isn't afraid to hold me and other staff members accountable." Several other NPs emphasized the need to receive constructive criticism. Several NPs reported having supervisors who were reluctant to confront problems, which resulted in creation of even worse situations.

- *Listen.* As an NP stated, "Most importantly, I want a supervisor to listen to what I have to say and respect the insight that I can provide as someone new to both the profession and the campus." Another NP put it this way: "I want a supervisor that asks me about 'problems' and then listens to what I have to say before telling me what to do. I have a right to be heard. My ideas should count for something."

Consistency

Numerous NPs mentioned the importance of supervisors treating all staff in the same way. When asked about the areas of greatest difficulty with supervisors, NPs identified inconsistent treatment or favoritism as their principal complaint. One NP said: "The biggest . . . [criticism of my supervisor] is simply inequality of treatment. It is very frustrating to hear peers being praised for their efforts, but never to hear it yourself." This is somewhat echoed by another NP who stated that her principal complaint about her supervisor was "not holding everyone to the same standards, that is letting some get away with things that I wouldn't get away with." Another difficulty was identified when supervisors formed closer personal relationships with some staff member than with others. "No matter whether there is actually favoritism involved, it usually looks that way when there are those kinds of relationships," explained an NP.

Role Modeling

Numerous NPs expressed the desire to have a supervisor who could be viewed as a role model of a "competent, involved student affairs professional." As one NP put it: "A supervisor must 'walk the walk,' if he/she is going to 'talk the talk.' The old adage 'lead by example' is the best and most important thing that a supervisor can do." Or, as another NP put it: "Don't expect something from me if you aren't doing it."

Other NPs considered it important that their supervisors were knowledgeable about the latest literature in the field and wanted them to be able to help NPs translate theory into practice. "Anyone can recite theories. I need a supervisor who knows how to take it from theory to practice," stated one NP. Another noted that in two years he never heard his supervisor mention theory once. "As a result, I had no idea why he did the things he did nor did I understand why some things worked and others did not. [But] . . . at last I have a supervisor who can do that [use and explain theory]. Unfortunately, I wasted most of the first two years of my professional career." Other NPs expressed the desire to have a supervisor who is active in professional organizations and who guides NPs into active professional involvement.

Having a positive attitude was important to several NPs. A few described supervisors who did not enjoy their work, were sour on the field, and/or were pessimistic about the institution. When this occurred, the NPs reported feeling discouraged, unappreciated, and devalued just as they were beginning their careers. One NP described a supervisor who "showed a complete unconcern for her position, the field, and the university," which resulted in the NP feeling "isolated, abandoned, and frustrated." Supervisors who are unhappy with their work or the institution can easily infect everyone with whom they have contact but especially those they supervise. It would appear that NPs are especially sensitive to their supervisor's lack of enthusiasm and commitment to the profession.

Sponsorship

New professionals often mentioned that they wanted their supervisors to be "mentors." What they were asking for, however, seems to fall short of a true mentoring relationship (see Otto, 1994; Schuh & Carlisle, 1991; Winston & Creamer, 2002). NPs reported wanting supervisors who would introduce them to key individuals in the institution and professional leaders beyond the campus. They wanted encouragement to become actively involved in professional organizations, time to devote to professional association-related activities, and money (to the extent it was available within the institution) to attend workshops and conferences. One NP stated: " I want my supervisor to open the door of opportunity for me. Help me get connected professionally. I'll take it from there." Other NPs noted that they wanted supervisors who would help them identify learning opportunities and to incorporate them into their jobs.

POWER AND SUPERVISION

The very concept of *supervision* has built into it a power differential between the supervisor and his or her staff. In fact, the previous sentence demonstrates this power dynamic. The use of the possessive "his or her staff" suggests supervisors in some way control (no matter how benignly) the staff members who report to them. How well student affairs professionals understand and exercise the power inherent in their positions and the power attached to them as persons greatly influences their success as supervisors.

Yukl (1998, p. 177) defines power as "an agent's potential influence over the attitudes and behavior of one or more designated target persons." Power also may be seen as the ability to influence decisions, events, and material things, such as expenditures or use of facilities.

Ultimately, supervisory success depends on the ability to understand and use power wisely and to the benefit of the institution and the staff members the supervisor is charged to direct. For some in student affairs, it may be uncomfortable to think about supervision as the exercise of power because it smacks of authoritarianism and suggests a lack of appreciation of individuals. It also suggests that relationships are unimportant in supervision.

As French and Raven (1959) pointed out, however, power should not be thought of as a repressive force or the tool of totalitarianism. It is not antithetical to the student affairs field's humanistic values. Any organization that has a division of labor and a rudimentary hierarchical organizational structure has differing levels of power. This differentiation is intentional because it is thought necessary to organize resources (human and material) and to get work done effectively. The exercise of power has many constructive uses. The judicious exercise of power is essential for implementing synergistic supervision. To exercise power judiciously, it is helpful to understand the different forms power can take.

Kinds of Power

Over 40 years ago, French and Raven (1959) proposed a taxonomy of types of power that remains relevant today. They labeled the types of power as (a) legitimate, (b) coercive, (c) reward, (d) expert, and (e) referent. Synergistic supervisors need to understand and appropriately utilize each of these kinds of power.

Legitimate power influences people to comply because they believe that the agent (person possessing power) has the right to make the request and the target persons believe that they have an obligation to comply. This belief in the legitimacy of power is based largely on the generally implicit expectation that employees should show deference to those higher in the organization's hierarchy. Position invests formal authority in organization members—typically identified by title. "Authority is based on perceptions about the prerogatives, obligations, and responsibilities associated with particular positions in an organization" (Yukl, 1998, p. 179). Authority is also evident in a position holder's exercise of control over expenditures, resources, personnel, equipment, and facilities. A supervisor by definition is vested with legitimate power.

Coercive power is exercised through control of punishment or bestowing/withholding rewards such as promotions, salary, or lessened work loads. In higher education, coercive power is frequently disparaged as inappropriate—it is generally associated with the military and other more rigidly structured hierarchies such as large corporations. Yukl (1998) asserts that "coercion is effective only when applied to a small percentage of followers under conditions considered legitimate by a majority of them" (p. 183). In higher education there is considerable dependency between supervisors and staff; coercion is likely to provoke resistance that may escalate into open conflict that benefits neither party. Staff members at all levels have many overt and covert ways to impede or thwart supervisors' directives. An old adage in higher education is, "Never get your secretary upset with you because she [usually] has a thousand ways to make you look bad."

Reward power derives from control over tangible benefits, such as promotions, work schedules, operating budgets, travel funds, degree of authority and responsibility, and formal and informal recognition (Yukl, 1998). This kind of power has limited utility in higher education because organizational structures are relatively flat, thereby offering few opportunities to promote staff. Likewise, raises in salary are generally restricted by legislative and/or institutional guidelines or personnel classification systems (although much greater latitude is generally available in private institutions). Reward power depends on control of resources and the perception by staff that the assignment of rewards is feasible and if carried out will actually result in the promised benefit. In higher education, all supervisors are called on to dispense rewards routinely. They also on a nearly daily basis have the power to reward new professionals through special benefits, such as award of travel funds for professional development or providing opportunities to broaden experience through new assignments.

Expert power is a personal characteristic; supervisors with expertise can solve consequential problems, perform important tasks, or have exclusive access to certain information. As Yukl (1998) notes, however, "expertise is a source of power for a person only if others are dependent on the person for advice" (p. 185). Possessing expertise is a source of power only if staff members recognize the expertise and see the supervisor as a reliable source of information and advice. Consequently, reputation is crucial to having expert power, but ultimately it is necessary that the expert maintain her or his expertise through an ongoing process of education, research, and practical experience. In student affairs, supervisors are expected to have a better understanding of the field, greater experience dealing with the institution and its students, and a clearer understanding of student development and learning theories and their applications than the new professionals they supervise.

French and Raven (1959) labeled the final type of power as referent power, which is derived from the desire of others to please a person for whom they have feelings of friendship, affection, or admiration. Staff members are usually willing to do favors for friends or to carry out requests made by someone they admire and respect, even though the request exceeds usual job responsibilities. Referent power "depends on feelings of friendship and loyalty that are usually developed slowly over a long period of time. Referent power is increased by acting friendly, . . . [being] considerate, showing concern for the needs and feelings of others, demonstrating trust and respect, and treating people fairly" (Yukl, 1998, p. 186). In synergistic supervision, establishing a caring, trusting, and responsive relationship with staff is essential. This kind of relationship is a necessary condition for effective supervision: that is, supervision that addresses the twin goals of promoting the accomplishment of the institution's mission and fostering individual staff members' personal and professional growth.

Consequences of the Exercise of Power in Supervision

Table 3.1 offers examples of effective uses of power in staff supervision and also identifies how power can be abused and thereby dissipated. Just as there are ways to enhance one's power to promote the interests of the institution and its students, supervisors can lose power and become impotent as supervisors. The use of power or influence produces three qualitatively distinct outcomes—commitment, compliance, and resistance. These outcomes are not produced categorically. Rather, each is produced as a matter of degree.

If a staff member responds to a supervisor with *commitment*, she or he agrees with a decision or request and makes a great effort to carry out the request or implementation of the decision effectively. In other words, the staff member is supporting an approach that he or she believes is the correct course of action. "For a complex, difficult task, commitment is usually the most successful outcome from the perspective of the agent who makes an influence attempt" (Yukl, 1998, p. 176).

Another outcome produced in staff by an exercise of power is *compliance*. When a staff member complies, he or she is willing to do what is requested but is phlegmatic, rather than enthusiastic, in performing tasks and will make only a minimal effort. Yukl (1998) points out that this exercise of influence affects behavior, but not attitudes. In the performance of simple tasks compliance may be all that is necessary. The more complex the tasks, however, the greater the need for commitment from the staff member.

The third consequence of the attempt to exercise influence over staff is *resistance*. If staff members respond to a request by resisting, they actually oppose the proposal or request (rather than just being indifferent) and actively try to avoid carrying it out. Staff responses (Yukl, 1998) may include:

- Making excuses about why the request cannot be carried out.
- Trying to persuade the supervisor to drop or alter the request.
- Asking higher authorities to overrule the request.
- Delaying action in the hope that the supervisor will forget about the request.
- Appearing to be complying, but trying to sabotage the effort.
- Refusing to carry out the request.

Using Power in Synergistic Supervision

All supervisors have power to influence staff and to create environments that promote goal achievement, dedication, and amicable working relationships. How sensitively, carefully, and thoughtfully supervisors use their power, however, determines their ultimate effectiveness as supervisors.

TABLE 3.1. Examples of Using Power in Staff Supervision

Types of power	Ways to use power effectively	Ways to abuse or dissipate power
Legitimate power	Make requests for what is needed, politely and clearly	Demand services or action in demeaning or disrespectful way
	Explain reason for requests and intended use or purpose of what is requested	Issue commands without explanation or rationale
	Be sensitive to staff's concerns and interests	Appear self-centered or interested primarily in self-promotion
	Follow up to verify compliance or execution	Scapegoat staff for errors or mistakes in judgment
	Relate requests to stated goals or institutional/unit mission	Make threats or promises that are outside the scope of authority to carry out
	Follow agreed-on procedures and proper organizational channels	Fail to support staff who make decisions based on institutional policy or agreed-on procedures
	Regularly require staff to report results of assignments and projects	Unpredictably and selectively critique performance
Coercive power	Inform staff of policies, rules, and penalties for violations	Inconsistently enforce rules or policies
	Give ample prior warnings to taking disciplinary action	Act impulsively or too severely for nature of current infraction
	Remain calm and listen to explanations when staff members violate policies/ instructions	Allow past behavior or poor performance to enter into treatment of immediate problem
	Understand situation and any extenuating circumstances before disciplining	Become emotional, verbally abusive, or demeaning when correcting staff
	Ask staff about ways to improve performance or situation or perceptions of the problem	Act without soliciting and considering staff's opinions or concerns
Reward power	Offer desirable rewards (find out what staff want and need)	Offer rewards that are beyond supervisor's ability to deliver
	Offer fair and ethical rewards based on performance and productivity	Allow personal relationships with individuals to influence allocation of rewards
	Deliver on promises	Use rewards in a personally manipulative way
	Use rewards symbolically to reinforce desirable behavior	Use rewards for personal benefit or ego gratification
Expert power	Demonstrate competence by solving difficult problems	Discount or belittle staff's attempts to solve problems
	Provide evidence that strategy or plan will be successful ("sell" plan or strategy to the staff)	Appear arrogant or overbearing

(*Continued*)

TABLE 3.1. Continued

Types of power	Ways to use power effectively	Ways to abuse or dissipate power
	Seek input from those closest to the problem or target population	Disparage staff's experience or insights
	Act confident and decisive	Make rash, careless statements (overreact)
	Remain steadfast, do not change positions frequently	Lie or misrepresent the facts
	Remain knowledgeable about current theories and professional practices	Try to distort the evidence or hide mistakes or errors
	Stay actively involved in professional organizations	Lose touch with today's students and their interests and concerns
Referent power	Show interest in each staff member's welfare and personal and professional development	Treat staff as expendables in the organization
	Develop supportive and friendly relationships with staff	Manipulate staff for personal advancement
	Keep promises and confidences	Demand unquestioning personal allegiance
	Make personal sacrifices to show concern for staff	Expect staff to do inconvenient personal favors
	Stand behind staff as they perform their duties or implement policy	Respond to staff based on political needs of the moment
	Indicate when requests are personally important	Expect things of staff that the supervisor is unable or unwilling to do
	Use sincere forms of ingratiation	Show favoritism or unequal treatment based on personal relationships

Note. Based on French and Raven (1959) and adapted from Yukl (1998).

Yet power can be squandered or used in unproductive and damaging ways as well. When supervisors are motivated primarily by self-interest and/or fail to show respect and concern for staff members, they frequently lose referent, expert, and reward power and are left only with legitimate and coercive power at their disposal. Supervisors who do not have the respect of those they supervise neutralize their legitimate power to a large extent, causing staff to seek ways of avoiding interaction, subverting directives, and making "end runs." Such supervisors are left only with coercive power, which is difficult to maintain in higher education. Using coercive power also requires considerable psychic energy to maintain a supervisory approach based on fear and intimidation.

The tenets of synergistic supervision advocate that supervisors should capitalize on the power they are given and the power they can earn to further the goals of the student affairs division and the institution, as well as promoting the welfare of the staff supervised. Using power in appropriate ways leads many professionals to other strategies related to effective supervision of NPs.

MICROMANAGEMENT: SCOURGE OF THE NEW PROFESSIONAL

When working with new professionals, it is important that they feel that their supervisor is accessible, supportive, and interested. But at the same time, the supervisor does not want to be seen as micromanaging the new professional's job and/or life. Almost universally, NPs report that micromanagement by supervisors has a debilitating effect on their capability to do good work and on their professional self-esteem.

A Self-Assessment

Following are a few questions that supervisors can ask themselves to determine the degree to which they are micromanagers. This inventory has no known reliability or validity, but is offered as a stimulus to aid supervisors in examining their approach to managing.

1. Do I require staff to get prior approval before taking new initiatives in their areas of responsibility?
2. Do I frequently check up on subordinates' preparations for programs and activities?
3. Do I frequently ask students how well staff members are doing their jobs?
4. Do I tell staff members to do things the way they were done last year?
5. Do I spend time in staff meetings having staff members provide the details for upcoming programs and activities?
6. Do I know the details of every staff member's job?
7. Do I require that minutes of meetings that subordinates attend, but I do not, be provided to me?
8. Do I keep staff members guessing about my evaluations of their work?
9. Do I make it a point to reprimand staff members every time they make a mistake?
10. Do I offer advice about how staff members should arrange their offices?
11. Do I tell professional staff members to clean up their offices?

If supervisors answer yes to more than two of these questions, they are probably micromanaging to some degree the staff with whom they work.

The more questions answered affirmatively, the more frequently supervisors probably use micromanagement techniques with their staff members.

If supervisors are seen as micromanagers, new professionals are likely to view those supervisors as lacking confidence in their abilities and as negative influences in the workplace. Often, one of the most difficult things a supervisor is called on to do is to do nothing, thereby allowing the new professional to make mistakes that the supervisor could have avoided because of her or his greater experience. Sometimes supervisors must make a choice between preventing mistakes before they occur and standing back until poor results have been experienced so that the situation can be used as a teachable moment for the new professional. There are times, however, in which the supervisor must intervene early because of the long-range negative consequences of failure for the unit or because of the high cost to the institution in loss of money or reputation.

Making the decision about when or whether to intervene is complicated by the fact that frequently what appears as a disaster in the making is nothing more than a difference in style or personality. New professionals, if they are well qualified, will invent new ways of dealing with perennial problems and issues. However, these might not be the ways that the supervisor has responded in the past or would have ever thought of. The sign of a supervisor who refuses to be a micromanager is a willingness to accept a modicum of risk by allowing NPs to find their own ways.

Resisting the temptation to micromanage new professionals' work takes considerable ego strength and impulse control by the supervisor. If an NP fails or comes up short of expectations, can the supervisor accept that without feeling diminished self-worth? The urge to micromanage may come from a sense of insecurity on the part of the supervisor. This can be made more complicated when the micromanager is higher in the organizational chart. Micromanaging on the part of chief student affairs officers can spread the virus throughout the organization, with crippling effects. "Micromanagement diminishes people and slows organization development." It destroys organizational commitment, trust in the relationship, and group cohesiveness. "Ultimately, it robs employees of their self-respect and organizations of their future" (Weyland, 1996, p. 62).

Weyland (1996), somewhat tongue-in-cheek, comments that "Micromanagers do have value. Why else would they continue to exist in an enlightened time, such as the one we are now in?" From a business perspective, he proposes a list of reasons why micromangers can be useful. They are presented here in an adapted form to fit higher education.

- No expensive training and development program is needed. There is also no need to cultivate new leaders.
- No one questions who is in charge.

- It cuts down on wasted time of seeking recommendations and suggestions or holding meetings. Just do it!
- There is no need for time-consuming performance reviews. Only one person needs to be evaluated.
- "Team" becomes just another four-letter word used in mission statements and strategic plans, to which no one pays any attention (p. 61).

Many new professionals attempt to deal with micromanaging supervisors by avoiding them and hiding problems and difficulties in order to keep supervisors "out of their hair." The ultimate effect is the creation of an atmosphere of mistrust and repeated crises when avoidable problems go unaddressed until they become near catastrophic. Because micromanagement may generate counterproductive results, a self-fulfilling-prophesy effect may be created. Supervisors doubt the ability of NPs to properly handle a situation or process, so they intervene by giving overly explicit instructions and closely monitor their implementation. The NPs feel that the supervisor lacks confidence in their abilities to handle a situation and resent the supervisor's intrusion into their "territory." The NPs, therefore, take the attitude that if the supervisor wants to do it, then we should stay out of the way; consequently, they make minimal efforts and attempt to psychologically withdraw, which seems to justify the supervisor's original diagnosis that the NPs were incompetent. A cyclical process kicks in: The more the supervisor intervenes, the more there seems to be a justification for doing so.

ADDRESSING THE CHALLENGES OF A DIVERSE STAFF

As higher education continues to address the problem of underrepresentation of students from many cultures, it has become clear that having staff members with characteristics similar to the target populations can increase the probability that minority students will feel welcomed and will be supported in meeting their educational and personal development goals. As Dixon (2001) notes, colleges need "employees who can demonstrate . . . [the] abilities . . . [of] working effectively on culturally diverse teams, or who can appreciate and value, but not be distracted by, difference in the workplace" (p. 68).

The introduction of staff members who do not come from the dominant culture in the institution presents an additional set of challenges to the supervisor of NPs. As noted earlier, NPs expect fair, even-handed, and equitable treatment from their supervisors, treatment that does not show unearned favor. (We suspect that many NPs actually expect *identical* treatment of all staff members.) Difficulty may arise, however, when NPs from minority backgrounds are introduced because they may need additional assistance in becoming acclimated to the institution and learning to negotiate the campus culture, especially if the NP is "one of his or her kind." As Janosik and Hirt (2001) note, cultural artifacts such as etiquette, values, language, traditions and customs, food, dress, musical tastes, belief systems, and worldviews may be the cause of conflict. From our experience, it seems that transparency on the part of supervisors is generally the best policy—that is, openly communicate the goals of increased multicultural representation on the campus and discuss what additional assistance underrepresented staff members may need to be successful.

Even though there are no absolute guidelines for dealing with these sensitive and complex issues, here are a number of suggestions for supervisors (Certo, 1994; Daddona, 2001; Karsten, 1994; http://filebox.vt.edu/users/dgc2/staffinghandbook/supervision.htm).

- Make understanding and working with persons from different cultures, sexual orientations, genders, handicapping conditions, and ethnicities a top priority for staff development, before and after the new NP arrives. (This is also valuable training for working with students.)
- Deal openly with the issues associated with increased diversity.
- Model open and accepting behavior.
- Provide coaching and support for women (in situations where they are minority or fulfill traditional male roles or functions), religious minorities, gay/lesbian/bisexual/transgender individuals, non-Whites, and staff members with disabilities—especially if the larger institution is not supportive.
- Become familiar with the communication styles and patterns of various cultural groups. Teach all staff about these differences.
- Avoid making generalizations and assumptions about specific groups of people. Remember that individual differences are almost always much greater than the common characteristics and attributes shared by the members of any group.
- Confront negative stereotypes and prejudicial statements whenever they occur, whether made by students or by other staff members.
- Be knowledgeable about the religious observances and holidays of various groups and make a concerted effort to avoid conflicts with planned events.
- Do not attempt to suppress conflict. Instead, recognize that conflict is natural and deal with it openly and honestly.

STRATEGIES FOR IMPROVING THE EFFECTIVENESS OF SUPERVISION

Successful supervisors take the initiative to create conditions that encourage and support NPs in fulfilling position expectations and developing professional skills, thereby increasing the likelihood that the most talented and gifted NPs will have long and rewarding careers in student affairs. Just as micromanagement generally has debilitating results, other strategies supervisors can adopt promote a positive experience for NPs. Listed next are a number of suggestions for implementing the synergistic supervision approach with new professionals in student affairs. Supervisors, however, should understand that supervision must be an individualized process that is constrained by many factors, including (a) the personalities of the supervisor and new professional, (b) the quality of professional preparation NPs have received, (c) the institutional type, history, and culture, (d) the organizational structure of the student affairs division and college or university, and (e) the expectations and demands of the NP's position.

Discuss and Provide Supervision Systematically

An obvious, but often overlooked, practice in supervision is to spend time actually talking about *supervision*: what it means from the supervisor's perspective and from the NP's perspective. Supervisors also need to spell out a systematic plan for implementing supervision—including regularly scheduled one-on-one sessions. One might think of this process as creating a supervision contract.

Successful supervisors (Winston & Creamer, 1997) and new professionals (Winston, 2001a) both advocate frequent supervisory sessions as the NP begins the position, and these may become less frequent in the second and subsequent years. Many advise scheduling weekly individual sessions for the first half year the NP is on the job (Winston & Creamer, 1997). After the first 6 months, supervision sessions may be held biweekly. The exact schedule depends on many factors, such as the NP's maturity, the number of problems the NP encounters in the work setting, how effective the NP is working with less direct input from the supervisor, the NP's understanding of the institutional culture and history, and the amount of psychological support and encouragement the NP wants or needs.

If supervisors intend to use the synergistic approach, then they need to discuss the responsibilities and contributions that both supervisors and supervisees will be expected to contribute. For synergistic supervision to work, supervision cannot be viewed as something *done to* or even *with* those supervised. Instead, both parties to the relationship have responsibilities to each other and to the process. The goals and processes of supervision need to be periodically appraised, especially during the first year the NP is in a position and at least twice a year thereafter. These discussions should solicit input from both parties about their perceptions of goal accomplishment, what has proven useful or helpful, what has been less helpful or even burdensome, and what new or different projects each party would like or feels compelled to tackle.

The supervision "contract" should be viewed as fixing responsibilities and making time commitments, but also as being open to review and modification as circumstances change or the NP gains confidence, skill, and knowledge of the institution. Changes in the contract, however, must always be negotiable by either party. Perfectly reasonable plans in September may be completely unrealistic in January due to situations such as changing institutional priorities, budget shortfalls, unexpected misfortunes, or abrupt departures by staff. Staff members and their supervisors both must be flexible. Even though flexibility is essential, there also needs to be a sense of accountability. Many NPs need the structure of timelines and the requirement that they explain or document how they have used their time and what they have to show for their efforts. (Setting and evaluating goals is dealt with in greater detail later in this chapter.)

Supervisory sessions should be planned for and "built in" to regular, ongoing interactions with new professionals. Some supervisors assume that they are providing adequate supervision because they have frequent interaction with those they supervise; some might even say that they "supervise" a lot because they see members of the staff several times a day. Having frequent social interaction, even if accompanied with enquiries, such as "how is it going?" or "Are there problems?," is not a substitute for systematic, planned supervision. Supervision sessions should have preestablished agendas (with opportunity to cover other matters too). Each session should connect with the previous sessions and should also focus on future activities and responsibilities.

Assess Knowledge and Skills

Assessment of a new professional's knowledge and skills begins during the job interview process. After NPs arrive and assume duties, the supervisor needs to continue to assess their knowledge, interpersonal and professional skills, and other skills that are needed to adequately meet the demands and expectations of the position.

Skills and knowledge assessment can be threatening for new professionals, who may be suspicious of how identification of areas of weakness or knowledge gaps are to be used. Will this information be used to belittle the NPs' efforts, cause them to appear to have less status than other NPs on campus, or mean that supervisors will feel the need to micromanage their positions? For these reasons, attention must first be focused on building a trusting, open, respectful relationship. Until NPs are made to feel comfortable in admitting shortcomings and lack of knowledge to the supervisor, assessment may be viewed as menacing. The assessment process also should focus on identifying the NPs' unique or exceptional skills and talents that can be utilized in the unit. Supervisors, however, should be cautious that NPs' special talents are not overused; for instance, if a NP has exceptional knowledge about computer applications, all technology questions should not be automatically assigned to her or him. Instead, it may be more appropriate to utilize the NP's computer savvy to teach others in the unit, thereby avoiding overworking the skilled NP.

If supervisors have the responsibility to manage "professional" staff members who lack professional academic preparation from a "good" master's degree program, they have a much larger responsibility. By hiring underprepared staff, the institution assumes the moral responsibility to provide what would have been included in a quality master's program in student affairs. It is the supervisor who must bear the brunt of the responsibility for providing this basic education. In our opinion, it is unethical to employ staff members who are not qualified to promote the personal and educational growth of students and to function and contribute within the institution's organizational structure. Because of a lack of availability of a sufficiently large pool of well-qualified NPs or inopportune vacancies, however, institutions may be forced to knowingly employ underprepared staff. When this happens, then the institution must assume the responsibility for providing basic education—either through systematic in-house programs and strategic use of professional development opportunities offered by professional associations or through support for the NP to enroll in a quality student affairs master's degree program, if one is available in the area. (The field is not well served by insisting that underprepared staff members obtain a master's degree in *any field*. In many—if not most—cases, master's degrees in fields not directly applicable to student affairs are of dubious value in equipping staff to carry out the mission of student affairs.)

MAKE DECISION-MAKING STRUCTURE APPARENT AND GENUINE

As noted earlier, NPs look to supervisors for structure. This, however, requires delicate treatment in creating a framework that steers a middle course between overprescribing procedures and activities (micromanaging) and providing insufficient guidance and direction, thereby leaving the NP uncertain about the supervisor's expectations and willingness to provide support. The director of housing at Samford University (Winston & Creamer, 1997) explained his approach to working with NPs: The supervisor and staff member need a clear understanding about which decisions are the sole province of the NP, which must be made by the supervisor (ideally with the input of the NP), and which should be made jointly. (As this director of housing put it, this involved a determination of which decisions *you* make, which *I* make, and which *we* make together.)

Yukl (1998) puts these distinctions in the context of participative leadership theory. He distinguishes four different kinds of decision-making process. *Autocratic decisions* are made by the supervisor without asking the opinion or suggestions of others. Decisions made through *consultation* involve asking others for their opinions and ideas, and then the supervisor makes the decision after thoughtfully considering others' input. *Joint decisions* are the results of the supervisor and others involved meeting and discussing the problem or situation and then making a group decision. In this kind of decision the supervisor's opinion carries no more weight than any others. Supervisors can *delegate decisions* to individuals or groups, which are given both the responsibility and authority for making decisions. Limits may be specified within which the final decision must conform, and the supervisor may require that the decision be approved before implementation. Making the decision-making process explicit helps NPs more clearly define their areas of responsibility and the limits of autonomous action. Strauss (1977) cautions, however, that it is important to clearly differentiate between overt procedures and actual influence. On occasion what appears to be participation is intended to simply inform or is only pretense. Generally, it is far better to forego requests for extensive input from subordinates if the supervisor knows what she or he is going do (or feels compelled to do by superiors). It requires only a few instances of sham participation requests to produce cynicism and even hostility from NPs. When decisions are handed down to supervisors to implement, ordinarily it is better for supervisors to explain the reasoning behind the decisions and the intended outcomes rather than convey the impression that staff members can have any real input into the decisions. Yukl (1998) observes that "consulting will not be effective unless people are actively involved in generating ideas, making suggestions, stating their preferences, and expressing their concerns" (p. 135).

Guidelines for Delegation.   When working with NPs, supervisors may be undecided about what responsibilities to delegate and when to delegate those responsibilities. Yukl (1998) offers some guidelines for making the determination about delegation.

- Delegate tasks that can be done better by subordinates (for instance, when the staff member has more expertise or is closer to the problem or the supervisor simply does not have sufficient time to do things properly).
- Delegate tasks that are urgent, but not high priority. The NP may not be able to do the tasks as well as the supervisor, but if the supervisor does

not have time to do them, it is better that they be done by a less experienced person than not done at all.

- Delegate tasks relevant to the NP's career development. "Developmental delegation is likely to include special projects that allow a subordinate the opportunity to struggle with a challenging task and exercise initiative and problem solving" (p. 141).
- Delegate tasks of appropriate difficulty. The delegated tasks should be difficult or novel enough so that mistakes are likely to occur, "because mistakes are an integral part of the learning experience. However, the task should not be so difficult and important that mistakes will undermine the subordinate's self-confidence and ruin his or her reputation" (p. 141).
- Delegate both pleasant and unpleasant tasks. If supervisors only delegate onerous or boring tasks, such tasks will not enrich the NP's work life and are likely to reduce job satisfaction. If, however, the supervisor delegates only "fun" activities, NPs may acquire a gap in their development that may impede their career advancement. NPs often need experience dealing with the unpleasant, such as disgruntled parents, and tedious, such as keeping records of staff conferences, because these activities are important even though not fun.
- Delegate tasks not central to the supervisor's role. Tasks that are symbolically important and central to the supervisor's role should never be delegated. These responsibilities include such things as setting objectives and priorities for the work unit, allocating resources among peers or subordinates not directly supervised by the NP, evaluating the performance of peers, making personnel decisions about pay increases and promotion of peers, and directing the unit's response to a crisis.

Establish Goals

Following the assessment of knowledge and skills, supervisors should assist NPs in developing realistic personal and professional goals and goals directly related to job responsibilities. Figure 3.1 illustrates a conceptual framework for thinking about goals in the context of supervision. The basic tenet of synergistic supervision is concern for the accomplishment of institutional mission and the enhancement or enrichment of staff members' personal and professional lives.

The other axis of the figure relates to time frame. For new professionals, the time frames are immediate, near-term, and long-range. For the purposes of this figure, *immediate* may be operationalized as meaning goals to be accomplished, or at least addressed, within days or weeks. For new professionals in their first year on the job, initially these goals may well address things that need to be accomplished before the opening of the institution for

Time Frame	Goal Focus	
	Institution	**Personal and Professional**
Immediate	Maintenance / Aspirational	Maintenance / Aspirational
Near-Term	Maintenance / Aspirational	Maintenance / Aspirational
Long-Range	Maintenance / Aspirational	Maintenance / Aspirational

FIGURE 3.1. Conceptual framework for establishing goals in supervision. Based on DeCoster and Brown (1991).

the fall term or within the first month of the term. *Near-term* is a focus on goals that should be engaged or completed within the current academic term or calendar year. *Long-range* goals are those that require more than a year to accomplish. Following are examples of the types of goals that are intended to more fully explicate the model.

Types of Goals. There are two types of goals within each cell of the model: maintenance and aspirational. *Maintenance goals* relate to the efficient and effective functioning of one or more areas of responsibility. In residence life, a maintenance goal for a NP might be to have 80% of the residents in a hall participate in at least one program or other "nonfood" event during the fall semester. In student activities, a maintenance goal might be that at least 95% of the "scheduled" events in the student center are entered into the computer reservation system at least 24 hours before they take place. These are classified as maintenance goals because they represent achievements that need to be institutionalized or because they are the current norm, which is deemed "good practice." In other words, this is an activity that the supervisor and NP consider important and they want to ensure its perpetuation. All dimensions of an NP's position description are subject to maintenance goals. Through evaluation of past performance and analysis of current problems and issues, the NP and supervisor should identify a few areas that could benefit from close attention. Maintenance goals should then be formulated in those areas. For an NP new to a campus, the supervisor may want to recommend establishing maintenance goals in areas of recent success or in areas that have shown signs of deterioration during the tenure of the previous position holder.

The other category of goals is *aspirational goals.* These goals are associated with a desire to improve, transform, or modify existing practices or to create something new. In the student judiciary office, an aspirational goal for an NP might be to create a weekend retreat for the student justices that fully explicates the student conduct code, explores possible ethical difficulties associated with serving as a justice, and trains the justices in the proper procedures for conducting hearings. This could be aspirational if no such training program currently exists or if the present methods of operating have proved unsatisfactory, requiring substantial changes in structure or objectives.

One can establish both maintenance and aspirational goals in all cells of the model. Supervisors, however, should take care to ensure that NPs do not perceive them as imposing goals. To be effective, goals should be mutually derived.

During the early days of an NP's arrival on campus, focus should be on immediate goals. In other words, most NPs need to be told what needs to be done by what date. After the NPs have become somewhat acclimated to the institution, know the other players, and begin to grasp the culture, they can take a much more active role in selecting and designing goals. They also will be in a better position to begin serious dialogue about near-term and long-range goals.

Focus of Goals.   Goals may be focused on addressing institutional concerns or on personal and professional areas. Institutionally focused goals are directly related to getting the work that is needed at the time done. It may call on the NPs to use skills that they have already developed or may require them to learn new things or to take responsibility for functions with which they have no previous experience. In the latter case, the supervisor needs to assist in orienting or training the NP to a level that he or she can adequately perform the necessary tasks. Throwing NPs into the "deep end of the pool" is as poor a tactic for facilitating professional development as it is for teaching swimming.

Personal and professional goals are more directly focused on the needs of the NP. In the best of circumstances, professional goals and current position responsibilities are congruous. This, however, may not always be the case. NPs, especially in the second and third years in an entry-level position, may have career aspirations or personal goals that are not directly related to their current position. For instance, suppose an NP in residence life desires to move to another area of student affairs; his or her need may be to expand in professional experience beyond housing. Because there are a limited number of mid-level positions, there may not be adequate opportunity for the NP to advance in housing. Or, the NP may want to simply explore other functional areas as a means of broadening her or his area of experience in preparation for a move to a more generalist position. Synergistic supervisors will assist the NP in addressing these kinds of professional goals.

A more delicate matter is addressing personal goals. Generally, most supervisors are reluctant to address areas of an NP's life that are not directly related to job performance; many view attention to personal matters as an invasion of privacy. This is indeed a delicate matter, but in our view, supervisors need to be sensitive to what is happening to the NP on the job and outside of work. He or she should offer an empathic ear and be flexible. As Winston and Creamer (1997, p. 190) wrote: "Fostering personal development requires the supervisor to know what is going on in the lives of those they supervise and to make reasonable accommodation to support staff members in addressing developmental and personal issues." It is essential to respect the NP's desire for privacy, but it is equally important that the supervisor display interest and concern about the NP's personal life and a willingness to assist when asked. If the NP and supervisor begin to establish an open, caring relationship from the day the NP arrives on campus, it will be less difficult for the NP to tell the supervisor to "back off" or to share personal problems and triumphs.

Dalton (1996) underscored the importance of attending to staff members' personal issues: "Personnel issues can be highly deceiving. What appears to be a minor problem can mask a torment of feelings and complexity. Never underestimate an employee's problems. Treat every issue seriously until the nature of it is more fully known" (p. 507).

Integrate Goal Setting, Staff Development, and Performance Appraisal. It is primarily through the goal-setting process that supervision, staff development, and performance appraisal are integrated. Supervisors need to help NPs realistically assess their current level of experience, knowledge, and skills. They also need to help the NP formulate near-term and long-range career and personal goals. Once goals have been formulated, they should be analyzed to determine what skills, experience, and knowledge the NP will need to move up the career ladder and/or to realize a personal goal.

For instance, suppose an NP in residence life has a goal of moving to a mid-level position in student activities. Perhaps the most important thing that the NP will need to do to be competitive for a mid-level position in student activities is to get some work experience in student activities or student-activities-like work. This might be accomplished in a number of ways: (a) the residence life position description could be modified to include working part-time in student activities, or (b) an NP in student activities might want some experience in housing and a job-sharing arrangement could be effected, or (c) position responsibilities in residence life could be changed so that the NP spends more time doing student-activities-like work such as advising student organizations and organizing and managing large-scale programs such as "Diversity Week" or "Welcome Week in the Halls." Judicious appointment of NPs to department/division/institution committees can also be used to further career goals.

By integrating supervision, staff development, and performance appraisal, the needs of the institution can be well met and the institution can also contribute to the staff members' personal and professional growth and assist them in realizing their ambitions. (Staff development is more fully explored in chapter 4, and performance appraisal is dealt with in greater detail in chapter 5.)

Goal Accountability.   One of the most detrimental things that a supervisor can do is to devote time and energy to developing goals with staff and then not hold staff accountable for the accomplishment of those goals. We strongly advise supervisors not to enter into the goal-setting process unless they can make an absolute commitment to following through with staff. Frequently, staff members feel that they are wasting a valuable resource—time—when they devote energy to establishing goals and then work on accomplishing them only to discover that the supervisor has forgotten all about those goals. If supervisors fail to hold staff accountable for the goals they establish, it will be extremely difficult to hold staff accountable for anything else.

Accountability need not be thought of as an attempt to punish or "catch out" staff members who fail to reach goals. Instead, it should be thought of as a means of teaching. Celebrate successes; distribute praise appropriately; with the NP, analyze why some goal accomplishment fell short and assist the NP in learning from the experience.

Transparency and Explicit Values

The most successful supervisors are transparent and explicit about their own and the institution's values. As has been stated repeatedly in this book, establishment of an open, caring relationship between supervisors and those they supervise is an essential first step in implementing synergistic supervision. One of the most destructive forces in the supervisory relationship is a lack of candor and suspicion of ulterior motives. A lack of openness may be motivated by seemly "good" intentions, such as a reluctance to confront unsatisfactory behavior or to critique ideas honestly in order not to disturb relationships or cause ill will. Supervisors who are more concerned about staff members' feelings than they are about fair and honest evaluations of work performance are destined to cycles of crises and/or acceptance of substandard work.

It is absolutely essential that supervisors have the best interests of staff at heart in all interactions. There are times, however, when staff may be called on to make personal sacrifices for the good of the institution or department. When these occasions arise, supervisors need to explain to staff what is required and why. Acknowledge the sacrifices called for; do not attempt to disguise them or to lie about the situation. Generally, staff members will accept disappointment or hardship when they fully understand why. Of course, should these hardships continue for extended periods of time, many staff members may need to find employment at a more stable or nurturing institution. Good supervisors will attempt to assist staff members in making the move; they do not attempt to keep staff in the institution through emotional coercion or deceit.

Values may be thought of as "summaries of our beliefs—catchphrases that explain who we are. They are the backbone of our behaviors, the great simplicities that spring from the deepest wells of our experience" (Young, 1997, p. 3). Supervisors have a moral responsibility to be explicit about the institution's espoused values and, even more importantly, the values that are acted on and actively guide decision processes and treatment of students, faculty, and staff. On almost all campuses there is a disparity between the espoused values and the values that actually hold sway—at least on some occasions. A college may publicly espouse the values of individual freedom and student responsibility, but when a crisis arises (especially if it receives media coverage or influential individuals exert pressure), there may be considerable demand to assume a controlling or in loco parentis relationship with students or to "overlook" or modify established policy. New professionals should not be left to discover these proclivities on their own; supervisors need to openly communicate with staff, including being forthright about how the institution's leadership deals with high-profile, potentially emotion-charged, or divisive issues. New professionals should never be left "holding the bag."

Suspicion by NPs that they will be adversely evaluated because they enforced the institution's policy or acted in good faith in following instructions given by superiors can be highly detrimental to establishing and maintaining open and trusting relationships. New professionals because of their lack of experience may be disillusioned about apparent discrepancies between their idealism and the realities of organizational life. Supervisors can and should help NPs work through these feelings and help them place events in perspective. This advice, however, should not be interpreted to mean that we advocate that supervisors should rationalize away value conflicts or be seen as fighting rear-guard actions to protect institutional leaders.

Changing Work Ethic and Supervision

As noted earlier, when discussing supervisors' perceptions of supervision challenges, there seems to be a widely held view (based on anecdotal evidence alone) that today's new professional in student affairs is different from the previous generation—typically characterized as "lacking a work ethic." There is some evidence from the general population to support this belief (Coupland, 1991; Siegel, 1983; Yankelovich, 1979).

Today's supervisors of new professionals are largely Baby Boomers (born between 1946 and 1962), whereas most of the new professionals are Generation Xers (born between 1965 and 1977). There have always been generational differences, usually with the older generation concluding that the younger generation is "going to hell in a hand basket."

Generalizations about age cohorts must be viewed as stereotypes, which usually have some basis in fact, but which cannot be used with validity to characterize or label any given individual. As is true with most stereotypes, there are many individuals within an age cohort who fit the generalization but a substantial minority do not. The negative stereotypes of Generation X (Gen X) by managers in business include arrogance, disloyalty, short attention spans, and an unwillingness to "pay their dues" (Juriewicz, 2000). This, however, must be understood within the context of the Baby Boomer (Boomers) generation, whose members are today's supervisors. Juriewicz (2000, p. 59) contrasts the interests of Boomers with those of Gen X:

> Boomers are reported to be concerned with retirement issues, while Gen Xers focus on child care. . . . Boomers view Gen Xers as disrespectful of rules and authority, lacking employer loyalty, and scornful of paying dues to move up the ladder. Gen Xers see Boomers as overcautious and hierarchy-worshiping, and overly influenced by their parents' Depression mentality.

Gen X Work Values.   Hays (1999) rather succinctly summarized how Gen Xers view work.

- [Gen Xers] . . . like variety, not doing the same thing from 9 to 5 every day.
- Part of their career goals is to face new challenges and opportunities. It's not all based on money, but on growth and learning.
- They want jobs that are cool, fun, and fulfilling.
- They believe that if they keep growing and learning then that's all the security they need. Advancing their skill-set is their top priority.
- They have a tremendous thirst for knowledge.

- Unlike Baby Boomers who tend to work independently, Gen Xers like to work in a team environment.
- They prefer learning by doing and making mistakes as they go along.
- They're apt to challenge established ways of doing things, reasoning that there's always a better way.
- They want regular, frequent feedback on job performance.
- Career improvement is a blend of life and job balance. (p. 47)

This description of Gen Xers actually seems to embrace characteristics that many in student affairs would applaud. They do differ from the Boomers, but it seems to us that it is more a matter of degree than major substance. For instance, the desire to balance out-of-work life and work is a frequently heard anthem from new professionals. Many Boomers also sought that kind of lifestyle, but perhaps later in their professional lives. Numerous Boomer student affairs professionals were willing to make significant sacrifices in their personal lives during the early years of their careers, devoting long hours to their jobs and frequently foregoing marriage and/or starting a family. Gen Xers seem much less willing to make such a compromise, even for a few years in their early careers.

Gen Xers seem less willing to obediently accept the decisions of those in leadership positions. Boomers may have been willing to hold their tongues in the presence of superiors and to wait until they rose in the hierarchy to press their opinions and beliefs; whereas Gen Xers seek immediate freedom and autonomy to structure their lives and work responsibilities. Gen Xers resent and resist supervisors who guide with too heavy a hand. Such supervisors may well face high turnover rates among new professionals. Gen Xers seem less willing than earlier generations to endure intrusive supervision.

Tulgan (1995) identified a number of nonfinancial rewards that seem to hold motivational power for Gen Xers. They include (a) greater control over their own schedules, (b) exposure to decision makers, (c) the chance to put their names on tangible results or products, (d) clear areas of responsibility, and (e) creative freedom. All of these rewards are well within the control of synergistic supervisors. This also seems to clearly reinforce the importance that supervisors avoid micromanagement. It would seem to us that synergistic supervision is well suited to Gen Xers. Autocratic and laissez-faire styles of supervision (see Winston & Creamer, 1997), however, seem much less likely to produce desirable results with this generation of new professionals.

Money Matters

A popular refrain often heard in higher education is that "one does not go into the field for the money." As a general rule, that is correct; that is, most of the people who are attracted to careers in student affairs are generally motivated by intrinsic rewards such [as] the personal satisfaction of assisting students' development, the esprit de corps of shared achievement, relatively high levels of professional autonomy, and the freedom to exercise their creativity. One should not conclude, however, that extrinsic rewards such as salary, titles, and recognition by supervisors and peers are not important.

It is difficult for many NPs to retain their initial enthusiasm when they compare their salaries and hours worked with those of their former undergraduate classmates who are employed in the business world. When contemporaries make 1.5 to 2.0 times more money, many NPs in student affairs begin to reevaluate their career decisions. This is coupled with the phenomenon found in business settings of the U-shaped relationship between job satisfaction and age. Generally, new workers in all fields enter jobs with unrealistically high expectations, which are seldom met. Job satisfaction then declines, but subsequently increases as expectations are realistically matched with the demands of the position (Avery, 2001; Bourne, 1982). This initial disillusionment also comes at a time in the lives of many NPs when they are considering marriage or committed relationships and starting a family and may also have substantial debts incurred during college and graduate school. One should not be surprised at the relatively large number of NPs who leave the student affairs field after 2 or 3 years for financial reasons.

Money as a Motivator.   Salaries in student affairs, especially during the first half of staff members' careers, rarely will be on a par with similar positions in business. There is little likelihood that this situation will change in the foreseeable future. But because the field is unable to compete head to head or dollar for dollar with business, that does not mean that money is unimportant or does not affect motivation.

Several aspects of monetary compensation need to be understood. Money is rarely an end into itself, but rather it is a means to an end—the ability to purchase and to have a certain kind or level of lifestyle.

First, money means different things to different people. For instance, a $3,000 raise to a person making $35,000 a year means that the person would be able to maintain her or his current lifestyle because the effects of inflation probably have been neutralized. Indeed, such a raise may perhaps provide a slight improvement in buying power. The same raise for a staff member making $25,000 a year could mean a significant improvement in his or her standard of living. But $3,000 for someone making $75,000 per year would be almost unnoticed in terms of standard of living. "Money has the potential to motivate if individuals are seeking to maintain or improve their standard of living" (Rebore, 2001, p. 247). Almost all NPs are seeking to improve their standard of living.

Second, money has symbolic meaning attached to it in this culture. If one receives a raise equivalent to 4% of his or her salary and others receive raises equivalent to 3.5% of their salaries, that carries symbolic meaning, even though the actual dollar differences are minimal (perhaps as little as $700 to $800). In fact, somewhat ironically, the fewer the dollars available for raises, the more significance small differences among individuals may be perceived. In this context, perception means a great deal. In the short run, the amount of money available for salary adjustments based on merit in any given year is unpredictable. In most public institutions, the state of the economy, and thereby tax revenues, and the priority that education is given by political leaders determine the amount of personnel dollars available. In public institutions, a change in the occupant of the governor's chair, the political party in control of the legislature, and economic fluctuations can all contribute to uncertainty about higher education budgets from year to year. In private institutions, fluctuations in enrollment, the state of the economy, and unanticipated expenses—such as abrupt increases in the costs of utilities—make predicting budget revenues difficult. In some years, there may be funds available for very modest or no salary increases.

Staff members who may have performed at exemplary levels or who went well beyond normal expectations cannot be adequately rewarded for their contributions to the unit. (As a general rule, lost raises in one year can seldom be recouped in subsequent years.) Because NPs by definition have a short time frame to view their careers, such situations can be major deterrents to remaining committed to the field or continuing at an institution beyond 1 or 2 years. One should also keep in mind that a year of "no raises" means an actual deterioration in everyone's buying power due to the effects of inflation.

Merit pay systems can be pernicious. For the system to work, some staff members must be judged as performing poorly, at least in comparison to others. Therefore, to have the funds to reward high achievers, some others must receive subpar raises. If one has a poorly performing staff in general, then this is much less problematic. What becomes problematic is when the whole staff has been performing well. To single out some individuals on a team for recognition at the expense of other team members can be destructive to morale and ruinous to the team concept by introducing competition for salary into the system. To give everyone equal raises destroys the concept of merit, and may be prohibited by budget rules designed to force discrimination among staff members.

Compensation systems that do not have merit components are equally problematic. In systems where raises are based on longevity and educational level alone, as is typical in many public school systems and some collective bargaining agreements, the lack of discretionary salary funds denies the supervisor a valuable tool for recognizing extra effort and success. This also makes it difficult to retain talented new professionals in the institution. Schedule-based compensation systems can also lead to establishment of a cadre of mediocre-performing mid-level staff who impede change and act as "wet blankets" to initiatives intended to improve programs and services. As Rebore (2001, p. 247) stated, "If money is to motivate an individual within an organization to greater performance, it must be very clear that such performance is indeed rewarded with more money." Because of the uncertainty about institutional budgets from year to year in many institutions and the lack of merit pay provisions in others, salary adjustments are difficult for NPs to comprehend and frequently do not serve as effective reinforcers for desirable behavior patterns.

Entry-Level Salaries.   When working with new professionals in student affairs, one must remember that as a group they are woefully underpaid. In comparison with professionals in other fields with similar education levels, entry-level positions in student affairs are low-paying. It is difficult to determine exactly how entry-level student affairs staff salaries compare to others. For instance, in the biannual NASPA salary survey, no data were collected about entry-level professionals. Likewise, in the annual report about administrative salaries published in the special "Almanac" section of the *Chronicle of Higher Education* each fall, entry-level positions are not identified—only job titles are specified. Because position titles vary dramatically from institution to institution (an associate dean at an institution of 3,000 may be an entry-level professional, whereas at an institution of 20,000 such a title may be associated with a mid-level practitioner), little can be learned about entry-level salaries.

Understanding how many new professionals view money is important in developing strategies for supervision. Probably one of the least effective things a supervisor can do is to attempt to minimize the importance of money. Even though most new professionals did not enter the field with the expectation of becoming wealthy, they generally expect to afford a comfortable standard of living. Perhaps because many of them have just completed graduate school where they were expected to defer material gratification, it is difficult for NPs to continue with the "promise" of better income in the future. (This is dealt with in greater detail in chapter 5 in performance appraisal.)

Many campuses must find additional funds to raise the starting salaries for entry-level professionals if they expect to be able to attract and retain competent NPs. If that does not happen, supervisors will continue to experience very high turnover rates. In many cases, it may be the most talented and promising NPs who leave the field, which can have ruinous effects on the long-term vitality of the field as a profession.

Planning and Documentation

Good supervision requires careful documentation both as a means of providing structure for new professionals and for assisting staff and supervisors in building careful planning and accountability processes. As mentioned earlier, we strongly advocate that supervisors hold frequent one-on-one sessions with new professionals. These sessions serve multiple purposes, including acting as "guaranteed" occasions that NPs can ask questions and receive feedback about their performance, opportunities for supervisors to share knowledge of the institution and the field, time to share information and analyze the significance of events, and forums for planning work and distributing responsibility.

These individual sessions may not be replaced by the staff meeting. In our opinion, staff meetings serve useful purposes, but have limited value as a means of providing supervision. They are useful for building group cohesiveness and a sense of identification with the unit, sharing information about what individual staff members are doing and planning, making decisions about processes and procedures to follow, comparing notes and observations about happenings or problems, advertising upcoming events, communicating and explaining policies, making announcements, and soliciting assistance with projects or programs. Supervisors might consider if it is necessary to accomplish all these goals in a group setting. Perhaps much of the information sharing that does not require cooperative action could be more efficiently handled electronically.

We offer several suggestions for ways of effectively organizing individual supervision sessions.

- Always have an agenda of topics to be covered. Both the supervisor and staff member should have the privilege of placing items on the agenda. The supervisor can initiate the process or the supervisor and NP can alternate the responsibility. This is easily handled via e-mail.
- Make certain that all topics on the agenda are addressed to everyone's satisfaction.
- Following the meeting, share notes about what was covered, decisions

made, and instructions given. Either the supervisor or staff member can make the first draft of the notes that should be shared and edited until both parties agree as to their accuracy. This can be handled electronically. This is a particularly important way to ensure that all parties have a similar understanding about expectations and responsibilities.
- Make sure to note both successes and examples of good work as well as critiques of mistakes, errors, and miscalculations.
- Keep the notes on file. It may be wise to keep a paper copy to protect against computer failures.

These notes serve many useful purposes. Over time, supervisors have a record of their interactions with NPs and can see trends and patterns of growth. Notes are excellent, accurate sources of information that can be used in performance appraisals. Should it ever become necessary to discharge a staff member, the supervisor will have the necessary documentation to justify the personnel action to the human resources unit and to defend it in court should that be necessary. These notes also can help supervisors evaluate the content and quality of supervision provided. For instance, has the supervisor adequately and consistently offered a balance of praise for good performance and criticism? Is there evidence that the supervision process actually addressed both institutional and personal/professionals goals? Is there a record of goals established and their outcomes? Examining notes in light of these questions can provide valuable feedback to supervisors about their supervision styles.

Supervisor as Mentor

When NPs are asked what they want from their supervisors, many mention that they are looking to those who supervise them also to be their mentors (Winston, 2001a). On the surface that seems a reasonable expectation. Ideally, NPs should have someone whom they can admire, who is knowledgeable about the field, and who is concerned about their welfare. A mentoring relationship, however, entails more than that.

As Schuh and Carlisle (1991) note, mentoring relationships have two intertwined functions or areas: career and psychosocial. Career functions include:

- *Sponsorship.* Serving as a sponsor entails opening doors within the institution by making introductions to decision makers and influential persons and to fellow practitioners beyond the institution, primarily through professional organizations. Sponsors can also assist NPs by helping them become actively involved in professional association committees, commissions, and task forces.

- *Coaching.* This might best be characterized as helping NPs "learn the ropes," through furnishing feedback about performance, providing opportunities for NPs to observe the mentor work and to analyze what was done and why, and having frank discussions about events and their causes and implications.
- *Protection.* Mentors can act as a buffer for protégés from forces outside their control. For instance, mentors can confront institutional authorities who are unhappy or concerned about a facet of the protégé's responsibility by insisting that the novice professional is following the mentor's instructions. "If a problem needs to be addressed, tell *me.*"
- *Exposure.* Protégés can be given opportunities to expand their horizons and to experience things not usually afforded persons with such a short tenure in the field. For example, the protégé may accompany the mentor to a high-level meeting within the institution or a professional association. This provides opportunities to introduce the protégé as a competent professional whose career is accelerating upward and can be an eye-opening, demystifying learning experience for the protégé.
- *Assignment of challenging tasks.* Through the institution or professional organizations, protégés can be assigned tasks that require them to stretch their skill levels beyond what is normally expected of professionals at early stages of their careers. Success can be a powerful boost to a new professional's visibility and career trajectory. On the other hand, it may require considerable time for a NP to recoup from a failure; consequently, mentors need to be careful not to put their protégés into situations for which they do not have the needed skills and experience.

Psychosocial functions of mentors include:

- *Role modeling.* Mentors teach by example. They demonstrate attitudes, skills, and other behaviors associated with being a competent student affairs professional. By allowing close observation and honest discussion, mentors help their protégés vicariously acquire new knowledge and skills and to visualize "success."
- *Counseling.* Mentors make themselves available to discuss problems, ethical dilemmas, professional concerns, and personal problems confidentially. Protégés need to feel that they can discuss anything with their mentors and that the mentors are invested in their being successful and happy. They also need to feel confidence in the advice and guidance mentors offer, being convinced that the mentors have no self-serving interests.

Mentoring relationships require high levels of nonsexual intimacy. Mentors and protégés must self-select each other. Assigning mentors to new professionals has the same chance of success as one would have in assigning new professionals marriage partners. There must be a mutual attraction, and the relationship must be entered into voluntarily. It also requires time to mature. There is no reason to believe that because one is an NP's supervisor that he or she should, or even can, be the NP's mentor.

Problems of Combining Roles. There are several problems that supervisors should consider before undertaking the role and functions of a mentor for someone they directly supervise. First, if the supervisor has responsibility for more than a single professional staff member, there may be problems with the appearance of favoritism. One of the most destructive dynamics in a staff group can be the appearance of unequal treatment (reality does not really matter that much). "Why did Juan get assigned that project rather than me? It was because of Juan's special relationship with the supervisor."

Another consideration is that mentoring can be a time-consuming activity, for which few supervisors can handle more than one or two individuals at a time. Not being available to protégés when needed destroys the efficacy of the mentoring relationship.

Supervisors who undertake the role of mentor for those they supervise run the risk of being caught in a dual relationship. For instance, Tamika is a member of the staff supervised by Maria; Tamika is also Maria's protégé. Tamika has had very little experience working with budgets and that would be a good skill to list on her vita. As the supervisor, Maria must select a staff member to oversee the budget for a new project. Tamika is not the most experienced staff member and is not the only one seeking budget management experience. If the assignment is given to Tamika (no matter how rationally defensible), the decision will be suspect because of Maria's perceived "special relationship" with Tamika. No matter how objective the supervisor attempts to be, decisions involving protégés will frequently be disputable.

Often it becomes difficult for supervisors to evaluate protégés' work performance fairly, especially if they are called upon also to award merit pay increases. Because of the nature of the mentoring process, mentors are predisposed to view their protégé's work favorably. To avoid that problem, there may be a tendency to be overly critical when evaluating protégés.

The mentoring relationship also encounters problems when people cross gender or sexual orientation boundaries. Because of the intimate nature of mentoring relationships, they can become the topic of campus gossip, suspicion, and resentment, which can impede organizational functioning and create awkward social situations. This becomes compounded when a person functions in the dual roles of supervisor and mentor.

There are aspects of mentoring that supervisors can and should provide to those they supervise, such as sponsorship, protection, exposure, coaching, and role modeling. These are important aspects of being a supervisor. (See chapter 1 of this volume and Winston and Creamer, 1997.) Care, however, should be exercised to ensure that these benefits are offered to all staff members supervised, not just a select few. The problematic aspect is the depth and intensity of the personal relationship. Generally, it is much less problematic to serve as a mentor for someone for whom one does not have direct supervisory responsibilities. In many instances, established student affairs professionals are effective mentors for emerging professionals who work at other institutions.

CONCLUSION

In conclusion, supervision of new professionals is a complex and cumulative process. In this chapter, we provided suggestions on the types of issues and interactions that can lead to a positive, synergistic supervisory model as well as to describe the pitfalls that supervisors may wish to avoid. In the end, though, it is a combination of personality and institutional characteristics, coupled with the quantity and quality of interactions between supervisors and NPs, that dictates the success of the supervisory experience.

REFERENCES

Arminio, J., & Creamer, D. G. (2001). What supervisors say about quality supervision. *College Student Affairs Journal, 21*(1), 35–44.

Avery, C. M. (2001). Developing recognition programs for units within student affairs. *College Student Affairs Journal, 21*(1), 64–72.

Bourne, B. (1982). The effects of aging on work satisfaction, performance, and motivation. *Aging and Work: A Journal on Age, Work and Retirement, 5*, 37–47.

Certo, S. C. (1994). *Supervision: Quality and diversity through leadership.* Burr Ridge, IL: Irwin.

Coupland, D. (1991). *Generation X: Tales for an accelerated culture.* New York: St. Martin's Press.

Daddona, M. F. (2001). Hiring student affairs staff with disabilities. *College Student Affairs Journal, 21*(1), 73–81.

Dalton, J. C. (1996). Managing human resources. In S. R. Komives, D. B. Woodard, Jr., & Associates, *Student services: A handbook for the profession* (3rd ed., pp. 494–511). San Francisco: Jossey-Bass.

DeCoster, D. A., & Brown, S. S. (1991). Staff development: Personal and professional education. In T. K. Miller & R. B. Winston, Jr. (Eds.), *Administration and leadership in student affairs: Actualizing student development in higher education* (2nd ed., pp. 563–613). Muncie, IN: Accelerated Development.

Dixon, B. (2001). Student affairs in an increasingly multicultural world. In R. B. Winston, Jr., D. G. Creamer, & T. K. Miller (Eds.), *The professional student affairs administrator: Educator, leader, and manager* (pp. 65–80). New York: Brunner-Routledge.

French, J., & Raven, B. H. (1959). The bases of social power. In D. Cartwright (Ed.), *Studies of social power* (pp. 150–167). Ann Arbor, MI: Institute for Social Research.

Hays, S. (1999). Generation X and the art of reward. *Workforce, 78*(11), 45–48.

Janosik, S. M., & Hirt, J. B. (2001). Resolving conflicts. In R. B. Winston, Jr., D. G. Creamer, & T. K. Miller (Eds.), *The professional student affairs administrator: Educator, leader, and manager* (pp. 269–286). New York: Brunner-Routledge.

Jurkiewicz, C. L. (2000). Generation X and the public employee. *Public Personnel Management, 29*(1), 55–74.

Karsten, M. F. (1994). *Management and gender.* Westport, CT: Quorum Books.

Otto, M. L. (1994). Mentoring: An adult developmental perspective. In M. A. Wunsch (Ed.), *Mentoring revisited: Making an impact on individuals and institutions* (pp. 15–26). New Directions for Teaching and Learning No. 57. San Francisco: Jossey-Bass.

Rebore, R. W. (2001). *Human resources administration in education: A management approach.* Boston: Allyn and Bacon.

Schuh, J. H., & Carlisle, W. (1991). Supervision and evaluation: Selected topics for emerging professionals. In T. K. Miller, R. B. Winston, Jr., & Associates, *Administration and leadership in student affairs: Actualizing student development in higher education* (2nd ed., pp. 495–561). Muncie, IN: Accelerated Development.

Siegel, H. (1983). Work ethic and productivity. In J. Barbash, J. Lampman, R. J. Levitan, & G. Tyler (Eds.), *The work ethic: A critical analysis* (pp. 27–42). Madison, WI: Industrial Relations Research Association.

Strauss, G. (1977). Managerial practices. In J. R. Hackman & J. L. Suttle (Eds.), *Improving life at work* (pp. 101–130). Santa Monica, CA: Goodyear.

Tulgan, B. (1995). *Managing generation X: How to bring out the best in young talent.* New York: Nolo Press.

Weyland, J. (1996). Micromanagement: Outmoded or alive and well? *Management Review, 85*(1), 62–63.

Winston, R. B., Jr. (2001a). *New professionals' views of supervision.* Unpublished document, University of Georgia.

Winston, R. B., Jr. (2001b). *Supervisors of new professionals: Observations about supervision.* Unpublished document, University of Georgia.

Winston, R. B., Jr., & Creamer, D. G. (1997). *Improving staffing practices in student affairs.* San Francisco: Jossey-Bass.

Winston, R. B., Jr., & Creamer, D. G. (2002). Internship supervision: Relationships that promote learning. In D. L. Cooper, S. A. Saunders, R. B. Winston, Jr., J. B. Hirt, D. G. Creamer, & S. M. Janosik, *Learning through supervised practice in student affairs* (pp. 64–96). New York: Brunner-Routledge.

Yankelovich, D. (1979, 6 August). Yankelovich on today's workers. *Industrial Week,* pp. 61–68.

Young, R. B. (1997). *No neutral ground: Standing by the values we prize in higher education.* San Francisco: Jossey-Bass.

Yukl, G. (1998). *Leadership in organizations* (4th ed.). Upper Saddle River, NJ: Prentice Hall.

Chapter 4

PROFESSIONAL DEVELOPMENT

Its Integration with
Supervision Processes

Joan B. Hirt
Roger B. Winston, Jr.

The previous chapters in this book have explained the importance of supervision and the roles that supervisors play in assisting new professionals (NPs) to become successful, contributing members of the student affairs division. We have also discussed the importance of assuring that NPs receive a thorough orientation to the institution, the student affairs division, departments in the division and other units of the institution, and their positions. In chapter 3, we described some of the issues that one should consider in providing daily supervision to NPs and some techniques and strategies that can be used to enhance supervisory practice.

Supervisors might conclude at this point that they had fulfilled their responsibilities and that it is now up to the new professionals to prove their worth. We, however, are of the opinion that still other obligations need to be addressed to provide good, high-quality supervision for new professionals.

Once NPs are fully engaged in their new positions, the supervisor can evaluate whether earlier assessments made when the NPs were candidates were accurate. Of particular interest are the new staff members' skills, knowledge of the field and the functional area for which they were hired, personal maturity, interpersonal skills, work ethic, and professional judgment. These assessments and the actions taken by supervisors and NPs to address any weaknesses form the basis for performance appraisal. Professional development, on the other hand, focuses on actions taken to improve performance.

Professional development is a major link between performance assessment and performance appraisal. When handled well, a good staff development plan can address employee and organizational needs, expand a staff member's professional horizons, and improve both individual and organizational performance. If handled poorly or haphazardly, staff development can become nothing more than a series of trivial activities for employees that squander the individuals' and the organizations' most precious resource—time.

In this chapter, we start by describing four scenarios that reflect some typical NP situations. Then we explore how various scholars have interpreted staff development to arrive at a working definition of the concept. Next, we describe a conceptual model of staff development that can guide professional practice. Suggestions about implementing professional development are offered, along with some caveats about implementing such programs. Finally, the connections between the staff selection, orientation, supervision, and professional development components of the staffing model presented in this book are described, and the link between professional development and performance appraisal, is explored.

FOUR NEW PROFESSIONALS

Consider the following scenarios, which are referred to throughout this chapter in an attempt to mirror supervisors' everyday experiences.

The Case of Jessica

Jessica is a 24-year old, entry-level staff member who reports to you. She graduated with a BA degree in psychology from a small liberal arts school. As an undergraduate, she was a resident assistant and very active in student government. She enrolled in a student affairs master's program immediately after completing her bachelor's degree and served as a graduate assistant in the student activities office while completing her degree. Jessica's skills in working with students are excellent. She relates well to all types of students and has introduced several new programs that are very popular with the undergraduates with whom she works. In her zeal to be creative, however, she has a tendency to overlook some of the basic procedures the department has developed to ensure that major programs are not scheduled on the same day, have sufficient funding, and meet safety and security standards.

The Case of Tarik

Tarik is a new member of your staff who is 27 years old. He graduated from a community college and worked as a lab assistant in a chemical factory for 3 years before returning to school to complete his BA in biology. His original plans included medical school, but while an undergraduate he served as president of his fraternity and of the interfraternity council. Upon graduating, he took a job as a field representative for his fraternity and decided he wanted to pursue a career in student affairs. Tarik has developed exceptionally strong relationships with the students with whom he works. They are candid with him about their successes and concerns. He has clearly defined his role as a student advocate and articulates their concerns exceptionally well. His supervisor has noticed, however, that in voicing the concerns of the students he serves, Tarik can become myopic, only seeing the student perspective on many issues. In his efforts to excel in his areas of responsibility, he has begun to earn a reputation among other student affairs staff members on campus as a "hot shot" who is more concerned with his own agenda than the collective efforts of the staff team.

The Case of Shawn

Shawn is a new member of the staff whose performance has met or exceeded her supervisor's highest expectations. She relates equally well to students, subordinates, and senior-level administrators. She is well organized, attends to detail well, and has taken what once was a less-than-successful program and turned it around in the few short months she has been on campus. The students she serves both respect and admire her and frequently report how delighted they are to have her on staff. Her supervisor's concerns about Shawn are not performance related, per se. Rather, the issue is the degree of challenge she may be finding in her job. Her supervisor is worried that she might become bored and choose to move to another position at the end of the academic year. The unit would very much like to retain her for at least one more year, but there are no other more challenging positions anticipated to be open in the near future.

The Case of Will

Will is also a new staff member. He graduated from a prestigious university with a degree in political science and had originally intended to go to law school. But his involvement as an orientation leader and student government officer as an undergraduate prompted him to go to graduate school in student affairs. He took a position on a campus but his significant other works in a city about two hours away. They plan to wed next summer. Both enjoy hiking and camping and have spent several weekends together away from campus. Will's performance in the few months he has been on staff has been excellent. He is energetic, articulate, well organized, and manages his job responsibilities exceptionally well. Students respect and like him. Recently, however, Will has begun to make comments about whether he can afford to stay in the profession. He is concerned about his fiancée finding a job in the local area and about the demands the profession makes on his time, especially at night. His supervisor thinks he has excellent potential in the field and would like to encourage him to remain in the profession.

These four scenarios although completely fictional, reflect some of the issues that supervisors may face when directing staff. Despite thorough screening, extensive selection procedures, and detailed orientation programs, if supervisors are carefully monitoring the progress of NPs they are probably going to notice weaknesses in their performance that need to be addressed or concerns about the duration of their tenure with the institution. In fact, a good supervisor will look for gaps in the employees' performance so that the supervisor can assist them to become fully functioning and effective practitioners. Good supervision goes beyond providing daily oversight. It requires supervisors to help NPs assess their overall potential—strengths and weaknesses—and to design opportunities for them to take steps in realizing their potential. This ongoing process we refer to as professional development.

DEFINING PROFESSIONAL DEVELOPMENT

The concept of professional development is not unique to those who work in higher education or student affairs. Anywhere from 25% to 50% of practicing professionals in the United States engage in some form of continuing education each year. This includes professionals in architecture, engineering, accounting, law, social work, and health care, and any number of other fields. Indeed, it is estimated that nearly 17% of all people who are employed engage in some form of professional development each year. Many professions require members to participate in development activities to maintain licensure or registry while others simply encourage professional development so that members stay current in their field (Nowlen, 1988).

Professional development experiences can take any number of formats. In some cases, they are classes or seminars. In other instances, ongoing education is offered through individualized programs of study or tutorials. Participating in conferences and executive development programs are standard formats for many professionals. These programs can last anywhere from a few hours or several days, to weekly sessions for several months. They can be non-credit-bearing, credit-bearing, or part of a degree or certification program. The delivery of information can also vary, from live presentations, or film and video approaches, to more recent applications of technology that deliver programs through web pages or interactive teleconferencing (Nowlen, 1988).

Within the higher education arena, even larger numbers of practitioners engage in professional development activities. Winston and Creamer (1997) reported that up to 75% of student affairs professionals attend off-campus workshops, 75% participate in professional conferences or conventions and 20% attend preconference workshops, summer programs, or institutes in any given year. Similar to other professions, these staff development activities assume a variety of formats. Results of their study revealed that 60% of student affairs divisions sponsor social events for staff at least once per year, and most offer programs in which they invite speakers to campus. Institutionally sponsored workshops are also a regular feature on most campuses.

Not only do the form and format of professional development vary widely, definitions of staff development are equally as diverse. Some of these definitions come from outside the arena of higher education and student affairs but are relevant for those in the academy. For Filby (1995), professional development involves collaborative reflection that links theory and experience. It is designed to enable staff to act appropriately in complex situations and promote ongoing learning.

Others assume a broader perspective. They describe staff development as "mechanisms for improving the continuing development of professionals by stimulating demand, through enhancing motivation, increasing flexibility, extending networks, and improving support" (Geale, 1995, p. 6). Definitions that parallel the tenets of holistic education suggest that professional development entails promoting the social, emotional, spiritual, intellectual, and occupational wellness of employees (Hubbard & Atkins, 1995). Those definitions that emerge from organizational theory suggest that staff development involves the convergence of institutional policies, programs, and procedures to support staff so they may fully serve personal and institutional needs (Webb, 1996).

The literature on staff development in higher education and student affairs is somewhat more sparse and sporadic. There was a spate of research on the topic in the late 1960s and early 1970s, as the profession came into its own and numbers of professionals grew rapidly. One thorough discussion was offered by Truitt and Gross (1970), who described 10 characteristics of staff development programs and argued that programs should be related to the objectives of the student affairs division, should address short-term and long-term needs, and should be coordinated by a single person on campus. Many of the characteristics they describe are still relevant today. For example, they suggested that planning development activities should involve staff, should address the needs of staff at varying levels of responsibility, and that the activities themselves should include presentations by staff as well as by outside experts.

Other scholars during this early era focused their attention on the types of programs student affairs practitioners preferred. The most popular forms of in-service training are off-campus workshops or on-campus programs that use outside experts. Less popular formats include on-campus programs featuring on-campus staff and programs sponsored by graduate preparation programs. Interestingly, attending national conferences and conventions was rated relatively low among the preferences of respondents, although participation in such conferences has grown steadily over the years (Miller, 1975). For instance, in 2000 more professionals attended the ACPA and NASPA national conferences than ever in the history of the field.

From the mid-1970s through the 1980s, much of the literature on staff development consisted of articles about successful programs that had been implemented on different campuses. Although interesting, they do not provide reflective, thoughtful research on the topic. However, the 1990s witnessed a resurgence in attention to this important issue. DeCoster and Brown (1991) identified objectives of staff development programs. They argued that such programs should promote interaction among professionals and should be designed to provide staff with cutting-edge information about the profession. There is also a personal component in this model, and the authors suggest that staff development programs should offer an opportunity for self-actualization and professional renewal.

Dalton (1989) also identified the personal nature of the staff development process. He argued that the goals of development programs include benefiting students, enhancing individual performance, and improving institutional performance and his definition of staff development focuses on improving individual performance through a series of purposeful activities.

Although there are many other descriptions of professional development in the literature, perhaps the most thorough and recent review is offered by Winston and Creamer (1997). Their chapter on the role of staff development in the overall issue of staffing practices provides a historical overview of research on the topic and summarizes the common elements of these various perspectives.

Further work by Winston and Creamer (1998) goes a step beyond previous work by describing the fundamental elements of staff development and the connection between development and supervision of NPs. Moreover, this work provides frameworks that can be used to assess developmental needs of staff members and to identify appropriate mechanisms through which to address those needs

What Staff Development is Not

Before examining those common elements, however, it is instructive to consider what professional development does not include. For example, as noted in chapter 3 of this volume, professional development does not typically include the notion of mentoring. Mentoring has been defined in its own right. Some characterize a mentor as a parental figure who is concerned with all aspects of a staff member's life (Levinson, Darrow, Klein, Levinson, & McKee, 1978). Others suggest that mentoring is related more to the availability of effective role models who assist protégés in achieving their career goals (Blackwell, 1989; Dreher & Ash, 1990). Bruce (1995) blends these definitions to identify the three components of mentoring: social support, role modeling, and professional development.

Regardless of definition, there are important distinctions between mentoring and staff development. Mentoring implies a personal, one-on-one relationship between an experienced professional and one who is new to the profession. Although this relationship may foster a staff member's development, it typically goes beyond that to promoting career aspirations and personal interests. Mentoring relationships may not be available to all staff members on a campus. And, as noted in chapter 3 of this volume, it may be unwise for supervisors to attempt to undertake the role of mentor for NPs they directly supervise.

Staff development, on the other hand, is typically a program available to all members of a staff. Supervisors need to be aware of this subtle yet important distinction. Even though they are not expected to be (cannot be) mentors for all the staff members they manage, supervisors are expected to provide opportunities for staff members to broaden their professional experience, acquire new skills, pursue new professional challenges, increase their knowledge base, and expand new personal dimensions and horizons.

Finally, it is important to mention the relationship between professional development and career anchors. *Career anchors* is a term that refers to the different values, motivations, and needs of staff. Schein (1996) has identified eight such anchors. For example, people who value autonomy are likely to be drawn to jobs that allow them to act independently, whereas those who prefer stability may seek positions that promise long-term employment. Other anchors in the model include technical competence, managerial competence, entrepreneurial creativity, dedication to a cause, high challenge, and lifestyle issues (Schein, 1996). Winston and Creamer (1998) offer a thorough description of each of these anchors and provide examples of how each may affect student affairs professionals. As they noted, the notion behind career anchors rests on the assumption that understanding what motivates staff enables supervisors to provide motivators, or anchors, that are more highly valued by employees, thus maximizing productivity and satisfaction.

Again, the distinction between career anchors and professional development needs to be made clear. Supervisors should understand that staff members are motivated by different values, and they may wish to identify what motivates staff. However, providing motivation is only part of a supervisor's role. Staff development, on the other hand, goes beyond merely identifying motivators for staff. It involves identifying areas that need improvement and areas that will benefit the employee's overall professional development.

A Definition of Professional Development

Given this understanding of what does not constitute professional development, then, it is important to examine what the various definitions of staff development have in common and how they can be used to shape the definition of staff development used throughout the remainder of this chapter. First, most scholars seem to concur that staff development programs should be designed to promote individual and organizational effectiveness (Dalton, 1989; DeCoster & Brown, 1991; Nowlen, 1988; Truitt & Gross, 1970; Winston & Creamer, 1997, 1998). Nowlen (1988) also believes that staff development promotes development of a given profession. Additionally, Sanford (1980) has argued that personal development is an important component of any staff development program. Finally, scholars nearly universally suggest that staff development needs to be intentional, purposeful, and integrated into an overall program of support for staff.

These four factors comprise the definition of staff development we employ. Staff development refers to an intentional program of intervention that is designed to improve individual, institutional, professional and personal effectiveness. This program must be linked to individual, organizational, and professional performance standards, and evaluated as part of the performance appraisal procedures. To elaborate on this definition, we offer a model of professional development that might assist supervisors in shaping such programs for the staff they manage.

MODELS OF PROFESSIONAL DEVELOPMENT

There are nearly as many models of professional development programs as there are authors on the topic. Some of these come from the literature outside of higher education and student affairs. Nowlen (1988), writing from the perspective of adult education, describes three groups of models. Update models are those that provide cutting edge information to professionals in short, concise formats. Competence models are broader than update programs and are designed to identify the competencies needed by professionals. These competencies are used to derive a series of development activities to ensure that members of the profession possess the competencies deemed necessary for successful functioning. Professional development programs assigned to the third group, performance models, are designed to consider even a broader array of issues, including institutional culture and practice, life skills, individual and organizational learning skills, and needs for current information.

The apprenticeship model (Kraus, 1996) describes four characteristics of development programs. First, such apprenticeships are grounded in a culture of expert practice that engages participants in problem-solving tasks and reflective practice. Second, programs employ modeling and coaching to promote motivation and learning. The third characteristic relates to collaborative working relationships among participants. Finally, the model rests on providing opportunities for staff to compare not just the outcomes of the program, but the learning processes they experienced while participating in the program.

Other experts have employed what are collectively referred to as reflective professional development models. Three approaches characterize reflective programs. Case methods use case studies as the basis for the program so staff members are exposed to real-life situations that prompt extended problem solving and reflection. Peer-assisted programs rely on a system in which partners are assigned to observe one another, conduct interviews, construct models, and explore alternate ways to address dilemmas they face in daily practice. The third model is based on research efforts by professionals (Filby, 1995).

In the arena of higher education, Boud and McDonald (1981) take a somewhat different approach by identifying three types of professional development programs that are defined by the role the facilitator of the program plays. In professional service programs, the facilitator provides special services like computer-assisted programs or multimedia presentations. In this case, the facilitator serves as an expert and provides technical support. In counseling programs, the facilitator creates conditions that enable participants to explore the nature of their problems and look for solutions to those problems. Collegial programs are those in which the facilitator collaborates with the participants on projects designed to improve practice. Given the advantages and disadvantages of any single approach, Boud and McDonald advocate for an eclectic approach to staff development that employs all three types of programs.

A review of the literature on staff development in higher education also reveals a fascinating discussion of the relationship of current models to biological determinism. Webb (1996) discusses developmental theorists commonly associated with student affairs work and points out the weaknesses in these theories when considered from a staff development perspective. For example, he summarizes the premises of Kohlberg and Perry and suggests that they are based on the "echoes of the Enlightenment's 'good' and rational man" (p. 27). Even Gilligan, another well-known theorist, he suggests, bases her model on an evolutionary endpoint, albeit one that differs from theories normed on men. He argues that we need to view development from a phylogenic perspective, so that development "has no predetermined direction, no preplanned purpose, and no necessary stages along the way" (p. 32).

Winston and Creamer (1998) support most of Webb's (1996) contentions, although perhaps unwittingly. They assert that staff development, although purposeful, is an ongoing and continuously evolving process. Changes in personnel, organizational objectives, and individual interests dictate that staff development efforts be routinely reassessed and redesigned.

Finally, it is important to examine models of professional development offered by those with expertise in the area of student affairs administration. Interestingly, recent models in the literature might be described in terms of the Goldilocks fable—some are too broad while others are too narrow and none seems to fit "just right." For example, Young (1987) identifies three constructs around which to build a comprehensive staff development program. The first construct calls for the supervisor to identify the developmental stage of the staff member (formative, application, or additive). Next, the supervisor identifies the focus of the intervention (staff only, students only, or both students and staff). Finally, the supervisor selects a method of delivering the program (inquiry, application, performance, or instruction). Young suggests that by identifying the appropriate form for each construct, practitioners can design both comprehensive programs of staff development as well as individual developmental activities. But the model does not provide sufficient details on how to appropriately identify these forms, rendering it somewhat vague and difficult to apply.

Another model (Creamer, 1988) is grounded in three assumptions. First, in-service education should be based on individuals who articulate their needs and initiate a process to address those needs. Second, institutions should provide support for those individual initiatives, and third, the institution should adopt methods that will enable individuals to address those needs. The model is theoretically sound, but limited. It focuses only on the notion of staff development to improve individual performance.

In contrast, Burke and Randall (1994) present a model that focuses primarily on organizational needs at the expense of individual development. They juxtapose roles (e.g., staff, supervisors, or senior student affairs officers) against the purposes of staff development (e.g., job opportunities, performance review, or career development programs). Even though they argue that the model serves a number of purposes, including promoting development on a division-wide basis and generating loyalty to the division and institution, the model seems to favor institutional development and the benefits to the individual are somewhat limited.

The model that most closely approximates our assertions in this chapter was designed by Winston and Creamer (1998) who offer both a philosophical rationale for staff development as well as pragmatic suggestions on how to approach development. Again, however, Winston and Creamer focus on personal and institutional development. The definition we suggest for staff development focuses not only on individual and institutional, but on professional and personal development as well.

What is needed, then, is a model of professional development that incorporates all the concepts identified in the definitions of professional development cited previously in this chapter. We suggest that such a model would consist of four components: development in the functional context, development in the institutional context, development in the professional context, and development in the personal context. All four components can be addressed reactively and proactively and all four components can be designed to promote individual and organizational effectiveness. Table 4.1 illustrates the model.

The Functional Context

Functional development refers to individual growth that focuses on improving performance in a specific department or unit. As we suggested at the start of this chapter, a supervisor can use the best search and selection procedures and still not be assured that every employee will perform at expected levels in all areas of responsibility all of the time. Typically, as one begins to provide daily supervision to staff members, he or she will notice some gaps in their performance that may be addressed through development activities within the functional context.

Consider, for example, the scenario involving Jessica. She is not meeting

TABLE 4.1. A Model of Professional Development Activities by Arenas and Approach

Developmental Arena	Reactive Approach	Proactive Approach
Functional	Activities that address NP deficiencies to improve job performance in the unit	Activities that expand NP's knowledge/skills related to the unit
Institutional	Activities that address NP deficiencies and performance at the institutional level	Activities that expand NP's contributions to the institution
Professional	Activities that enable NPs to learn from other professionals	Activities that enable NPs to contribute to the profession
Personal	Activities that enable NPs to address personal concerns	Activities that enable NPs to expand personal interests/ abilities

expectations with respect to notifying others in the department of her plans for major programs. There are many ways the supervisor might address this problem in her performance, ranging from the simple to the more complex. Initially, one might try reminding her of the needs of others in the department to know about programmatic efforts to see if such a discussion influences her behavior in the future. Alternatively, one may suggest that she interview selected staff in the department about the roles they play in programming efforts. The supervisor might also refer her to articles that describe unsuccessful events so that she might examine more objectively the potential implications of her oversights. In all these instances, the supervisor is adopting a reactive approach to development in the functional context. That is, a problem is detected and addressed retroactively.

But functional development can also occur in a proactive manner. Take the scenario related to Shawn, whose performance is excellent but who may not be sufficiently challenged in her position. If the supervisor is interested in providing Shawn with additional challenges, she or he may consider the type of job to which Shawn would logically progress in her next position. Then, together the supervisor and Shawn might design activities that would expose her to the responsibilities such a position might hold. For example, many entry-level staff like Shawn are responsible for managing funds allocated to their areas of responsibility. Managing such funds can teach staff members about the accounting procedures of the department—how to request funds, document expenditures, and reconcile balances. Typically, however, such tasks do not expose the staff member to the budgetary processes of the department—how revenues are generated, how expenditures are estimated, and how revenues are allocated to cover those expenditures. By creating opportunities to involve Shawn in the budgeting process, the supervisor adopts a proactive approach to development and provides her with additional challenges to engage her in work.

These examples are provided to offer a general idea of how supervisors might approach the issue of staff development in the functional context from both a reactive and a proactive perspective. Clearly, any number of other activities could be designed to promote development for either Jessica or Shawn. At issue here is the need for supervisors to understand the notion of staff development in the context of the functional area unit.

The Institutional Context

Although many supervisors are aware of the implications of a staff member's performance at the functional level, it is also important to remember that the department is only one of many administrative units on campus. Professional development, in the definition used here, also refers to improving performance at the institutional level. How can supervisors attend to both departmental/divisional and institutional needs?

Just as synergistic supervision is concerned about both the productivity and welfare of individual staff members and the efficiency and effectiveness of the organization, professional development also may be focused on individuals or on the organization itself. Most of what is generally considered professional development is concentrated on helping individual staff members acquire new skills, modify ineffectual behavior or attitudes, or increase knowledge. That focus is maintained in this chapter as well. However, we also want to mention some kinds of professional development activities that are primarily focused on the organization as the target of intervention and secondarily on individuals. The target may be a functional unit at [a] large institution or the total division. These activities have special relevance for new professionals, because through them they can gain broader experience and can serve career exploration functions for those who are unsettled about the specific career directions they want to pursue.

Social Events.   When Winston and Creamer (1997) conducted case studies of staffing practices of student affairs divisions with reputations for high-quality programs at diverse types of institutions, many of them identified social events as being an important type of professional development activity. Social events, such as holiday parties, summer ice cream socials and picnics, and celebrations of birthdays and service anniversaries can serve several important functions. They can (a) encourage cross-functional/departmental interaction among staff who may not interact regularly (this is particularly important on large campuses where staff may speak to each other on the phone frequently, but never actually meet or on campuses where the student affairs division is the home to widely disparate functions), (b) supplement formal organizational relationships by encouraging formation of informal personal relationships, (c) contribute to development of a sense of identity and affiliation with the larger unit (these events may be the only times everyone in the student affairs division actually sees the whole staff in one place, even on small campuses), (d) promote esprit de corps (especially if the occasions are used to highlight accomplishments or recognize outstanding performance by units and/or individuals), and (e) humanize senior administrators by allowing staff members at all levels to have informal, social interaction with them.

Social events in themselves may accomplish few or none of these objectives, however, unless they are carefully planned to promote interaction among individuals outside their usual work units. In other words, if there is a social event and everyone only talks with her or his usual coworkers, then the event as a professional development activity will have minimal value. Use of ice-breakers and games to promote interaction and break down social barriers should be carefully considered, however. These kinds of activities may be viewed as somewhat threatening by some staff members and as trivializing the event by others. If such activities are used, they should be low threat and short in duration.

For new professionals, these social events can have particular significance because it allows them to broaden their professional networks and to see the institution through lenses different from the ones they encounter daily. These events can also serve as indirect links to the local community and as means of expanding the NPs' professional networks.

Cross-Functional Projects.   Another approach to promoting professional development focused on the organization, which has been used successfully for many years at the University of Tennessee, involves creating activities that cross usual organizational lines. For instance, each year the division could address an important institutional problem or concern, such as racism, low student involvement, alcohol abuse, relationship violence, student attrition, international education, or accommodations for students with disabilities. Using a single issue as a theme, speakers and resource persons could be brought to campus to educate the staff about the issues and possible responses; teams that cut across functional lines could be charged with addressing different aspects of the problem; some staff members could be sent to conferences and workshops that focus on the issue to gather information to share with the whole staff; faculty and other sources of expertise could be recruited to join the effort; and on-campus workshops could be conducted that help staff members acquire new understanding and/or skills. This ap-

proach to professional development has the triple benefits of focusing attention on a critical issue for the institution, bringing together expertise and
resources from varied perspectives, and promoting cooperation within the
student affairs division and integration of the division into the total institution. For this approach to be effective, however, it is crucial that (a) the division sees the issue as important and strategic to the institution, (b) there is a
creditable evaluation component, and (c) teams be held accountable for documenting the results of their efforts. It also is desirable that this activity have
its own budget line; otherwise, units within the division may come to feel
that they are being penalized for participating because part of "their" budgets are being "usurped." This approach can also work for individual departments on campuses that have a large cadre of professional staff, such as
counseling and career centers, housing, and student activities. It is probably
most effective, however, when diverse units are brought together for this
activity.

Due to the complexity and obstinacy to solution of many of these issues, it may be advisable to devote 2 years to a given topic, thereby allowing
for research, planning, skill building, and pilot testing the first year and implementation and evaluation the second year. Two years is also a more realistic
time frame allowing for experimentation and learning from mistakes and
producing measurable results.

Cross-Training. Another useful approach to professional development that
focuses on the organization is cross-training staff in different functional areas or responsibilities within a functional area. This is a particularly valuable
tool for new professionals in their second and third years in a position. It
allows NPs to broaden their area of experience, thus better preparing them
for entry into middle management positions, and creates greater flexibility
for the institution to meet unexpected resignations or priority shifts by having staff on hand who can quickly step in. Cross-training in other functional
areas also introduces novelty into NPs' work. Some institutions that have done
this also report an unanticipated side benefit of creating more congenial relationships between units that have staff members who are cross training.

Team Building. Much of the work that staff are required to do entails cooperative action. Seldom are staff members able to act independently, without
regard for how other members of the unit are doing their work. As a consequence, team building or development is a popular activity in many units.

Reilly and Jones (1974) identified 10 reasons for using team building:

1. Promote a better understanding of members' roles within the unit.
2. Develop a better understanding of the team's role and function in the
   larger organization.

3. Increase communication within the team.
4. Enhance support for members of the team.
5. Increase the team's understanding of group process.
6. Find effective and efficient ways of dealing with tasks and interpersonal problems.
7. Find ways to use conflict constructively.
8. Promote collaboration over competition.
9. Increase the team's effectiveness in dealing with the larger organization.
10. Enhance interdependence among group members.

As Winston and Creamer (1997) pointed out, however, there are several conditions that need to be met for team building to be an effective staffing approach. First and foremost, the activities that the team addresses need to be of a type that requires the involvement of multiple staff members. "It makes no sense to build a team to do work that could be accomplished by an individual" (p. 191) or several independently functioning individuals. Second, there must be opportunities for members of the team to make meaningful, independent decisions that do not require approval by the supervisor. Just because several staff members are needed to accomplish a task does not mean there is a need for team-building strategies. Without considerable freedom and decision making and action, teams are of limited functionality. Third, team building must be directly related to accomplishing work/task goals. Even though improved morale and a friendlier environment may be desirable by-products, they should not be the principal reason for using team building. "Team building and maintenance is not a feel-good prescription. There are less time-consuming and less expensive ways to address interpersonal relationship issues" (p. 191).

Team building can be an effective professional development approach. However, it requires careful conceptualization and skilled implementation. Through the functioning of effective teams, NPs have many informal and formal opportunities to acquire new knowledge and skills and to model the behaviors of successful colleagues.

Conferences.   An effective approach to staff development is through the organization and presentation of professional conferences. For example, the Student Affairs Division at the University of Maryland at College Park (UMCP) has sponsored for a number of years a professional development conference to which practitioners from across the state are invited to participate. The planning and execution is the responsibility of the professional staff at UMCP, which is organized into a structure similar to that used by national professional associations for their conferences. Such an approach has multiple benefits to individuals and the institution, such as allowing NPs to work with established professionals outside their functional areas, requiring the adoption of broad perspectives in looking at the field and contemporary issues, and the educational value of attending and presenting sessions. In the UMCP example, the profession in the whole state also benefits from the opportunity to participate.

TQM/CQI. Use of management approaches such as total quality management (TQM) or continuous quality improvement (CQI) is a systematic way of looking at supervision and professional development. As defined by Bryan (1996), TQM (CQI) in the college setting is:

> a comprehensive philosophy of operation in which community members (a) are committed to . . . [continuous quality improvement (CQI)] and to a common campus vision, set of values, attitudes, and principles; (b) understand that campus processes need constant review to improve services to customers; (c) believe the work of each community member is vital to customer satisfaction; and (d) value input from customers. For TQM to exist in the campus culture, there must be a commitment to CQI and the training and development of faculty, administration, and staff as a team dedicated to customer service. (p. 5)

This approach clearly requires extensive ongoing professional development and training to be effective. As Bryan indicates, however, such an approach needs to be a total institution (at least division) commitment. It is not an approach that can be implemented piecemeal, although some of the concepts, such as Deming's (1986, p. 24) principle of "institute a vigorous program of education and self-improvement," clearly have applicability in many different approaches. One of the most appealing aspects of TQM is its integration of employee training, feedback, and supervision.

Division Committees. On many campuses the division committee structure in student affairs somewhat parallels the institution's governance structure, which typically involves use of cross-disciplinary committees composed of faculty. Many student affairs divisions appoint a number of committees whose membership is drawn from the staff across departmental lines in areas such as professional development, awards and recognition, research and evaluation, and facilities. These committees, if appropriately charged and held accountable, can render effective professional development for their members by requiring them to extend their usual range of activities and to interact cooperatively with numerous segments of the campus that they do not regularly encounter. Without a clear charge and accountability, however, these committees frequently do not produce anything that is valuable to the institution or to their members.

Other Institutional Interventions.   Tarik's scenario is a good example of a staff member who might benefit from other developmental activities at the institutional level. Recall that Tarik is an excellent advocate for students, but at times fails to see perspectives other than those of the students. As a result, he is gaining a reputation among other staff on campus that may not serve him well. As his supervisor, one may want to consider some sort of reactive staff development activities that would assist Tarik in seeing the bigger picture. This may involve asking him to coordinate a program for staff in other units, or talking with those staff members in other units that may be affected by his advocacy role. In either case, the goal would be to improve relations between Tarik and staff in other units, thereby improving both his individual performance and the organization's performance overall.

Development at the institutional level can also be proactive. Take, for example, the case of Will, the new staff member who is questioning whether he should remain in student affairs as a career. As his supervisor who perceives his remarkable potential to contribute to the profession, one might suggest that he spend some time talking with staff in other units to see if the lifestyle issues he is dealing with can be addressed through a position in a different unit. Such a course of action may provide opportunities for Will while simultaneously introducing other staff on campus to a potential colleague. Again, the interests of both the individual and the organization are well served.

The Professional Context

The third component of the model, staff development in the professional context, is one that is frequently overlooked by supervisors. Many supervisors realize the importance of a staff member's performance in the department and appreciate the role a staff member can play on the campus. But it is also incumbent on supervisors to realize the need for the profession to benefit from new staff and for new staff to benefit from professional opportunities. Again, promoting professional development can be reactive or proactive.

Tarik might be a candidate for some activity related to professional development. If the assessment of Tarik's performance suggests that he needs to broaden his perspective on the student issues he handles, perhaps encouraging him to interact with professionals in an association setting might expose him to others who have a broader vision of higher education or student affairs. Tarik might benefit from the wisdom and experience other professionals might offer, whereas other professionals might benefit from the passion that Tarik brings to his job. Both the individual and the profession can be well served through experiences such as this.

Professional development can also take a proactive form. Consider

Shawn, the new staff member who excelled in her position but worried her supervisor who feared she might not be sufficiently challenged in her position. One way to promote individual development might be to encourage Shawn to become more actively involved in a professional association. Serving on an association committee or working on a program outside of her immediate area of responsibility might provide her with the challenge she seeks in her work. It should also expose her to new programming ideas and different perspectives on students' development and interests. At the same time, the profession gains from the expertise that Shawn develops through association involvement.

There are some other considerations when dealing with the issue of development in the professional arena. There are literally hundreds of professional associations at the local, state, regional, national, and international levels. Staff members may have varying needs, interests, and strengths that are better served by different associations. As a general rule, NPs should be encouraged to hold membership in and seek involvement in at least two different kinds of professional associations. The first should be a generalist, broad-based association (such as ACPA and/or NASPA) that provides exposure to the totality of the profession and many of higher education's current issues and problems. The second should relate to a functional area (e.g., Association of College and University Housing Officers-International [ACUHO-I], National Association of Campus Activities [NACA], or the Assocation for Student Judicial Affairs [ASJA]) that focuses on the specifics of practice in specialty areas. State and regional association involvement can also be valuable because NPs have many opportunities to get involved quickly and to assume significant leadership experiences. Other staff may benefit also from affiliating with an organization that is outside their functional area but relates to another professional interest they have.

Membership in professional organizations can be costly from the perspective of a new professional's salary. At institutions that can pay annual dues, we strongly encourage them to do so, especially for NPs. At institutions that cannot pay professional dues because of state law or institutional policy, supervisors should strongly encourage NPs to join professional associations, facilitate their active participation through introductions and release time, and give public recognition for their involvement. We believe that membership in professional associations is an essential element of professionalism for which there is no substitute. From our experience, institutions are almost always beneficiaries of staff involvement in professional organizations both directly and indirectly. Perhaps it does not need to be stated, but supervisors cannot promote professional association involvement if they themselves are not involved. Likewise, they cannot promote involvement if they use a disproportionate amount of resources to support their own involvement at the expense of the involvement of their staff.

Many supervisors are active members of professional associations. Their own experiences with those associations may prompt them to encourage the staff they supervise to affiliate with the same associations. But this may not serve staff members as well as other options. If staff members have interests or need to join organizations with which the supervisor is unaffiliated, the supervisor should help the NP make contact with other staff on the campus or in the state who can help the NP become involved in the appropriate organization.

Appendix F provides a partial listing of just some of the many professional associations in higher education and student affairs. We encourage readers to review this list, and add to it, when considering the issue of staff development in the professional arena.

The Personal Context

The final component of this model focuses on personal development. Interestingly, this component is perhaps the most difficult for supervisors to address, yet it is the component most closely related to the values of higher education and student affairs professionals. One of our historic missions is to take a holistic approach to education—to address not only the intellectual but the social, emotional, spiritual, and physical needs of students. One form of delivering those lessons is through role modeling. If professionals lead well-rounded lives, students are more likely to follow suit. Yet many who work on campuses do not have the kind of balance in their lives that they encourage students to pursue. "Do as I say, not as I do" may not be the most effective approach to promoting personal development.

Addressing personal development is further complicated by some of the proscriptions of supervision. There are fairly clear lines between the personal and the professional realms that we are reluctant to cross. Clearly, it may not be appropriate to question staff members about personal issues if those employees have not volunteered information about their situations. However, it may be equally appropriate to address employee concerns if they have talked about those concerns. In these instances, supervisors can and should consider the issue of personal development.

For example, revisit the scenario of Will, a new staff member struggling to balance his professional interests, his impending wedding, and his love for the outdoors. As his supervisor, one may want to create some developmental activities that allow Will to examine other career opportunities in higher education (e.g., campus recreation, university attorney) that would enable him to blend his varied interests. By encouraging Will to explore other options, the supervisor is promoting Will's individual interests while simultaneously promoting the interests of higher education by suggesting he remain in the larger field.

Personal development also can be addressed proactively. Remember Jessica, the staff member whose inattention to detail was causing some problems for others in the department. Her supervisor may have the opportunity to identify how this lack of attention is impacting her personal life. For example, if Jessica relates stories about missing car payments or forgetting her mother's birthday, her supervisor may have an opportunity to address her personal development proactively. One might encourage her to avail herself of programs or workshops offered by the human resources office or continuing education center on campus that address personal financial management or organizational skills. As she attends to such issues in her personal life, she may also begin to attend to them in her professional life, so the supervisor has addressed both her individual needs and some organizational needs.

In summary, the four components of the staff development model—development in the functional, institutional, professional, and personal contexts—suggest a holistic approach to professional growth. On the surface, the model makes intuitive sense. But is it practical? Models are not very useful unless people know how to use them. So it is important that we suggest a method to use when designing professional development plans.

DESIGNING PROFESSIONAL DEVELOPMENT PLANS

There are four important elements to remember when designing professional development plans with staff members. The first is to recognize the role that staff development plays in the overall model of supervision described in this book. Good staffing practices start with well-constructed search and selection methods, and thorough orientations for new staff. Once this groundwork is laid, effective supervisory practices are required to ensure employee and organizational success. It is through supervisory practices that professional developmental needs can be identified. Once the supervisor has had an opportunity to observe staff members in their jobs and to get to know them on a more personal level, the gaps in their performance can be addressed reactively and their future growth can be addressed proactively through staff development plans.

Second, it is important to remember that professional development plans need to be individualized. What is relevant for one employee may not be relevant to another. Moreover, activities that are successful for one staff member may not have the same affect for another member of the team. It is important to tailor each plan to the individual employee's needs and interests.

Individualizing development plans is closely related to the third important consideration for supervisors: involve staff members in the process. One of the keys to successful supervision is recognizing that staff members have a vested interest in their own success. They may have ideas about how to improve their performance or advance their professional skills that the supervisor might have overlooked. In practice, involving staff in designing their own development plans is not that different from involving students in their own learning, a philosophy widely embraced by those in higher education. If we are committed to engaging students in the learning process, we should be equally committed to engaging staff in their learning process.

Finally, and perhaps most important, it is crucial to remember that professional development plans need to be intentional if they are to result in improved individual and organizational effectiveness. Plans should connect individual and institutional needs to meaningful activities and the outcomes associated with those activities should be evaluated. Sending a staff member to a workshop or a professional conference does not ensure that learning has occurred. Often, staff development activities are disconnected from performance issues. Indeed, more and more frequently staff, particularly entry-level staff, view development opportunities as an entitlement rather than a mechanism to further their education and develop new skills. They inquire about financial support for staff development during interviews and assess job opportunities based on the availability of such support. Professional development plans that are not closely associated with performance issues are likely to result in experiences that have little meaning in the context of the job. Plans that do not include an evaluation component are likely to cost precious time and resources without resulting in improved performance at either the individual or organizational level.

So how can supervisors design professional development plans that are both effective and meaningful? We suggest a four-step approach. Each step should take into consideration the four components of the staff development model: the functional, institutional, professional, and personal contexts (Figure 4.1).

Assess Personal and Professional Skills

The first step in designing robust and powerful professional development plans is to conduct an initial assessment of NPs' strengths and weaknesses. This assessment should be conducted as soon as possible after the NP starts working. We also need to emphasize that the assessment conducted as part of the professional development process is different from the assessment conducted as part of the performance appraisal process. Clearly, staff development and performance appraisal are connected, particularly in our model

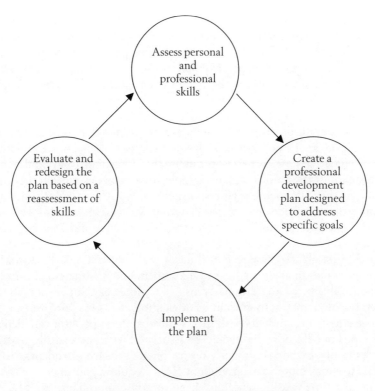

FIGURE 4.1. Designing professional development plans.

of synergistic supervision. Performance appraisal, however, can involve any number of approaches. Indeed, widely varied of performance appraisal processes are described in another chapter of this book.

The appraisal associated with professional development plans, on the other hand, is conducted with the specific intent of using the results to design a staff development plan. The supervisor assesses the areas where staff members are performing well and areas where performance could be improved and/or expanded. The importance of having a direct connection between performance and development cannot be overemphasized. The assessment step of designing a plan also presents an opportunity for supervisors to review the other components of the supervision model: selection, orientation, and evaluation. We recommend that supervisors develop detailed position descriptions prior to conducting selection processes. Each position description should clearly identify the tasks for which the incumbent employee will be held responsible. (See Raetz, 2001, for guidelines on conducting comprehensive position analyses in student affairs.) Moreover, we encourage supervisors to include a thorough review of that position description when orienting new employees to the job. Finally, the model of supervision calls for careful evaluation of employee performance. Two of the documents necessary to enact this model of supervision are the job description and the evaluation form. Both are used in performance appraisal, but both can also be used when conducting an assessment to create a staff development plan.

The position description can serve as a starting point. If well constructed, the position description provides a list of the responsibilities a staff member is expected to assume. Supervisors can use this list as a starting point in their assessment of the employee. For example, a position description may indicate that the staff member is "responsible for assisting students with academic, social, and personal concerns." Other typical responsibilities include "advising student groups" and "serving on departmental and university committees."

At first glance these responsibilities seem fairly straightforward, but when it comes to assessing how well a staff member is meeting his or her responsibilities, some additional steps will be necessary. Supervisors should operationalize each responsibility. For example, to assess how well an employee is assisting students with their concerns, the supervisor can identify the kinds of behaviors that would be associated with successfully assisting students. Staff who (a) promptly return phone calls from students, (b) respond to e-mail inquiries from students, (c) schedule appointments with students in a timely fashion, (d) can diagnose student problems, and (e) can assist students in developing effective strategies to deal with them or can make successful referrals to appropriate campus resources are likely to meet their responsibilities in this area. Likewise, NPs who (a) regularly attend student group meetings, (b) routinely meet with leaders of those groups to discuss issues and plans, (c) provide training for both leaders and group members, (d) educate members about the import of organization activities, and (e) assist organizations in evaluating their programs and activities are likely to succeed in their role as advisors to student groups. In terms of committee service, attending meetings, reporting results of meetings to other staff, volunteering to take responsibility for some activities, and circulating minutes of meetings to keep others informed are all behaviors that might suggest successful fulfillment of these duties. Notice that all these behaviors are activities that supervisors can observe within a month or two after an NP assumes a position. That is, they are behaviors that can be assessed early on in the NP's tenure and hence can serve as the basis for a professional development plan.

The second tool that can be useful in the assessment stage of developing a plan is the evaluation form that guides the employee's performance evaluation. Again, there are any number of performance appraisal methods employed on campuses. It is incumbent on supervisors to become acquainted with the system employed on their campus, and it may behoove supervisors to subsidize that process if it is found to be lacking. In most instances, though, evaluation forms provide criteria around which to evaluate a staff member's performance. Typical criteria on such forms include "relates well to supervisors and subordinates," "meets deadlines," and "is knowledgeable about current issues in the field." Again, the supervisor must translate these expected outcomes into behaviors that can be more readily assessed and assessed early on in the NP's tenure. For example, relating to subordinates may be assessed by student responses on evaluation forms or keeping a log of verbal comments made to the supervisor about the staff member. Relating to supervisors may be measured by the frequency with which the staff member seeks advice from the supervisor and whether those requests are appropriate. Tracking whether the employee submits paperwork in a timely fashion, arrives promptly for meetings and appointments, or asks for extra time to complete tasks may be indicators of the extent to which the NP meets deadlines. Talking about articles in current publications, raising questions about incidents that have occurred on campus or at other institutions, or developing programs about emerging issues may be measures of how current a staff member is with respect to issues in the field.

These two tools (the job description and the evaluation criteria) form the basis of the assessment stage. If they are well constructed and thorough, the supervisor should be able to generate a fairly extensive list of behaviors that can be assessed soon after an employee begins work. If they do not lend themselves to generating this list, it may behoove the supervisor to revise either or both documents so that they can be clearly linked to behaviors.

The next step is to group these behaviors according to the components of the staff development model: functional, institutional, professional, and personal. For example, assisting students with concerns may fall into the functional context, whereas serving on campus committees may reflect the institutional context. Staying current with issues in the field is probably most closely related to the professional context. By assigning each task on the job description and each criterion included in the evaluation to one of the four contexts of the development model, one can create a list of behaviors to assess.

This initial assessment need not be complicated. Indeed, we encourage supervisors to keep it fairly simple and save more elaborate assessments for the performance appraisal of the staff member. Indicating whether the employee "exceeds expectations," "meets expectations," or "does not meet expectations" is probably sufficient. Remember, the purpose of this exercise is to enable the supervisor and the NP to identify those areas where professional development activities may be warranted. To assist the supervisor in conducting this assessment, he or she may need to create a matrix similar to the example in Table 4.2. The four components of the staff development model are listed. Under each component, the relevant job responsibilities or evaluation criteria are listed. Under each responsibility or criterion, the behaviors associated with that task or criterion are listed. Across the top of the matrix, the rating system is described. This enables the supervisor to consider each behavior and rate it. Those behaviors rated as not meeting expectations are clear targets for professional development activities. Others may warrant developmental activities.

Once areas of needed improvement or development have been identified, a short list of personal and/or professional goals needs to be developed jointly by the supervisor and the NP. The goal statements need not be exhaustive or highly technical. The goal statements are to assist in the process of developing professional development plans and identifying criteria for evaluating success. As suggested in chapter 3 of this volume, there should be maintenance goals and aspirational goals related both to current position responsibilities and to professional ambition and aspirations. For example, the assessment in Table 4.2 suggests the NP needs to improve in the area of "knowing resources." The supervisor and NP may elect to identify a maintenance goal with respect to improving performance in this area: The NP will be able to name the resources on campus related to advising by the end of the term and will know the basic functions of each resource. But they may also design an aspirational goal in this area as well: The NP will spend 150 hours over the next year working in an advising office to gain a better understanding of the advising function. Such an aspirational goal would be particularly helpful if the NP aspires to an advising position in the future.

Designing a Professional Development Plan

The design of a staff development plan is crucial if the plan is to result in improved personal, institutional, professional, and personal effectiveness. As noted earlier, the supervisor should involve the NP when developing the plan.

No matter how accurate a supervisor's diagnosis of an NP's needs, unless the NP understands and agrees with the analysis, he or she is unlikely to be committed to pursuing the plan. It will remain the supervisor's plan, which will benefit the NP minimally or not at all. After all, it is the NP who must invest the time and energy in the activities designated on the plan.

A second key to successful plan design is to be creative. There are literally scores of programs and services provided by departments, institutions, local organizations, and professional associations that may be helpful to employees. Activities can range from fairly simple, individual efforts like reading a book, viewing a videotape, or conducting a search for information on

TABLE 4.2. **Staff Development Assessment Matrix**

Context/Responsibility/Behavior	EE	ME	DNME
Functional			
Assist students			
Returns calls	x		
Returns e-mails	x		
Timely appointments		x	
Knows resources			x
Advise student group (name)			
Attends meetings		x	
Meets with leaders		x	
Provides leader training	x		
Provides member training			x
Department committee 1			
Attends meetings	x		
Reports on meetings		x	
Circulates minutes			x
Department committee 2			
Attends meetings		x	
Reports on meetings		x	
Circulates minutes			x
Relates well to supervisors			
Frequency of advice seeking	x		
Appropriate requests for advice	x		
Relates well to subordinates			
Student evaluations		x	
Student comments		x	
Meets deadlines			
Timely paperwork			x
Prompt for meetings/appointments	x		
Completes tasks on time			x
Institutional			
Campus committee 1			
Attends meetings	x		
Reports on meetings		x	
Circulates minutes		x	
Campus committee 2			
Attends meetings		x	
Reports on meetings			x
Circulates minutes			x
Professional			
Knows current issues			
Talks about articles	x		
Raises questions about incidents	x		
Devel. progs. on emerging issues		x	
Personal			
Job for spouse			
Reads local ads			x
Checks with local companies		x	
Maintains outdoor life			
Hikes			x
Camps		x	

Note. EE = exceeds expectations, ME = meets expectations, DNME = does not meet expectations.

the Internet, to more structured activities like attending seminars, classes, workshops, or conferences. When considering professional development activities, one should not limit the possibilities to only formally programmed, group-oriented activities. Some of the most effective professional development choices may be one-on-one activities with the supervisor or other staff member in the department or division. This is especially true when NPs need help in sharpening interpersonal skills or dealing with particularly thorny problems in the work site, such as difficult student paraprofessionals or support staff or student organizations that have developed poor relationships with the institution.

DeCoster and Brown (1991) and Winston and Creamer (1997) offer extensive inventories of activities that may be considered when designing a professional development plan. Supervisors and NPs may wish to consult these resources to ensure that they are considering the widest range of options available.

The third issue to keep in mind when designing a staff development plan is the degree of improvement that is needed or warranted. A staff member who submits paperwork on time but has difficulty meeting deadlines when completing tasks may not benefit from a semester-long class on time management. A short workshop on the topic may suffice, or a plan that keeps the NP's attention on this aspect of the position by reporting on progress during weekly supervision sessions might be all that is required. On the other hand, the NP who consistently asks for more time to complete assignments, whose reports are always submitted after deadlines, and who routinely arrives late for meetings and appointments may truly benefit from an extensive intervention on time management and ongoing attention from the supervisor.

The fourth consideration when designing developmental plans is individualization. Each staff member is unique and has unique skills, needs, and interests. An activity that is effective for one staff member may not have the same effect on another employee. For example, suppose that the staff member who has some trouble meeting deadlines attends a workshop on time management and returns raving about the experience. Subsequently, that employee exhibits marked improvement in meeting deadlines. It might seem reasonable to send another staff member who has trouble with timeliness to the same workshop. But that second staff member may not learn well in workshops and might benefit more from reading a book on time management or independently conducting a series of interviews with those who exhibit strong time management skills. By individualizing each staff member's professional development plan and consulting with each NP when designing those plans, supervisors can tailor activities to meet the unique needs of individuals.

It is also important to keep in mind that staff development can be proactive as well as reactive. Remember the scenario about Shawn, the superior staff member whose supervisor was concerned about providing a sufficient challenge. In Shawn's case, an assessment of performance might reveal that she is meeting or exceeding expectations in all performance areas. Hence, workshops, conferences, or other activities designed to improve performance may not be relevant for Shawn. Earlier, we suggested that Shawn might benefit from becoming actively involved in a professional association and assuming some sort of responsible position within that association. But simply providing her with that opportunity may not be sufficient. It is important that the supervisor establish some standards by which to measure the degree of challenge the activity provides to Shawn and the extent to which individual and professional performance is enhanced as a result of her participation in the association. In short, professional development activities should not be treated as perks for employees who are performing well. Even proactive development activities should be intentional and include an evaluative component to ensure that they are meeting the goals of the plan.

This evaluative component is the final key to designing sound staff development plans. As mentioned earlier, simply attending a workshop or conference does not guarantee that the employee has learned from that experience or will make use of that learning in the near future. For a staff development plan to be successful, the supervisor and staff member should include some sort of evaluative component associated with each activity. Certainly, improved performance might be one indicator of the effectiveness of the developmental activity. But improved performance should not be the only indicator. If a staff member receives coaching on a particular skill, for example, requiring that staff member to submit a written report of what was learned as a result of the coaching might be appropriate. Or, the supervisor might ask the staff member to present a brief report on the coaching at a staff meeting. Another option might include asking the NP to demonstrate the knowledge gained from the coaching by sponsoring a program for other staff or students on the topic of the coaching. In all three instances, the supervisor is asking the staff member to demonstrate that some professionally relevant learning has occurred as a result of the activity. This is really no different from the expectations we hold for students who participate in programs or make use of services. We hope that those students benefit from their experiences in some positive, demonstrable ways. The same is true for staff development activities. Supervisors need to be assured that the activities in which NPs participate lead to some demonstrable learning, and they should incorporate some way of assessing that learning into the development plan.

Once the professional development plan is designed, it is time to implement it. Implementation of staff development plans is the third step in the model, and there are issues to keep in mind when acting on plans.

Implementing the Staff Development Plan

The most thorough staff development plan will be of little use to the individual or the institution if it is not implemented with an equal degree of care. Staff members, particularly those with performance deficiencies, need supervisors to do more than simply identify with them the kinds of activities they can undertake to address their performance. They often need assistance in determining how to carry out those activities. We offer several suggestions to supervisors when implementing professional development plans.

It is important for both the staff member and the supervisor to be realistic. If there are several activities identified in the plan, it may not be feasible for the NP to engage in all those activities as soon as the supervisor and the staff member agree on the plan. Nor is it realistic to assume that performance in a given area will change immediately upon completion of any given activity. Keep in mind that improving performance requires learning. As theories suggest, learning varies from person to person, and it takes time for people to integrate new information into their knowledge base and begin to make use of that information in daily practice. Setting up realistic expectations for accomplishing the activities on the plan enables both the supervisor and the staff member to maintain realistic expectations about the anticipated outcomes associated with that plan. Being realistic also requires both supervisors and staff members to prioritize and balance the activities in the plan. There may be multiple activities in the plan that the supervisor and NP have agreed are important, but for a variety of reasons it may not be feasible for the NP to engage in all the recommended activities at once. In such cases, it is important to prioritize developmental activities. Are there certain performance areas that are more important and therefore should be addressed first? Are there activities on the plan that require longer periods of time (e.g., completing a class) and that therefore should be a priority on the plan? These questions should be answered so that the plan can be implemented in a purposeful fashion.

Prioritizing activities should be a negotiated process between the supervisor and the staff member. Although the supervisor may have an opinion about what areas of performance ought to be addressed most immediately on the plan, it is likely that the NP will also have an opinion about what is most important to address first. At times, supervisor and staff opinions about these priorities may differ. In such cases, it is important to weigh both sides of the issue and provide some balance in the priorities on the plan. Addressing some of the supervisor's priorities and some of the employee's priorities may balance the overall plan to maximize its effectiveness. Keep in mind that it is the NP who must participate in and learn from the activities. If all those activities are imposed on the NP, that person's willingness to actively engage in the staff development process and learn from the targeted activities may be diminished.

Resources. To prioritize and balance activities in the developmental plan, we encourage supervisors to consider three final suggestions, all of which relate to the resources required to conduct the activities identified in the plan. The most obvious of these resources is funding. Although some activities in the plan may be offered at no cost (e.g., workshops offered through a student affairs department or other departments on campus, coaching received from another professional on campus), other activities can be much more expensive. Winston and Creamer (1997) report that only about half of the campuses they studied had budget lines that were dedicated to student affairs staff development activities, and the figure varied considerably by institutional type. If supervisors expect or require new professionals to engage in an activity designed to improve individual or institutional performance, they have an obligation to identify the sources of funding to support staff's activities. This may not always mean that the department covers the full cost of the activity. Indeed, if staff members are going to benefit from the experience, and the experience will make them more marketable for future jobs, it may not be unreasonable to ask them to assume some of the financial responsibility for the experience. But it is important to determine this in consultation with the staff, particularly if the plan calls for staff members to participate in multiple activities that call for extensive financial resources. As noted in chapter 3 of this volume, consistency is important—in both reality and perception. Supervisors are urged to develop clear, widely communicated policies about who receives financial support and under what conditions. The appearance of incongruity between stated policy and individual treatment can cause dissent within a staff group and ultimately hostility toward the supervisor.

Another resource required when implementing a staff development plan is less obvious than financial support, but perhaps equally if not more important—time. It takes time for staff to engage in activities that go beyond their assigned job duties. If one expects a staff member to actively engage in an activity and benefit from that activity, it is crucial that the staff member be provided with adequate time to engage in the learning promoted by that activity. It is usually unreasonable to expect staff to participate in professional development activities above and beyond a full schedule of other responsibilities. Professional development should be identified in the position description; expectations should be established and NPs should be given a reasonable amount of time to accomplish those expectations.

It is important to work with the staff member to identify how to provide that time. Perhaps there are other staff members who can assume some of the NP's duties, or perhaps the supervisor can assume those duties from time to time. Exchange programs, where one staff member covers for another for certain activities and the roles reverse during other activities, are another option. The bottom line is that it is incumbent upon the supervisor to ensure adequate time for staff development activities if those activities are to be effective.

Finally, there may be other resources that one can provide to staff members to assist them in the developmental activities. These may include equipment, tools, facilities or other items that are directly associated with a given activity. These resources are best identified in the planning stage and in consultation with the staff member, but, again, the important point is to recognize that staff members cannot benefit from professional development activities if they are not fully equipped to learn from those activities.

Evaluating and Redesigning the Staff Development Plan

The final step in implementing the staff development plan involves evaluating its effectiveness. If supervisor and NP have carefully designed the plan, this step should be relatively straightforward. It makes use of the matrix developed in assessing the NP's effectiveness and the materials used to create that matrix, specifically, the position description and the performance evaluation form.

The professional development plan was designed to intentionally improve individual, institutional, professional, and personal effectiveness. It targeted certain behaviors that the supervisor and staff member agreed merited improvement. These behaviors were identified on the matrix developed with the NP in the assessment stage. If the supervisor and NP have carefully targeted behaviors on the assessment matrix, then it should be fairly easy to go back to that matrix after the staff member has completed the designated activity to see if performance with respect to that behavior has improved. If the supervisor cannot easily evaluate whether there has been a change in behavior, it may mean that the behavior was not clearly identified on the matrix in the first place. The stages in the model are closely linked—a weakness in one stage will likely result in difficulty completing subsequent stages. If the supervisor was not careful in operationalizing the behaviors associated with each task on the job description or each criterion on the performance evaluation form, it may be difficult to evaluate that behavior after the staff member has engaged in an activity to improve performance.

It is also important to consult with the NP when evaluating the outcomes associated with professional development activities. The staff member's perceptions of what has occurred in terms of performance are indicative of whether genuine learning has taken place as a result of the staff development activity. As mentioned, sometimes it takes time for learning to be integrated into daily behavior. If the NP can articulate the kind of learning that has occurred, that could influence the assessment of the staff member's performance with respect to a certain task. Perhaps the NP has had insufficient time to integrate the learning into routine performance. It is possible the NP knows what needs to be done, and is working on accomplishing that, but has not yet had an opportunity to demonstrate that to others. Talking with staff members is one way to check whether the supervisor's observations of their performance fully reflect their abilities in that area.

Finally, once the supervisor has evaluated the effectiveness of the professional development activities completed by the staff member, it is important to revisit the overall plan and reassess it. If the supervisor and NP prioritized certain activities and those activities have been conducted and have resulted in improved performance, it is time to prioritize the next series of activities. If the staff member's performance has not improved, the supervisor may wish to identify additional activities targeted at that performance area. Additionally, both people and jobs change over time. It is possible that different responsibilities have emerged since the plan was originally designed and those need to be included in the assessment and planning stages of future staff development activities. The important issue here is that professional development is a continuous process. There are always new challenges and opportunities for individuals and institutions. Routinely evaluating and redesigning the staff development plan allows supervisors and employees to ensure that continuous growth and development can occur.

It is essential that supervisors and NPs regularly and realistically communicate about the professional development plan. For most student affairs professionals, that means that it first must get on the calendar; otherwise other responsibilities will push this activity aside. We recommend that supervisors and NPs schedule a meeting specifically to address the professional development plan's implementation once every two months. These dates should be scheduled near the beginning of each academic term.

CAVEATS ABOUT PROFESSIONAL DEVELOPMENT

The importance of professional development is unquestionable. Good development plans can enhance performance at the individual, institutional, professional, and personal levels. But improved performance for multiple constituencies requires supervisors to balance the needs of those constituencies. If developmental activities focus too exclusively on individual performance, improved effectiveness at the institutional or professional level may be sacrificed. If activities focus exclusively on institutional or professional needs, there may be a cost in terms of individual or personal development. Many supervisors have a proclivity to focus on improving or advancing individual performance. But improved individual performance may come at a cost to institutional effectiveness. For example, when NPs are away from campus engaging in professional development activities like conferences and seminars, the work of the unit or the campus can suffer. It is incumbent on supervisors to recognize the need for balance between individual, unit, and institutional effectiveness.

Closely associated with the need for balance is the need to recognize issues of diversity when designing and implementing staff development plans. Characteristics, backgrounds, and experiences prior to assuming their current job shape staff members. Factors such as gender, ethnicity, physical capacity, intellectual ability, religious beliefs, and sexual orientation have all shaped staff and need to be considered when assessing NPs' needs and designing staff development plans with them. Moreover, people learn in different ways. Recognizing and appreciating individual differences, and incorporating those differences into assessing, designing, implementing, and evaluating professional development plans is essential if those plans are to succeed.

This appreciation for differences leads us to a last piece of advice—making sure to address one's own developmental needs at the same time the supervisor addresses the needs of those she or he supervises. Even though it is important to balance individual and institutional needs in the staff development process, it is equally important to balance one's own needs as a supervisor with the needs of staff. Remember that modeling is an important component of supervision. The supervisor can provide that modeling by designing one's own professional development plan and engaging in one's own developmental activities. Indeed, the model we have described in this chapter applies as much to the supervisor as any other staff member. The supervisor can design his or her own plan in consultation with his or her supervisor. At times, consulting with one's staff about supervisory activities that might improve the supervisor's performance can be advantageous when designing plans. It models the process for NPs and suggests that one is equally concerned about his or her own performance as about their performance. Finally, it encourages NPs to learn to address their own needs when they move into supervisory positions.

CONCLUSION

We have stressed the importance of employing intentional developmental activities in one's role as a supervisor. The proposed model is purposefully broad, and designed to remind supervisors that development is important in the functional, institutional, professional, and personal contexts. The suggested steps taken to design, implement, and evaluate professional development plans are intended to provide details about how to address needs in all of those contexts. But staff development alone is not effective if it is not tied to the overall model of supervision presented in this book. It is important to examine staff development in the context of the other components of that model.

First, successful staff development programs depend on the degree to which expectations in the previous stages of the model have been met. In the selection stage, it is important to assess the skills of candidates relative to the requirements of the job and the needs of the institution. The more accurately one assesses these skills, and the more closely these skills match the requirements of the job, the more likely one is to hire a candidate whose performance will meet expectations. The degree to which a candidate meets expectations dictates the degree to which reactive or proactive staff development activities will be needed.

The orientation stage of the synergistic model of supervision is equally important to the issue of staff development. A thorough orientation process can accomplish two things. First, it ensures that the staff member fully understands the responsibilities of the position, the scope of the position, and the role of the position within the departmental and institutional setting. Supervisors cannot expect staff to meet their responsibilities if those responsibilities have not been fully and carefully explained. Second, the orientation stage allows the supervisor some initial assessment information about the new professional's performance. The kinds of questions the NP asks and the issues the NP raises can provide insights into that person's strengths and weaknesses.

These initial assessments can then be carried into the supervision stage of the synergistic supervision model. Good supervision is an essential component of the model and the basis for the professional development component of the model. Through supervisory activities, one can home in on the NP's abilities and compare those with the responsibilities assigned to the position. The assessment of those abilities is directly linked to the needs the supervisor identifies in a staff development plan and the activities he or she creates to address those needs.

Finally, it is critical to remember that staff development is the link in the model that connects supervision to performance appraisal. Performance expectations are reliant upon the talents the staff member brings to the position and the efforts the supervisor makes to expand those talents through intentional professional development activities. If professional development efforts are not part of the evaluation process, they become less meaningful.

Professional development cannot stand alone in staffing practices. It is inextricably linked to the selection, orientation, supervision, and performance evaluation components of our staffing model. We would argue, however, that carefully crafted professional development programs are an essential element of strong overall staffing practices. When planfully implemented and evaluated, professional development activities can result in increased effectiveness at the individual, institutional, professional, and personal levels.

REFERENCES

Blackwell, J. E. (1989). Mentoring: An action strategy for increasing minority faculty. *Academe, 75*, 8–14.

Boud, D., & McDonald, R. (1981). *Educational development through consultancy.* Guilford, England: SRHE.

Bruce, M. A. (1995). Mentoring women doctoral students: What counselor educators can do. *Counselor Education and Supervision, 35,* 139–149.

Bryan, W. A. (1996). What is total quality management? In W. A. Bryan (Ed.), *Total quality management: Applying its principles to student affairs* (pp. 3–15). New Directions for Student Services No. 76. San Francisco: Jossey-Bass.

Burke, T. H., & Randall, K. P. (1994). Developing an organizational commitment to employee success: The student affairs staff development model. *College Student Affairs Journal, 13,* 73–81.

Creamer, D. G. (1988). A model of in-service education: Professional initiative for continuous learning. In R. B. Young & L. V. Moore (Eds.), *The state of the art of professional education and practice* (pp. 62–70). Washington, DC: American College Personnel Association.

Dalton, J. C. (1989). Enhancing staff knowledge and skills. In U. Delworth, G. R. Hanson, & Associates, *Student services: A handbook for the profession* (pp. 533–551). San Francisco: Jossey-Bass.

DeCoster, D. A., & Brown, S. S. (1991). Staff development: Personal and professional education. In T. K. Miller, R. B. Winston, & Associates, *Administration and leadership in student affairs: Actualizing student development in higher education* (2nd ed., pp. 563–613). Muncie, IN: Accelerated Development.

Deming, W. E. (1986). *Out of the crisis.* Cambridge, MA: MIT Center for Advanced Engineering Study.

Dreher, G. F., & Ash, R. A. (1990). A comparative study of mentoring among men and women in managerial, professional and technical positions. *Journal of Applied Psychology, 75,* 539–546.

Filby, N. N. (1995). *Analysis of reflective professional development models.* Washington, DC: Office of Educational Research and Improvement.

Geale, J. (1995). *Achieving growth: Stimulating the demand for continuing professional development among young professionals in north west England.* London: Training, Enterprise, and Education Directorate, Employment Department.

Hubbard, G. T., & Atkins, S. S. (1995). The professor as a person: The role of faculty well-being in faculty development. *Innovative Higher Education, 20,* 117–128.

Kraus, C. M. (1996, April). *Administrative training: What really prepares administrators for the job?* Paper presented at the Annual Meeting of the American Educational Research Association, New York.

Levinson, D. J., Darrow, C., Klein, E., Levinson, M., & McKee, B. (1978). *The seasons of a man's life.* New York: Knopf.

Miller, T. K. (1975). Staff development activities in student affairs programs. *Journal of College Student Personnel, 16,* 258–264.

Nowlen, P. M. (1988). *A new approach to continuing education for business and the professions: The performance model.* New York: Macmillan.

Raetz, T. K. (2001). Job analyses and position descriptions for professional student affairs staff. *College Student Affairs Journal, 21*(1), 26–34.

Reilly, A., & Jones, J. (1974). Team building. In J. Pfeiffer & J. Jones (Eds.), *The 1974 annual handbook for group facilitators* (pp. 227–237). LaJolla, CA: University Associates.

Sanford, N. (1980). *Learning after college.* Orinda, CA: Montaigne.

Schein, E. H. (1996). Career anchors revisited: Implications for career development in the 21st century. *Academy of Management Executive, 10*(4), 80–88.

Truitt, J. W., & Gross, R. A. (1970). In-service education. In O. R. Herron (Ed.), *New dimensions in student personnel administration* (pp. 209–229). Scranton, PA: International Textbook.

Webb, G. (1996). *Understanding staff development.* Bristol, PA: Taylor & Francis.

Winston, R. B., Jr., & Creamer, D. G. (1997). *Improving staffing practices in student affairs.* San Francisco: Jossey-Bass.

Winston, R. B., & Creamer, D. G. (1998). Staff supervision and professional development: An integrated approach. In W. A. Bryan & R. A. Schwartz (Eds.), *Strategies for staff development: Personal and professional education in the 21st century* (pp. 29–42). New Directions for Student Services No. 84. San Francisco: Jossey-Bass.

Young, R. B. (1987). A model of professional education. In L. V. Moore & R. B. Young (Eds.), *Expanding opportunities for professional education* (pp. 19–25). New Directions for Student Services, No. 37. San Francisco: Jossey-Bass.

Chapter 5
PERFORMANCE APPRAISAL
Accountability That Leads to Professional Development

Don G. Creamer
Steven M. Janosik

Setting performance goals, overseeing performance-related activities, performing performance assessments and reviews, and revising performance goal contracts are ongoing responsibilities of supervisors of new professionals. The total process falls under the rubric of *performance appraisal*, which has as its principal purpose the assessment of performance as an approach to improving staff performance (Creamer & Winston, 1999).

PERFORMANCE APPRAISAL AND THE NEW PROFESSIONAL

New professionals must be properly taught or oriented to a culture of collaborative performance evaluation or appraisal. It cannot be assumed that new professionals understand or expect such conditions in the environments in which they work. Many new professionals may come from cultures where evaluation of performance is unidirectional. Professors, based on their individualistic judgments of performance on specific tasks, for example, generally conduct the evaluation of graduate student performance. Further, the professor normally assigns these tasks, and professors possess their own interpretation of the meaning or purpose of the assignment. In this case, the professor is uniquely qualified to judge graduate student performance. Even though examples exist of collaborative evaluations of performance in graduate preparation programs, such as might be required by group assignments supervised by a team of professionals, normally graduate students play minimal roles in establishing the conditions under which they will be judged or evaluated. In the graduate school environment, the unidirectional approach to performance appraisal may be justified, but it seldom is in modern student affairs divisions in the nation's colleges and universities.

The work environment in modern student affairs units or divisions for new professionals should be different from the graduate school culture or, for that matter, from any work environment where human capital is treated casually or with less respect than is demanded in viable teaching/learning environments. Supervisors should involve new professionals in the design of systems under which they will be evaluated. From day one, the relationship between supervisor and staff members should be based on a concept of synergistic supervision as described by Winston and Creamer (1996). In their view (described more fully elsewhere in this volume), supervision should be

- Focused on dual accomplishments of organizational and individual goals (including personal and professional development goals).
- Based on joint effort between staff member(s) and supervisor.
- Sustained in an environment of two-way communication between supervisor and staff member(s).
- Dependent on competence of staff members (not on personal traits alone).
- Centered on a growth orientation.
- Premised on proactivity of individual staff members and their units.
- Established in goal-based contexts for evaluation.
- Reliant on systematic and ongoing processes.
- Directed toward holistic views of people in the organization.

The principal cornerstones of this approach to supervision are duality of purposes and processes, collaboration and mutual trust among all stakeholders, open and ongoing communication, and developmental orientations to the evaluation or appraisal system. Essentially, this approach calls for the establishment of partnerships among staff and supervisors that enable more fully functional operations in student affairs units.

Consistent with this synergistic approach to supervision, new staff members must be taught processes of self-appraisal. If other dimensions of the advocated system of appraisal are to work well, they must be joined by staff member knowledge of self-performance that is trustworthy and that is accounted for in appraisal processes and events. New professionals may not be accustomed to self-appraisal, but they can and must be taught to engage in the process.

New professionals must be fully empowered negotiating partners with supervisors if an effective system of synergistic supervision is to be achieved. To accomplish this partnership status, new professionals must know and be fully confident in their knowledge of how well they are performing. Such knowledge cannot be based solely upon individualistic interpretations of competence and performance; rather, it must be fixed in contextual knowledge of institutional, division, and unit cultures and their established purposes and missions. In other words, the fully empowered staff member is culturally competent (Kuh, Siegel, & Thomas, 2001), and it is from this competency that an empowered partnership status is grounded.

Cultural competence is gained, according to Kuh, Siegel, and Thomas (2001), by "experiencing the campus as well as an on-going process of discovery and rediscovery by which one enhances the capacity for creative, appropriate responses to a new or dynamic environment" (p.55). The culturally competent professional learns to see the campus environment and to act on discoveries, observations, reflections, and evaluations or assessments in ways appropriate to the subjective reality of the environment.

New professionals should be taught to constantly reevaluate their job descriptions and their performance. This ongoing process should be conducted in full cooperation with the supervisor and should become a normal behavior for both. Position requirements change for many reasons and this should not surprise the new professional; rather, the new professional should learn to expect these changes in a dynamic culture filled with emerging needs and demands for performance.

Great pains should be taken to avoid negative consequences of performance appraisal of new professionals. They must not be inculcated into a system of performance appraisal that discourages them or robs them of their pride. Any system that uses scores or ratings may lead staff to conclude that anything below average is failure or anything above average is success. Judgments about performance should be expressed in terms that acknowledge contributions to unit goals and that suggest ways to constantly improve for both personal and institutional benefit. Yet even the notion of constant improvement can hang over the head of staff and diminish their pride. Better approaches to performance appraisal should mobilize pride in quality results and reinforce a sense of strategic membership in the organization.

DEFINING THE PROCESS

Most modern definitions of performance appraisal include an assessment of accomplishments and staff improvement components. For example, Mosley, Megginson, and Pietri (1993) see performance appraisal as a process of empowering and developing people, and they define the concept as "the process used to determine to what extent an employee is performing a job in the way it was intended to be done" (p. 364). Similarly, Schneier and Beatty (1982) see performance appraisal or evaluation as "the process of identifying, measuring, and developing human performance in organizations" (p. 4). Daughtrey and Ricks (1989) characterize the process as "measuring and reporting employee behavior and accomplishments for a given period of time for the purpose of improving job performance" (p. 248). Brown (1988) describes the process as "assessing and recording staff performance for the purpose of making judgments about staff that lead to decisions. Its primary purpose is as a tool for staff development" (p. 6). In all of these definitions, performance appraisal is seen as a process that is ongoing. *Performance appraisal is not a single event, such as completing a standardized performance review form.* It may include this activity but to accomplish the goal of improved staff performance it must include much more. The new professional especially needs the process to be personal and interactive.

This chapter uses the definition of performance appraisal provided by Winston and Creamer (1997), embodying all of these components in the definition of the process. Their definition emphasizes systems thinking about the process and is "an organizational system comprising deliberate processes for determining staff accomplishments to improve staff effectiveness" (p. 244). This definition underscores the ongoing nature of performance appraisal, connects the appraisal processes to organizational functioning, and requires supervisor focus on staff improvement as the primary purpose of performance appraisal—not just salary adjustment or disciplinary action.

UNDERSTANDING THE PROCESS

Supervisors of new professionals must carefully determine their approach to carrying out the essential functions of performance appraisal. Grote (1996) describes a useful model for comprehension of performance appraisal systems. He describes the performance appraisal processes as an appraisal cycle including (a) performance planning, (b) performance execution, (c) performance assessment, (d) performance review, and (e) performance renewal and recontracting. In the performance planning phase, the supervisor and staff member set measurable goals and determine how the goals will be met. The performance execution phase includes five steps for the staff member and six steps for the manager or supervisor.

New Professional's Responsibilities. First, the staff member must commit to goal achievement. Next, performance feedback and coaching are solicited. Open communication on a regular basis with the supervisor is included in this phase, followed by collecting and sharing performance data. The process for the staff member concludes with preparation for the performance reviews. All of these processes call for the new professional to be cognizant of competencies and skills and able to articulate them to the supervisor. The new professional must be open and receptive to input and prepared to process such input in ways that promote further learning and development on the job. The new professional must be ready to hear about his or her performance and to act on information provided.

Supervisor Responsibilities. The supervisor's responsibilities in Grote's model include (a) creating the conditions that generate subordinate motivation, (b) observing and documenting performance, (c) updating and revising initial objectives, performance standards, and job competency areas as conditions change, (d) providing performance feedback and coaching when problems or opportunities arise, (e) providing developmental experiences, and (f) reinforcing effective behavior and progress toward goals. In the performance assessment and review phases, judging of staff member performance occurs, as well as coaching or personally tutoring the staff member through developmental, mentoring, career planning, and recognition activities. Grote's model concludes by recycling the process, beginning with what he calls renewal and recontracting.

Brown's Model for Student Affairs. Brown (1988) sees performance appraisal in a student affairs division as a system of activities that are conscious and deliberate. Variations occur within institutions; however, certain commonalities should exist in all performance appraisal systems:

1. A student affairs staff and management team coordinates development of the system and monitors its effectiveness.
2. A purpose statement links the appraisal system to the student affairs unit's mission and to its organizational style.
3. A behavioral job description derived from an adequate job analysis serves as the basis for setting goals with each staff member.
4. Job standards provide guidelines for determining adequacy of performance.
5. Top management, middle management, and staff support the system.
6. Appraisal tools and procedures are accurate, reliable, and credible.
7. The appraisal process focuses on behavior rather than on personality traits or attitudes.
8. Training programs exist both for staff involved in conducting appraisals and for those appraised.
9. Management and staff engage in an ongoing process of setting goals and providing feedback, rather than depending only on end-of-the-year review sessions.
10. The interview process focuses on problem solving and staff development.
11. The pervasive orientation is that performance appraisal is an educational and developmental process (Brown, 1988, p. 7).

Winston and Creamer Model.   Winston and Creamer (1997) enlarge on both Grote's and Brown's views by demonstrating the application of their staffing model in which performance appraisal is seen as containing eight components or vital concepts essential for a quality system. Their model is based on a core belief that staffing practices in student affairs should attend to both meeting the needs of the organization and facilitating the personal and professional development of staff members. Performance appraisal systems, therefore, should both accurately and fairly evaluate staff performance for the purpose of providing staff members feedback that can increase their contribution to the institution and simultaneously further their effectiveness as members of the student affairs division. This dual purpose of performance appraisal was noted in all definitions of the process. Winston and Creamer caution supervisors about the difficulties of evaluating staff in ways to avoid negative results. This problem is discussed further later in this chapter. This approach is depicted in Figure 5.1.

"Performance appraisal systems are related to the institution's productivity requirements," according to Winston and Creamer (1997, p. 265). In

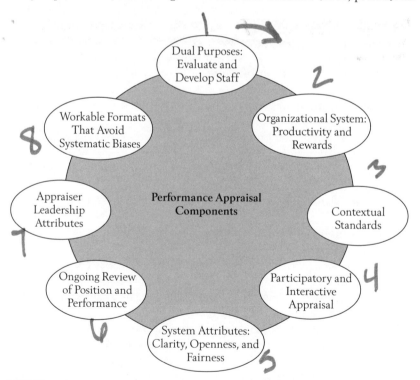

FIGURE 5.1. Performance appraisal components. Adapted from Winston and Creamer (1997) model of staffing practices. Reproduced by permission of Jossey-Bass Publishers.

this aspect of a performance appraisal system, the connection between productivity and rewards are noted. The system is designed to identify underproductive units or people and to address the problems in ways to correct the problems. This is often accomplished by the application of institutional rewards; that is, staff members who perform well are compensated, often in salary adjustments, while the underproducing staff members are requited in other ways such as reassignment, withholding of recognition, and strategic isolation from the unit's most important activities. It must be acknowledged that supervisors who are responsible for performance appraisal in higher education do not always have multiple options to deal with underperformance. They certainly do not have the options available to appraisers in corporate sectors. Still, they can make clear the extent to which they are satisfied with performance and can exercise some authority over institutional recognition and rewards.

The application of contextual standards is the third aspect of the Winston and Creamer approach to performance appraisal. This process refers to the acknowledgment that the nature of a particular position is derived from the context of the organization and its culture. Further, requirements for jobs change over time and often during a particular period of review of the staff member occupying the position. Supervisors also must keep in mind that the performance of an individual sometimes cannot be judged solely on observable manifestations of performance; that is, the effect of the environment may override all that is within the control of the individual staff member. Consider, for example, the difficulties of appraising the work of a fraternity advisor. This professional can directly affect policies and many external manifestations of fraternity conduct, but can hardly be held directly accountable for every instance of irresponsible behavior of fraternity members such as those driven by peer pressure and spontaneous, moblike acts arising from parties (something out of control). Finally, motivations of staff members change, sometimes by the intrusion of major life events or by a realization of an interest for further job-related training or education.

Participatory and interactive appraisal is considered next in the Winston and Creamer model. In this dimension of a quality process of performance appraisal they call for full participation in planning the process to be used by all staff members affected. It is far more likely that an appraisal process will be effective if staff members feel some ownership of or investment in the process. This aspect of performance appraisal leads naturally to the next dimension of a quality process—clarity, openness, and fairness. The agreed-on processes for performance appraisal should be clear. There should be an atmosphere of openness between supervisor and staff member, and the plan for appraisal should be fair to all parties. Beyond the self-evident nature of these conditions, it should be noted that they are anything but simple to create and sustain in a complex organization of any kind, and student affairs organizations are no different in this regard. Thus, great care must be taken to ensure that these system attributes are operational.

In their next dimension of a quality appraisal system, Winston and Creamer call for ongoing review of both positions and the performance of the persons occupying them. The guiding principle in this dimension of the quality model is that there should be no surprises at the "end" of the process. If the processes are operational all of the time, it is unlikely that either supervisor or staff member will be disconcerted by the outcome of the review process. Winston and Creamer also note in their approach that the appraiser should be a leader—that is, someone who can model the behaviors sought from other staff members. This attribute may be especially important for new professionals.

Finally, Winston and Creamer note that a quality performance appraisal system must use workable formats that avoid systematic biases. They make no case for a particular format for carrying out performance appraisal systems. In fact, they acknowledge that any system can be effective if it contains the other elements of their model; however, they alert users to scrupulously avoid formats with built-in biases such as rating all staff members the same, being overly lenient or harsh, or unconsciously practicing racial or gender prejudice.

Using the Winston and Creamer Model with New Professionals

Let us consider a likely scenario in a student affairs division where one midlevel administrator in campus activities employs two new professionals on her staff, both assigned to student organization advising and to campus-wide programming. The administrator, acting as supervisor and performance appraiser, knows that special attention needs to be given to these two new professionals. Both were selected because they possessed the professional competencies needed for the two jobs, and all members of the staff seem enthusiastic about their joining their unit. Although the salaries of the new professionals are not high, they nevertheless represent a significant long-term investment of unit financial resources. The administrator in charge is determined to nurture this investment.

The administrator is careful to thoroughly orient the new professionals to the culture of the unit, the student affairs division, and the institution as a whole. She is especially careful to provide detailed information about several recent events that have caused challenges to the unit's standing within the institution. Serious racial disturbances occurred last year and it is widely felt that staff members of this unit should have handled them better. Additionally, some new programs were added last year dealing with leadership training of organization officers and controversy arose because this program seemed to conflict with an academic program that offers a minor in leadership studies. The administrator of the unit wants the new staff members to be fully knowledgeable of these and other instances, to give them an opportunity to pick up where professionals actions left off last year, rather than allowing them to stumble blindly into emotionally charged cultural "potholes" in the path to full productivity.

The administrator shows the new professionals how to succeed in the unit, both by example and by conceptual plans. Processes used to appraise performance are clearly explained and the new professionals are invited to critique the process until they are in agreement with it. Job expectations are discussed, both from perspectives of the new professionals and from the supervisor. Aspects of the job that are clear and concrete are detailed; all parties agree to aspects that are vague and uncertain and how they will be addressed in ongoing appraisal. Goals for performance are established and agreed to. Plans are made for formal, regular meetings to discuss progress toward achievement of goals, and agreements are reached that informal processes will be practiced on an ongoing basis. The supervisor agrees to constantly teach the new staff members about the institutional culture and to keep them fully apprised to ongoing developments in the institution that may affect work in the unit. Both parties agree to open and candid conversations, in both formal and informal settings, about the work of the new professionals. Likely scenarios of performance appraisal are discussed. Alternatives available and not available to the supervisor are clarified. Groundwork is laid for an ongoing relationship between the staff members and the supervisor that includes knowledge of professional and personal plans and ambitions.

Although the work of the new professionals and of the supervisor throughout the year is hectic and very time-consuming, all parties know that their early agreements must be met. Time must be made to talk about achievements and about frustrations, about motivators and inhibitors, and about surprises that need to be dealt with along the way. Conversations must be open and two-way; judgments must be fair. Records are kept and reviewed as the relationship between new professional and supervisor matures and flourishes.

Thus, the components of the Winston and Creamer model—dual purposes; workable formats; systems-oriented productivity requirements and rewards; appraiser acting as leader; contextual standards being applied; ongoing appraisal; participatory and interactive processes; and clear, open, and fair procedures—are accomplished, not through some rigid application of a textbooklike process, but through an intuitively human and sensible process. Good supervisors and appraisers pay attention to their staff members and they help them achieve their goals in straightforward, nonthreatening, human ways.

Using the Brown Model of Performance Appraisal

Brown (1988) argues that the performance appraisal system should be deliberately and collaboratively constructed. Brown also makes specific suggestions to augment the process. Certain recurring or cyclical events are necessary, for example, and they include

1. Selecting a design team (note the emphasis on team).
2. Setting team goals (if the process is to be collaborative, the goals must be determined by all stakeholders).
3. Tying organizational goals to staff evaluation system (the appraisal process has dual purposes and must meet certain institutional demands as well as individual performance demands).
4. Matching evaluation system to organizational climate (the performance appraisal system must fit the institutional culture).
5. Specifying the purposes of the evaluation system (preferably, the system will focus of institutional and individual development or improvement), which include conducting job analyses (individuals cannot be evaluated well when they occupy positions with unclear purposes) and writing job descriptions (job descriptions must be clear, but they also must be revisited frequently).
6. Setting job standards (be explicit about threshold and aspirational criteria for judging performance), such as those advocated by Winston and Hirt in chapter 3 of this volume.
7. Designing evaluation strategies and tools (note the emphasis on designing these strategies that must fit the situation and the organization culture).
8. Obtaining top management support (appraisal systems tend to be directly connected to institutional-level policy and should be authorized by those representing this level of endorsement).
9. Obtaining staff support (the workability of the system depends largely on the extent to which staff members buy into the process).

One of the serious challenges to applying the Brown model is that most supervisors of new professionals do not have the opportunity to create the performance appraisal system from whole cloth. They must use an existing system that sometimes places specific duties on the appraiser and requires specific processes. Under such conditions, it probably will be necessary to take gradual steps toward the model advocated by Brown. A definite advantage of gradualism is that it gives the appraiser the opportunity to involve all parties in decision in a deliberative manner. Few existing systems leave no room for change or improvement.

STRATEGIES FOR PERFORMANCE APPRAISAL

Several approaches to performance appraisal are reviewed here, although not all are recommended for use with new professionals. The approaches that are recommended include an illustration of the types of performance indicators associated with the method.

Cummings and Schwab (1978) suggest that approaches to performance appraisal can be subsumed under four headings: (a) comparative methods, (b) absolute standards, (c) management by objectives, and (d) direct indexes. This is the approach taken by Sims and Foxley (1980), who borrowed heavily from the Cummings and Schwab categories and methods. Brown's (1988) approach is not much different, although he simplified the categories into ranking approaches, behaviorally anchored rating scales (which he strongly favors), and goal-attainment scales.

Grote (1996), who describes several popular approaches to performance appraisal in three categories, uses a more functionally distinct conceptual scheme: (a) performer-focused appraisals, (b) behavior-based appraisals, and (c) results-focused appraisal techniques. Each of these categories of appraisal methods, approaches, or techniques requires some elaboration and some specific examples to permit full understanding. The elaboration of Grote's appraisal approaches includes approaches and methods described by Cummings and Schwab (1973), Sims and Foxley (1980), and Brown (1988).

Performer-Based Appraisal

Performer-based approaches to performance appraisal normally employ a trait scale. They may include only personal attributes such as honesty, loyalty, cooperation, and adaptability. Such scales answer the question: What type of person is the staff member in the eyes of the evaluator? These scales may be more sophisticated than simply listing personal traits. They can, for example, include performance indicators such as quality of work produced and knowledge and skills indicators such as knowledge of the job, problem-solving ability, and oral and written communications. Such scales also may include managerial or executive abilities such as planning and organizing abilities, exercise of authority, and delegation and control.

Performer-focused methods may employ comparative methods and absolute standards. In the comparative methods, each staff member is compared to all other staff members in some manner. This approach normally focuses on some single global trait, such as overall competence or effectiveness, on which to base the comparisons. These methods may use:

1. Straight ranking (all staff members are ranked from the best performer to the worse).
2. Alternative ranking (staff members are alternatively chosen for being the best and then the poorest performer from a list that is reduced in size by two with each round of ranking until all performers have been ranked).
3. Paired comparison (each staff member is paired with every staff member and the evaluator chooses the best performer from each pair).
4. Forced distribution (the evaluator is forced to assign all staff members to categories such as top 10%, above average 20%, average 40%, below average 20%, and bottom 10% and may employ several traits).

The actual form on which performer-based rating systems are produced can be visualized as a matrix in which the trait to be evaluated (such as "attitude toward work" and "relationship with staff") is displayed vertically and the rating scale (such as excellent, very good, good, fair, and poor) is displayed horizontally. In this approach, each trait may also be assigned a weight; thus, "attitude toward work" might be weighted 4 and "relationship with staff" might be weighted 5.

Even though there may be good reasons to choose a performer-based approach to performance appraisal, there are several apparent weaknesses that should be taken into account. First, these methods generally (with the exception of the forced distribution method) focus on one global trait. To assume that all performance issues can be reduced to one factor may be unrealistic or may disallow valuable, but unconventional, contributions of staff members. Further, such evaluations provide little basis for feedback to staff members about how they might improve their performance. Because they are based on comparisons of one staff member with others, conversations about them may lead to very personal debates and thus lead to ill effects of the appraisal process, such as hurt feelings, poor morale, or a decline in group cohesion. In this situation, a major purpose of performance appraisal—staff development—will be lost. Second, comparisons of different groups within a department may be difficult if ranking techniques are used. The work performed in two units simply may not be easily compared, and one high performer in department A might be a mediocre performer in department B. Third, trait-based performance appraisals may have questionable legal authority. Reliability and validity may be difficult to prove and job relevance difficult to demonstrate. This weakness may be especially problematic when a trait-based form is used in several units with widely varying duties. These methods of performance appraisal are not recommended for use with new professionals. They are reviewed here because they are often found to be widely used and supervisors should know about them and, except for special purposes, avoid them with new professionals.

Behavior-Based Appraisal

Techniques that focus on behavior also normally use a concept called *performance factors* in whatever device is used. They might pertain to managerial performance, such as financial planning, staff development, or achieving quality goals, or other factors, such as staff relations, communications, decision-making, and problem solving.

There are, of course, a variety of methods of evaluating these performance factors. According to Cummings and Schwab (1973), they can be classified into quantitative and qualitative approaches. Quantitative approaches include conventional rating scales and behaviorally anchored rating scales. Qualitative approaches include critical incidents, weighted checklists, and forced choice.

Conventional rating scales are constructed to include several statements about staff member behavior and a continuous or discrete scale is provided for each item. Using the matrix visualization scheme as described earlier for performer-based systems, performance factors (such as "understands department functions" and "uses participative management techniques") might be displayed vertically on a form used to evaluate staff members. Horizontally, the form might include factor response options (such as high, above average, average, below average, and low). See Figure 5.2 for an illustration of this approach.

The behaviorally anchored rating scale approach is strongly favored for use in student affairs divisions by Brown (1988), who reports that these scales use words or phrases to identify the degree to which a behavior or characteristic is present in the person being rated. He explains their use in this manner: "A behavior such as being on time is listed, and raters are asked to indicate on a 1-to-5 scale (where 1 equals 'never' and 5 equals 'always') how frequently

Performance Factors	Performance Rating				
	Low	Below Average	Average	Above Average	High
Understands department functions					
Uses participative techniques					
Engages in long-range planning					

FIGURE 5.2. Illustration of behavior-based appraisal using conventional performance factors.

the individual exhibits that behavior" (p. 29). See Figure 5.3 for illustrations of this approach to performance appraisal.

Developing behaviorally anchored rating scales is not easy, and this is one of their major drawbacks in practice; however, Brown (1988) describes how they should be developed and he portrays a very straightforward process. First, Brown suggests that a team that is preparing the evaluation instruments gather critical incidents. Examples of exceptional, good, average, and poor performance are identified as a part of the process. They might be identified as a part of a brainstorming activity, for example, or during a staff meeting called especially for this purpose. Maintaining logs or having someone shadow a person doing the job under study might also be used to collect the critical incidents.

Next, Brown suggests that the incidents be categorized into what he calls performance dimensions. These dimensions might be staff training, staff supervision, or maintenance in a residence hall position. They might be budgeting, staffing, or programming in a campus activities position. Perhaps the categories already exist on job descriptions, but if not, they need to be created. Within these categories, the team needs to identify behaviors that characterize exceptional to poor performance. The team must match job behaviors within the categories. Conducting a reliability check is the next step, according to Brown (1988). The categories and the job behaviors need to be double-checked. This might be accomplished by asking another group or team to go through the same process as the original team to be sure that there is sufficient agreement on the categories and the levels of performance (such as which behaviors represent good, average, and poor).

Henderson (1980) points out that job performance dimensions or categories for professional positions usually yield similar broad categories including:

- Planning, organizing, and setting priorities.
- Technical knowledge and ability to apply knowledge.
- Proficiency in supervising staff.
- Responsiveness to supervision.
- Proficiency in handling administrative detail.
- Personal commitment.

Perhaps these categories could be used as the framework for categorizing the critical incidents derived from the job behavior descriptions or as a check to decide whether or not the critical incidents are comprehensive. Whatever process is used, a high level of confidence should exist at this point that the correct categories and performance behaviors are identified.

Finally, assigning numerical weights must be completed. Brown (1988) suggests the use of a 5- or 7-point scale where the high point represents ex-

Job Dimension: Uses Collaborative Methods in Meeting Unit Goals	
Rating	Behavior Anchor
5 [ ] Very Good	Develops workable plans for collaboration including timelines and budget and works regularly with others to achieve goals. Gives credit to others for their contributions and provides supportive written materials of the work. Always follows up on agreements.
4 [ ] Good	Plans for collaboration usually carried out. Helps all members of team make meaningful contributions. Experiences some difficulties in full collaboration among identified team members.
3 [ ] Below Average	Has a plan for collaboration, but experiences delays and frustrations with the nature of the collaboration.
2 [ ] Poor	Has no effective plan for collaboration, but expresses interest.
1 [ ] Unacceptable	Show no interest in working with others. Does not seek direction on how to improve.

FIGURE 5.3. Illustration of a behaviorally anchored scale.

cellent performance and the low point represents poor performance. In this form of appraisal, the matrix visualization scheme must be seen in performance categories. For example, one category might be using collaborative methods in accomplishing goals of unit. See Figure 5.3 for an illustration of this approach. Obviously, this same type of scale must be prepared for each performance factor or dimension identified in the developmental phase of the design process.

Grote (1996) takes the behaviorally anchored scale to another level that he calls a behavioral frequency scale. This scale differs from the behaviorally anchored scale in that it does not attempt to label good and bad behaviors in a staff member; rather, it describes the kind of behavior that is sought in staff members and asks how often the behavior occurs.

Using a staff supervision job dimension for an illustration of this approach, Arminio and Creamer (2001) studied successful supervisors who were believed to offer high-quality supervision to their staff members and developed a definition of quality supervision:

> Quality supervision is an educational endeavor focused on the essential functions of the institution: promoting learning and personal development of students. Quality supervision requires (a) synergistic relationships between supervisor and staff members, (b) ubiquitous involvement with and constant nurturing of staff members, (c) dual focus on institutional and individual needs, and (d) a stable and supportive institutional environment to be effective. (Arminio & Creamer, 2001, p. 42)

Job Dimension: Staff Supervision				
Behavior	**Frequency**			
	Always	**Frequently**	**Occasionally**	**Seldom**
Engages in synergistic relationships between supervisor and staff members				
Is ubiquitously involved with and constantly nurtures staff members				
Focuses on institutional and individual needs				
Provides a stable and supportive institutional environment				
Comments/Examples:				

FIGURE 5.4. Illustration of a behavioral frequency scale.

This definition can be converted into a behavior frequency scale, Grote's (1996) preferred approach, such as is shown in Figure 5.4.

Other behaviors, such as accountability, innovation, creativity, and interpersonal skills, could then be added to this instrument using the same format as is suggested for the staff supervision function. The most desirable behaviors in each category would be described, and then an opportunity for a rater to indicate how often the behavior is observed would be provided.

Other behavior-focused appraisal approaches include the use of critical incidents, weighted checklists, and forced-choice methods. Critical-incident approaches involve a process very similar to the behaviorally anchored scales without the weighting component. Weighted-checklist approaches involve a list of performance related statements that are collected and weighted; then each staff member is judged on a scale to indicate the degree to which the statement accurately describes staff member performance. Thus, scale value times performance weight yields a total scale score. See Figure 5.5 for an illustration of this approach.

The forced-choice method provides a list of performance-related statements about job performance that are collected and evaluated for their discrimination value (how well they discriminate among staff) and desirability (how beneficial the factor is to the job description). The discrimination value

Item	Scale Value	Individual Performance
Interprets institutional culture to staff	4	Accurate (3); Mostly Accurate (2); Mostly Inaccurate (1); Inaccurate (0)
Work results are high quality	5	Accurate (3); Mostly Accurate (2); Mostly Inaccurate (1); Inaccurate (0)
Holds high expectations for staff members	5	Accurate (3); Mostly Accurate (2); Mostly Inaccurate (1); Inaccurate (0)

FIGURE 5.5. Illustration of a weighted checklist.

indicates the ease with which each factor differentiates among staff members. The desirability value indicates the importance of the factor to unit or institutional performance. Both the discrimination and desirability values can be determined by consensus among existing staff members. These statements then are placed on an instrument in clusters that differ on discrimination but are similar on desirability and are shown in Figure 5.6. The product of discrimination and desirability value yields a total scale score.

Conventional rating scales are subject to several limitations (Cummings & Schwab, 1973), including errors of leniency, strictness, and central tendency. Evaluator bias can easily infect these types of scales, and they may focus on personality characteristics rather than performance behavior.

Behaviorally anchored scales and behavior frequency scales overcome many of the problems of convention ratings; however, they are challenging and time-consuming to develop. One of their strongest advantages, on the other hand, is their potential for feedback to staff members. The scales themselves address specific behaviors and the staff member can easily see what they are perceived to be doing right and wrong.

The behaviorally anchored scales, behavior-frequency scales, critical-incident methods, weighted checklists, and forced-choice approaches are

Item	Discrimination Value	Desirability Value
Work always is completed on time	4.5	4.8
Maintains excellent relations with staff	3.9	4.5

FIGURE 5.6. Illustration of a forced-choice method based on discrimination value and desirability.

similar in their advantages of discriminating among staff members based on their performance. The forced-choice approach adds a dimension of desirability to the discrimination feature and thus makes it a useful alternative in performance appraisal schemes.

Results-Focused Appraisal Techniques

There are two principal techniques in this type of appraisal—management by objectives (MBO) and accountabilities and measures—according to Grote (1996).

Management by objectives is to a considerable extent a philosophy of management and contains certain core elements that emphasize participation by all members of the organization. Grote (1996) describes these core elements as follows:

- Formation of trusting and open communication throughout the organization.
- Mutual problem solving and negotiations in the establishment of objectives.
- Creation of win–win relationships.
- Organizational rewards and punishments based on job-related performance and achievement.
- Minimal uses of political games, force, and fear.
- Development of a positive, proactive, and challenging organizational climate (Grote, 1996, p. 61).

Grote also delineates the steps in the MBO process:

1. Formulate long-range goals and strategic plans.
2. Develop overall organizational objectives.
3. Establish derivative objectives for major operating units.
4. Set realistic and challenging objectives and standards of performance for members of the organization.
5. Formulate action plans for achieving the stated objectives.
6. Implement the action plan and take corrective action when required to ensure the attainment of objectives.
7. Periodically review performance against established goals and objectives.
8. Appraise overall performance, reinforce behavior, and strengthen motivation. Begin the cycle again (p. 62).

An MBO rating form needs simply to provide space for listing staff member objectives in order of importance and a space for the evaluator to

Objective 1: (State the objective here.)

Accomplishments:

Performance Rating: _____

Objective 2: (State the objective here.)

Accomplishments:

Performance Rating: _____

Objective 3: (State the objective here.)

Accomplishments:

Performance Rating: _____

FIGURE 5.7. Illustration of a management by objectives rating form.

describe the staff member performance using some agreed-on scale for distinguished performance, superior performance, competent performance, provisional performance, and inadequate performance. See Figure 5.7 for an illustration of this method.

The accountabilities and measures approach entails supervisor and staff member agreeing on the accountabilities or performance factors and including them in the position description. Further, this process requires a forecast of performance on the factors to enable quantifiable measures on each. Assuming that the performance factors for a position description could be classified into three categories of administrative, supervisory, and programming, a form might look like the one shown in Figure 5.8.

Results-based approaches to performance appraisal have clear advantages and disadvantages. On the positive side, they produce both short- and long-term results within the confines on the original objectives, generally are perceived to be fair, tend to generate high levels of commitment to the organization, and are defensible in that a high level of participation is involved. On the negative side, they may be overly results oriented, especially in educational organizations, and they may be inflexible. They are not easy to develop or easy to use, and they may not fit all aspects of complex jobs.

Principles Accountabilities	Performance Value (Forecast)
Administrative: 1. Prepares reports in a timely fashion 2. Manages budgets effectively	1. 2.
Supervisory: 1. Creates a climate for high productivity 2. Provides opportunities for staff development	1. 2.

Programming:
1. Provides appropriate educational
    programs
2. Conducts programs that meet the
    needs of diverse clients
	1.
	
	2.

FIGURE 5.8. Illustration of accountabilities and measures approach to appraisal.

Appraisal of Team Performance

Increasingly, units of organizations require their staff to function in teams for part or all of their work. The evaluation of team performance is even more difficult than the evaluation of individual performance, and it also demands application of some of the most viable and difficult to use components of performance appraisal, including collaboration and mutuality.

Appraisal of teams suggests, of course, that the purposes of the team are clearly established and that all members are committed to their achievement. The obvious solution (at least partial solution) to the evaluation of teams is to require the team to develop its performance dimensions or requirements and the method of determining its achievement. Although the team establishes these determinations, supervisors must be involved in their development and become equally committed to their achievement and evaluation.

In some fashion, team appraisal forms might list members on the vertical dimension of a matrix and tasks on the horizontal dimension. Information then would be gathered to fill the cells with indicators of individual accomplishment (perhaps with some indication of mutual dependence with other team members). Collectively, these completed cells reflect the overall accomplishments of the team.

Let's consider an assignment of a team to work collaboratively to assess leadership development initiatives in three administrative units of student affairs. Working with the supervisor(s) in charge, the team should determine its performance goals. For the sake of this illustration, let's assume that the team and its supervisors decide on three goals: (a) measure student learning about self-responsibility in leadership, (b) measure effects of student leader behavior associated with educational leadership initiatives, and (c) measure the effectiveness of processes used in each of the three administrative units. Evidence of the achievement of these goals might be presented in the form of a product (i.e., a way to accomplish the goals) and the process (i.e., the manner of contribution of each team member to the product). A schema to judge the performance of each team member might be devised in the form of a matrix that is shown in Table 5.1. In this scheme, the goals are displayed and each member of the team contributions are detailed. This results in both "objective" evidence (the product) and "subjective" evidence (comments from both team members and supervisors about the processes used and the contributions of each member to the team results).

One of the universal problems of teams is the underproductive member. Any system employed to evaluate teams must be sensitive to individual variations in performance along with overall sensitivities. The identification of individual deficiencies, as well as the determination of what to do about

TABLE 5.1. Performance Evaluation Schema for Collaborative Team

Team Member Name	Team Tasks		
	Measure Student Learning	Measure Effects of Leader Behavior	Measure Effectiveness of Educational Processes Used
Evelyn	Product shown with indications of appropriateness	Product shown with indications of appropriateness	Product shown with indications of appropriateness
	Comments about process:	Comments about process:	Comments about process:
John	Product shown with indications of appropriateness	Product shown with indications of appropriateness	Product shown with indications of appropriateness
	Comments about process:	Comments about process:	Comments about process:
Maureen	Product shown with indications of appropriateness	Product shown with indications of appropriateness	Product shown with indications of appropriateness
	Comments about process:	Comments about process:	Comments about process:

the deficiencies, suggests the constant and efficacious involvement of the team members themselves in the appraisal process. This involvement should include the development of mutually agreed-on approaches between all staff members (team members in this case) and supervisors. The team members might, for example, agree among themselves and with their supervisor on the procedures to be used to complete the assigned tasks and the roles to be played by each member in the processes. They also might agree on leadership roles, that is, who is to do what, in the management of the team and what actions will be taken when one or more members are unsuccessful in their responsibilities. Judgments about success might require agreement on some decision rules to be applied relative to task completion.

Appraisal of Quality Processes

Total quality management (TQM) and other quality-oriented initiatives (Freed, Khugman, & Fife, 1997) remind supervisors that performance is tightly connected to the system or culture in which staff members function. It is unfair, say advocates of quality-oriented approaches to improvement in organization performance, to judge staff members' performance without judging system conditions. Especially in state-supported institutions where bureaucratic rules and procedures are mandated by state agency and institutional policies and procedures, and individual staff member or a team of staff members may be severely restricted in what they can do and cannot do to accomplish assigned tasks. Rules pertaining to fund expenditures are classic examples of such environmental restrictions on individual performance. Student cultures also condition the environment in which student affairs administrators must function. Planned systems of performance appraisal may not match the intended results. Yet, perhaps paradoxically, having a viable performance appraisal system is absolutely essential to a quality staffing operation. We cannot operate without such a system, but we often are disappointed in the outcomes or results. Excellent ideas for promoting student learning and development sometimes are thwarted by low or unformed student motivation.

    The connection between results and rewards also is crucial to performance appraisal. Higher education institutions generally embody strong systems at least for teaching faculty members that suggest practices that will be accepted by supervisors. These reward systems prize activities and behaviors that bring recognition to the institution, such as through research and scholarship (especially if it carries outside funding with it) or through service that promotes the institution's engagement priorities. Such reward systems are not as clear for administrators; thus, efforts should be made to establish them and to enforce them uniformly and fairly to underscore commitment to quality educational practices. Determining the nature of quality educational practices is not easy, but a key to the process is to concentrate on student learning and development as an appropriate outcome of higher education and to distinguish between activities that clearly contribute to student learning and those that do not.

Working Within the Institutional Performance Appraisal System

Almost all performance appraisal systems are based on institutional systems, not on systems developed within the administrative units in which people are employed. Some of these institutional systems may be enlightened and based on the best practices that have been described in this chapter. Others are shallow, perfunctory systems that require ultimately that a form be completed on each staff member by a legitimate supervisor and placed in the staff member's personnel file located in an institutional personnel office. Any system maintained "at a distance" from the unit where staff members work can appear to thwart the development of a dynamic and interactive system such as is recommended by Winston and Creamer (1997). Supervisors of new professionals must not let this condition prevent them from doing the right thing about performance appraisal.

   We recommend some simple steps to overcome apparent difficulties associated with system maintenance far from administrative units:

1. Know the institutional system. Understand its requirements, but observe where latitude is possible. Generally such systems require something basic such as a process that enables a supervisor to complete a form at a prescribed time during the year.
2. Create compatible unit systems of performance appraisal that enable the supervisor to meet minimum expectations of the institution, but that are dynamic and interactive with staff.
3. Be sure that the unit system is focused on the dual goals of institutional and individual development. Institutional development may be linked to multiple layers of administration between the unit in question and the ultimate institutional system. Goals and missions of all of these layers must be attended to in the developed system. Individual development includes both professional development and personal development. Nurture both in the developed system.
4. Be sure that the developed system fits the culture of the unit and its larger cultural affiliations. Such a condition only can be met by creating a system with broad ownership among all staff in the unit—those who can articulate the lived culture, not just the imagined one.

5. Ongoing involvement between supervisor and all staff members should be employed to develop, then maintain, a system of performance appraisal in which there is a high level of ownership based upon participation. New professionals should be involved equally with longer serving professionals.

6. Make the developed system clear and fair. Openness may be a key to achieving these goals.

7. Create a system in which there are no surprises at the end of an evaluation period. The processes agreed on should be of such a nature that concerns about performance are expressed as they are observed. Concerns also should be addressed throughout the evaluation period, not just at the end of a period.

8. Make performance appraisal a regular agenda item on meetings. Priorities of an administrative unit tend to be expressed in the items that appear on meeting agendas. Make performance a regular agenda item. Talk about it regularly and openly. Fix problems in the system as they become obvious.

9. Build into the performance appraisal system a method of evaluation of the system. This evaluation system need not be separate and cumbersome. It might, for example, be achieved by faithfully carrying out the suggestion in item 7. If performance is a regular agenda item, judging the system would be automatic and ongoing. When the system is not achieving its purposes, it could be and should be fixed, and in this environment, repaired by all, thus creating a new level of ownership and commitment by all staff members.

Making Performance Appraisal Positive

As reported by Winston and Creamer (1997) and by others such as Blackburn and Pitney (1988), most performance appraisal systems lead to negative consequences, such as lower morale, reduced productivity, and commitment of staff members. The evidence of these results is compelling; yet there are ways to overcome such consequences. We recommend at least the following for supervisors of new professionals especially:

 1. Developing a workable, effective, and positive system of performance appraisal is largely a function of will. There are no magic bullets. No idealized system will work in every situation. Supervisors must want to create positive systems and must be willing to work constantly to make their systems work.

 2. Performance appraisal should be treated as if the issue were student learning. In this case, however, the issue is staff learning, but the processes and

the desired outcomes are the same. Teachers design teaching/learning environments specifically to promote student learning; supervisors should do the same—that is, design a teaching system (in this case understanding performance) that will result in staff members learning about themselves and their contributions to the unit and its objectives. If the developed system depends on self-assessment, then the system should teach these skills. If the developed system depends on performance behaviors, then the system should teach these processes to all staff members in the unit.

3. Performance appraisal systems that mirror the culture of the unit are much more likely to be positive and to produce learning than systems abstractly designed and remotely administered. Thus, the system should be constantly judged by its cultural affinity.

4. Performance appraisal should be routine. Everyone should expect it on an ongoing basis and should regularly participate in it. Remember: No surprises.

5. The most effective systems of performance appraisal are well integrated into other staffing systems, such as supervision itself and staff development. The staffing components of supervision, staff development, and performance appraisal should be so well integrated that members of the unit should express surprise when questioned about the processes separately. These three components must function as one.

6. Like other educational activities, performance appraisal works best when functioning from a plan. The plan should be obvious and should be created and maintained by all members of the unit. Staff development, for example, should be a logical consequence of ongoing supervision and performance appraisal.

7. Records should be kept that accurately reflect the judgments of supervisors and staff members about performance. Genuineness should guide these records. Neither gloss nor fluff should be included. Accuracy of perceptions is to be expected to the extent that any involved party would read these records and say, "Yes. That is what we concluded about the incidents being observed."

8. Performance appraisal must be real and it must be flexible. Everyone in the system must know that no games are being played and that the processes are not just related to fulfilling the requirements of an institutional system. They must know and feel that the local system is about them and their future in the unit. As a real, lived experience, the system also must flexible. Things happen within complex units that change the playing field and the rules. Things also happen in the lives of staff members that change their perspective on their jobs. All of these contingencies must be "on the table" for discussion and for action when the need arises.

9. Guard against all systematic biases.

When Performance is Not Satisfactory

Even in the best of staffing systems where supervision, staff development, and performance appraisal are well integrated and meet all of the requirements suggested in this and other chapters in this volume, some individuals may not perform up to expectation or to standard. Let's revisit two of the scenarios used in previous chapters.

Despite the supervisor's nurturing, coaching, supervising, and support for additional skills development, suppose Jessica fails to improve on meeting deadlines and her failure to follow procedures start to jeopardize the effectiveness of the department. Or in the case of Tarik, what if his desire to advocate for students becomes so strident that he creates a working environment where administrators in other offices no longer wish to cooperate with the department? Sometimes individuals do not adopt the behaviors that are required to be successful and must be involuntarily separated from the unit and possibly from the institution.

When involuntary separation is necessary, certain aspects of the performance appraisal system will be illuminated. They must stand the scrutiny to law, ethics, and institutional standards. If supervisors adopt the practices recommended in this volume, they would in most cases have fulfilled their obligation to the poorly performing staff member and to their institution. Feedback on the performance leading to termination would have been accurately documented and discussed on more than one occasion. The staff member would have received specific feedback on how to improve performance and given the opportunity to do so. Again, there would be no surprises. But in addition to these sound practices, supervisors planning to terminate a staff member must also remember the following:

1. At a minimum, terminations should be joint decisions between the immediate supervisor and the appropriate staff member at the next highest level of the organization.
2. Before a final decision is made, all documentation surrounding the staff member's unsatisfactory performance should be reviewed for accuracy and bias.
3. The policies related to employee termination and any relevant stipulations in the employment contract or the letter of appointment should be reviewed and followed with the utmost care.
4. Other appropriate staff should be consulted. Institutional policy, for example, may require the involvement of legal counsel or representatives from the office of human relations.
5. Once the decision is made, the termination notice must be prepared in writing and reviewed and approved by those required to authorize such action.

6. Care should be taken to deliver such a notice both verbally and in writing in the most humanistic manner possible.
7. Responses to questions and challenges from the staff member being notified should be anticipated. Although we would hope it not so, remember that if the staff member has not responded positively to previous efforts to improve performance, it is also likely that the staff member will not respond well to the notice of termination.
8. The staff member's right to confidentiality and expectation of privacy, as determined by state law and institutional policy, must be preserved.
9. Plans for the staff member's departure from assigned office space, the department, and the campus should be made.
10. Responses to the questions and rumors from other staff that will eventually come also should be anticipated.

Obviously, terminating a staff member at any level of an organization is a difficult task, both administratively and emotionally. It is also an extremely complex task. To meet the legal, ethical, and institutional requirements of such a decision, careful planning is essential.

SUMMARY

Performance appraisal involves the assessment of human performance and the intentional effort to improve individuals and the organization. New professionals especially need to understand the vital role of performance appraisal in their careers and that it is best carried out in partnership with their supervisor. Supervisors owe all staff members, but especially new professionals, quality engagement in judgments about their performance. It should be a dynamic and collaborative arrangement wherein new professionals are involved from the beginning with their supervisors to assess their position requirements and to plan for assessment of their individual or team performance.

There are many performance appraisal systems and potentially any system can be made to work; however, it is most likely that systems will be effective if they include dual purposes of individual and organization improvement and are participative and collaborative in nature. These systems are more likely to be fair and open and to focus on behaviors rather than personalities or even results.

Performance appraisal systems should not be rigid or overly bureaucratic. They should be flexible, adaptable, supple, and sensitive to the fact that invaluable people and their lives and careers are at stake. All effective performance appraisal systems require enormous work by the supervisor and staff member alike.

Winston and Creamer (1997) have pointed out that performance appraisal as it is currently practiced is the least effective component of student affairs staffing practices. It need not remain so if certain principles articulated in this chapter are followed sensibly. It certainly should not be so where new professionals are concerned. They should be carefully nurtured by wise and caring supervisors and inculcated from the beginning of their relationship with the institution to be a vital part of a synergistic relationship with colleagues, supervisors, and institutional culture. When these conditions exist, performance appraisal collaboratively designed and executed will work for the benefit of staff and organization.

REFERENCES

Arminio, J., & Creamer, D. G. (2001). What quality supervisors say about quality supervision. *College Student Affairs Journal, 21*(1), 35–44.

Blackburn, R. T., & Pitney, J. A. (1988). *Performance appaisal for faculty: Implications for higher education* (Tech. Rep. No. 88-D-002.0). Ann Arbor, MI: School of Education, University of Michigan. (ERIC Document Reproduction Service No. ED 316 066)

Brown, R. D. (1988). *Performance appraisal as a tool for staff development.* New Directions for Student Services No. 43. San Francisco: Jossey-Bass.

Creamer, D. G., & Winston, R. B., Jr. (1999). The performance appraisal paradox: An essential but neglected student affairs staffing function. *NASPA Journal, 36,* 248–263.

Cummings, L. L., & Schwab, D. P. (1973). *Performance in organizations: Determinants and appraisal.* Glenview, IL: Scott, Foresman.

Daughtrey, A. S., & Ricks, B. R. (1988). *Contemporary supervision: Managing people and technology.* New York: McGraw-Hill.

Freed, J. E., Klugman, M. R., & Fife, J. D. (1997). *A culture for academic excellence: Implementing the quality principles in higher education.* ASHE-ERIC Higher Education Report, Vol. 25, No. 1. Washington, DC: George Washington University, Graduate School of Education and Human Development.

Grote, D. (1996). *The complete guide to performance appraisal.* New York: American Management Association.

Henderson, R. I. (1984). *Performance appraisal* (2nd ed.). Reston, VA: Reston Publishing.

Kuh, G. D., Siegel, M. J., & Thomas, A. D. (2001). Higher education: Values and culture. In R. B. Winston, Jr., D. G. Creamer, T. K. Miller, & Associates, *The professional student affairs administrator: Educator, leader, and manager* (pp. 39–63). Philadelphia: Brunner-Routledge.

Mosley, D. C., Megginson, L. C., & Pietri, P. H., Jr. (1993). *Supervisory management: The art of empowering and developing people* (3rd ed.) Cincinnati: South-Western.

Schneier, C. E., & Beatty, R. W. (1982). What is performance appraisal? In L. Baird,

R. W. Beatty, & C. E. Schneier (Eds.), *The performance appraisal sourcebook* (pp. 4–10). Amherst, MA: Human Resource Development Press.

Sims, J. M., & Foxley, C. H. (1980). Job analysis, job descriptions, and performance appraisal systems. In C. H. Foxley (Ed.), *Applying management techniques* (pp. 41–53). New Directions for Student Services No. 9. San Francisco: Jossey-Bass.

Winston, R. B., Jr., & Creamer, D. G. (1997). *Improving staffing practices in student affairs*. San Francisco: Jossey-Bass.

Chapter 6
EMPLOYEE SEPARATION
The Role of Supervisors

Joan B. Hirt
Steven M. Janosik

The original model of staffing practices described by Winston and Creamer (1997) consisted of five stages: selection, orientation, supervision, professional development, and performance appraisal. Conley (2001) pointed out that employee departure from an organization should be the final step in the cycle of staffing practices. Other studies seem to support this notion. Attrition rates for the profession range from an estimated 39% (Burns, 1982) to 65% (Richmond & Sherman, 1991). Winston and Creamer considered this suggestion and determined that it was well founded and that their model should indeed be revised to include a component they call *separation*. It seemed appropriate, therefore, to include a discussion of the newest stage of the model in this book on supervising new professionals.

To start, we turned to the literature to see how that might inform us on issues of separation. We begin this chapter with a summary of what that literature review reveals. Then, we identify and describe three reasons behind voluntary employee separation and two reasons behind involuntary employee separation. Next we talk about the role that supervisors play in each type of separation. Finally, we draw some connections between the separation stage and the other stages in the model of staffing practices.

THE LITERATURE ON EMPLOYEE SEPARATION

Research on the issue of employee departure mirrors the fluctuations in the economy over the past two decades. Essentially, it can be conceptualized in four groups. First are manuscripts written from the organization's perspective that discuss how to terminate employees. In a second group, studies also serve organizational purposes by focusing on how to manage outplacement services for employees who are terminated. Next are works written for terminated employees that address how to cope with job loss and how to successfully find another position. All three of these clusters of literature come from the private sector. In the final part of this section, we explore the limited work on the issue of employee separation in higher education.

Employee Termination

The early 1980s ushered in an economic recession that affected staffing practices across many organizations, especially those in the private sector. As Coulson (1981) noted, "The rules of the workplace seem to be in flux. Some employers are voluntarily adopting restraints upon their right to discharge. Others continue to treat their employees as an expendable resource, discharging them whenever they decide to do so" (p. 215).

It is not surprising that the downturn in the economy led to a spate of publications about the termination process (Coulson, 1981; Finnie & Sniffin, 1984; Morin & Yorks, 1982). For the most part, these studies promote organizational interests and provide information to supervisors and management about termination processes that meet federal regulations while simultaneously limiting liability for the organization.

In general, these experts talk about different reasons that lead to termination but focus their attention on involuntary termination (Sweet, 1989). They urge managers to document performance, consult with legal counsel, and prepare for termination meetings (Coulson, 1981; Latack & Dozier, 1986). Employees should be told of their dismissal in a straightforward manner and should be informed of their severance package (if any), when they need to vacate their workplace, and any outplacement assistance that will be provided to them (Ensman, 1998). Some authors also discuss how to deal with different situations that may arise during the termination meeting (Sweet, 1989). For the most part, however, this group of manuscripts aims to direct management in appropriate ways to terminate employees and protect employer interests.

As the economy slowly turned around in the late 1980s and early 1990s, the literature shifted slightly from its focus on how to terminate employees to matters of assisting employees in finding alternative employment (Brammer & Humberger, 1984; Pedersen, Goldberg, & Papalia, 1991; Wynne, 1989).

Outplacement Services

Much of the literature on outplacement is couched in humanistic terms but the focus of this topic remains on protecting the organization. Remember that the early 1990s was an era devoted to increased productivity. Brammer and Humberger (1984, p. 5) summed it up nicely:

> Terminating employees is a stressful task for managers and executive officers. It is difficult to inflict the pain and hardship of termination on fellow employees. Yet, organizations are concerned about increasing productivity. Outplacement counseling is a management tool for improving organizational effectiveness with a minimum of stress to executives and employees.

Outplacement is a process designed to assist employees cope with a job loss, understand the job market, and develop the necessary skills to market themselves to potential employers. At the heart of the concept is the notion that market globalization, the shift to a service economy, and increased technology have generated a job market that is constantly changing and evolving. This means that people need to learn new job-seeking skills (Davies, 1996).

In many instances, corporations contract outplacement services to national organizations that have offices in most major metropolitan areas, although some argue that locally managed providers are a better option (Pedersen et al., 1991). In either case, outplacement programs are designed to build (or rebuild) the self-confidence and self-esteem of employees who have been terminated by enhancing their understanding of this changing job market and providing them the skills to cope with that market immediately after termination and in the future (Wynne, 1989). Such services not only responded to the needs of terminated employees in a humanistic manner but also tended to reduce the potential for disgruntled employees to sue for wrongful discharge and helped bolster the company's public image in difficult economic times.

This focus on the future turned out to be somewhat prophetic. Between 1985 and 1996, Fortune 500 companies alone eliminated more than 3.5 million jobs (Ambrose, 1996). Termination seemed to permeate every employment sector, including the Catholic church, which laid off priests (Ambrose, 1996, p. 4). Statistics like these led to publications written to promote employee interests.

The Role of Employees in Job Survival

The work on the role of employees in job survival denotes something of a paradigm shift in the literature. To recap, the issue of termination was initially addressed purely from a corporate perspective: How could managers fire employees with the least amount of difficulty while simultaneously protecting the organization's interests? Over time, this led to corporate sponsored outplacement programs. By the mid-1990s, however, the experts recognized that the changes in the economy had rendered the old paradigm on job security moot. The new paradigm shifted a great deal of the responsibility for job security to the employee:

> For all practical purposes, outplacement is dead. The stark fact is that employees are ever more likely to be blasted out into the ranks of the unemployed with no safety net, and it could happen over and over again. Today's new college graduates will, on average, have 8 to 10 jobs and as many a 3 careers in their lifetimes. Job seekers should look for employers willing to help them continuously develop and maintain skills that will make them more valuable. They offer employees training not just in skills specific to the job at hand, but also in those that can enhance careers over the long haul. (Morin, 1996, p. 222)

Some scholars attempted to relate the need for continuous improvement in the job arena to the need for continuous development as an individual. They argued that the distinctions between personal life and work life had blurred and that one way to respond to this blurring of roles was to develop skills that would serve one well in either arena (e.g., problem solving skills, using feedback in positive ways) (Lee, Guthrie, & Young, 1995).

Others took a self-help approach. These experts addressed the emotional turmoil that can accompany a job loss and provided guidance on how to deal with the resultant stress (Morin & Cabrera, 1991; Quittel, 1994). They provided those whose jobs had been terminated with checklists and worksheets to assist them in seeking new positions (Wolfer & Wong, 1988). In general, these experts tried to empower employees and encourage them to take greater command of their professional future.

The effects of termination were examined empirically in these works and differences among groups of employees were investigated. Some studies explored differences in the effects of job loss on blue- versus white-collar workers. Not surprisingly, the latter group was more optimistic about future employment opportunities (Leana & Feldman, 1990). Differences by sex were the focus of other studies that reported that different factors led to career growth for men and women after job termination (Eby & Buch, 1992) but that women and men approach the outplacement process differently (Phelps & Mason, 1991).

Given this attention to empowering employees, it may not be surprising that the most recent twist in the literature returns focus to the organization. Specifically, because some literature has informed terminated employees of their rights, there has been an increase in employment-related litigation. In response, some of the most recent studies focus on how corporations can protect themselves from termination-related lawsuits (Lyncheski, 1996, 1997).

This abridged summary provides an overview of the literature on employee termination in the private sector. But this book focuses on supervision in higher education, so it was important to review what has been written about employee termination in academia.

Employee Separation in Higher Education

The work on employee separation in higher education is very limited. It mirrors the work in the private sector in some interesting ways but departs from the corporate literature in other areas. Like the literature from the private sector, the earliest work was precipitated by the threat of significant downsizing in higher education. One hundred and forty-four institutions of higher learning closed during the 1970s. This led to predictions that up to 50,000 faculty (and a proportionate number of administrators) would lose their jobs in the 1980s (Abrell, 1981).

The early work in higher education departed from that in the private sector in one important way, however. Although articles were written primarily to protect institutions, there was a humanistic tone from the start. As Abrell (1981, p. 31) noted, "If we value our human resources and respect each person with whom we work, higher education must do all that it can to use compassion and concern in dismissing people."

As for the work in the corporate sector, by the mid-1980s attention had turned to the issue of outplacement services. Indeed, Abrell (1985, p. 248) holds the corporate approach up as a model: "While dismissing employees is still an imperfect art in industry and business, education would do well to consider the practice of outplacement counseling currently being used in the non-academic world." The early work, though, merely spelled out the benefits to institutions that employed humane techniques when terminating employees. For example, benefits included stress reduction for both the terminated employee and the person doing the firing and reduced threat of litigation.

By the early 1990s, however, the literature reflected a clearly organizational perspective:

> Due to continued declining enrollments, loss of public funding, and budget cuts, more and more university and college faculty and staff will be told that their positions are being eliminated. As one university administrator states, "The smart executives in colleges and universities are already making the tough decision to reorganize and downsize. These are the colleges and universities that will survive." (Logan, 1991, p. 17)

The approach in these works was prescriptive. The steps the institution needed to take to terminate employees and provide outplacement services were described. Ways to protect the institution from lawsuits were identified (Butterfield & Wolfe, 1994; Logan, 1991).

In summary, the work on employee termination in the private sector over the past two decades has employed both an organization and an employee perspective. The literature on termination in higher education, on the other hand, has adopted an organizational perspective exclusively. It would seem that there is a need to examine the issue of employee separation in academia from a more individual perspective. Although we do not claim to thoroughly address this perspective, we attempt in this chapter to look at the reasons behind employee separation and the role of the supervisor in each of those scenarios.

REASONS FOR VOLUNTARY SEPARATION

Conley (2001) identified five reasons that employees might separate from their institution of higher learning. Although we agree with her assessment, we believe these reasons can be further grouped into reasons related to voluntary separation and those associated with involuntary separation, and we have modified the Conley model accordingly. There are three reasons that staff members might voluntarily leave an institution: professional reasons, personal reasons, or issues related to retirement.

Professional Reasons

The first, and perhaps most obvious, reason for employee departure involves professional issues. Employees, particularly outstanding employees, will seek to expand their professional realms and develop their skills by seeking positions that offer them upward mobility and broader responsibilities. This type of advancement is more achievable in some functional areas than in others.

For example, entry-level positions for NPs in housing and residential life operations are plentiful. In fact, jobs in residence life represent up to 39% of all entry-level jobs (Janasiewicz & Wright, 1993). Positions one step above entry level are significantly less numerous, although still available to top-notch candidates. Beyond that, however, opportunities for advancement are very restricted and even the most qualified of candidates may find further promotion limited. Indeed, of all the student affairs jobs posted in the *Chronicle of Higher Education* in 1990, only 28% were for mid-level jobs and only 4% were for executive positions (Janasiewicz & Wright, 1993).

Those who pursue careers in other functional areas may find advancement through a different path. In the area of new student orientation, for instance, the number of entry-level jobs for NPs is much more limited. This suggests that only the most qualified candidates will be successful in breaking the initial barrier to gain access to the career ladder in orientation. Upward mobility, however, may be more achievable as there are fewer experienced staff members seeking mid-level jobs in orientation programs. Regardless of functional area, upward mobility is a concern for student affairs practitioners who report they are underemployed and that their mobility at their home institutions is limited (Cox & Ivy, 1984).

These variations in promotional possibilities among functional areas lead to another professional reason for separation: changing functional areas. Some NPs pursue entry-level jobs in functional units that are accessible to them, like residence life. They may aspire, however, to work in other areas where initial access is more limited (judicial affairs or Greek Life, for example) and they believe that the skills they can hone in residence life will prepare them, even make them more competitive, for those jobs. When opportunities arise in the functional area in which they aspire to work, these NPs will elect to terminate with one unit to move to another unit, either at the same institution or at another institution.

On a related note, another professional reason for separation is to leave the field of higher education entirely. Consider the situation of Will described in chapter 4 of this volume. Will had originally intended to go to law school on completing his undergraduate degree but elected to pursue a master's degree in student affairs instead. He is working in the profession and is engaged to a woman who lives two hours away. While he excels in his job, he is concerned about the demands the profession places on his time. He is also worried that the low salaries in the field will prevent him from supporting his family in the future. Will is an NP who may elect to leave the field of higher education administration to pursue the benefits available in the private sector.

If Will were to leave the profession to pursue his original professional aspirations and attend law school, he would exemplify yet another professional reason for separation: pursuing further education or job training. Those who work in higher education and student affairs administration are frequently individuals who are convinced of the merits of education and who are committed to the notion of lifelong learning. It is not uncommon, therefore, for employees to leave positions to pursue further education. For those with master's degrees, this may mean seeking doctoral study in higher education or an unrelated field. For those without the master's, it may involve a commitment to earning that degree to advance professionally. For some, the training will be in a completely new area. Regardless of which path is taken, the employee is leaving the institution to pursue further education.

In some cases the pursuit of additional education or training may be symptomatic of two other professional reasons to leave a job. These final two reasons are more negative than any of the first four professional reasons for separation. The first relates to earning potential. Many NPs work with students who earn bachelor's degrees in computer science, information management, business, or engineering and who command salaries two to three times higher than starting pay rates for those with master's degrees in education. Indeed, some professional fields offer starting salaries that exceed what many student affairs professionals can expect to earn at the peak of their professional careers. That may explain why 16% of those who left the profession did so because of limited salaries (Burns, 1982). On a related note, some institutions offer significantly higher salaries for the same type of work that merits lower pay at other schools. It should not be surprising, then, if employees leave to take a like position at another institution that pays more or if they leave to take a position outside of higher education where the earning potential is more promising.

The other negative reason employees may leave an institution is to escape. This may mean escaping a supervisor or colleagues with whom the NP is incompatible. It may relate to some sort of hostile environment in the workplace. When good employees leave a job to take a position that does not advance them in some meaningful manner, it may well be that they do so to escape some element of their jobs. Finding out exactly why a staff member is leaving a position may serve to uncover organizational problems that need to be addressed.

So there is an array of professional reasons that may prompt NPs to leave their jobs. But not all reasons for separation are professionally related. Personal issues can be equally as compelling for NPs.

Personal Reasons

There is a multitude of personal reasons that may affect an employee's decision to leave a position but we have elected to discuss three here. The first is marriage or commitment to a partner. Many NPs are aged 24 to 30 years, a prime time to seek a life partner. And marriage or commitment to a partner frequently involves couples in which both people work. Dual-income couples are emerging as a dominant form of family in the United States. Not only do many couples value the professional identity and concomitant self-esteem associated with successful individual careers, but salaries from two positions are often necessary to support the family. This may be particularly true for couples in which one or both partners work in higher education or student affairs administration. Notoriously low salaries are the norm in the profession, particularly at the entry and middle levels of management. Although salaries at the upper levels of administration are typically more lucrative, most professionals do not achieve higher levels of responsibility until they have been in the field for several years. Thus, the years when couples may be raising children, for example, and have higher expenses, may coincide with the years in which they are earning less money.

The issue of raising children is associated with a second personal reason for employee departure: family responsibilities. Most frequently, departures due to family responsibilities involve child rearing or caring for ill or aging parents. The NP who was a traditional-age undergraduate (18–22) and who pursued a graduate degree within a few years of earning the bachelor's degree will reach the age bracket typically associated with child rearing within the first few years of professional experience. Although women may be more affected by the issue of child rearing than men, professionals of both sexes need to grapple with the decision of whether to raise children, and if so when. If the NP is a woman who becomes pregnant or adopts, she may elect to leave her position after the arrival of the child, either on an extended maternity leave or permanently. If the NP is the new father, he may elect to take a paternity leave, or to leave permanently, either to seek a higher salary to support his family or to handle child-care responsibilities if his spouse or partner is the family breadwinner. All of these scenarios result in the departure of an employee, either temporarily or permanently.

A second form of family responsibility that can lead to employee departure is caring for ill or aging parents. We suspect this will be an increasingly frequent cause of separation in the future. The Baby Boom generation is the largest mass of people in a single age group in history. These Boomers, born between 1945 and 1961, started bearing children in the mid-1960s and just stopped bearing children at the end of the 20th century. This means that children of Boomers born in the mid-1970s are currently NPs. Those born at the end of the 1990s could become NPs two decades from now. Meanwhile, their parents are now between the ages of 41 and 56. As their parents age, these children, our current and future new professionals, will become caretakers. Between demands of children and demands of aging parents, we think it likely that family responsibilities will account for an increasing number of employee decisions to leave their jobs.

The third personal reason for job separation relates to some degree to all of the preceding reasons for leaving a job. We refer to it as issues of mobility and it affects (or is affected by) marriage, child rearing, and caring for parents. For example, career mobility among dual-income couples is much more complicated than for professionals who are single. Whether one or both partners work in higher education, when one person elects to leave a geographic region for a better job, the spouse or partner usually is going to leave as well. In a sense, then, NPs are doubly susceptible to separation due to marriage or partnership. First, many young professionals will elect to marry or make a commitment to a partner; this is a normal developmental activity for this age group. Second, those NPs who are married are more likely to have one partner seeking a more responsible position or higher salary. Because the upward mobility of one half of the couple affects both partners, it is not surprising that some employees leave positions for reasons related to relocation in their marriage or partnership.

Child rearing and caring for aging parents can also result in employee relocation. Young, single NPs often accept jobs that are geographically distant from immediate and/or extended family. Indeed, many undergraduates choose to attend a university that removes them from the immediate vicinity of family. But when NPs begin to raise children, they may prefer to live in closer proximity to family—at least the family of one of the two partners. Families can provide emotional and physical support to NPs struggling with the challenges of parenthood. Older parents know how to deal with sick children, can help with child care, and can provide emotional support to new parents when they reach their wit's end. And many new parents want to raise children in places where their children can spend time with grandparents, aunts, uncles, cousins, and other members of the extended family. So it should not be surprising if relocating to be closer to family prompts employee decisions to separate. Likewise, employees who have moved away from family for professional reasons may be required to leave their professional positions if they are needed to care for ill or aging parents.

Marriage, child rearing, and caring for ill and aging parents, then, are all personal reasons that may lead to employee departure. But there is a third and final reason for voluntary separation: retirement.

Retirement

Although it may seem that the issue of retirement is out of place in a book on the supervision of new professionals, we disagree. There are older individuals who pursue careers in higher education and student affairs administration later in life. Some are people who worked in nonprofessional careers until midlife when some sort of crisis (e.g., layoff, debilitating accident, divorce) prompted them to pursue a college and/or postgraduate degree. Others elect to work in higher education as a second career. In either case, it is possible that new professionals may leave a position to retire.

Moreover, there has been a dramatic shift in the onus for retirement in the past two decades. Retirement is no longer an institutional responsibility; it is a personal responsibility. As such, NPs need to be concerned with the issue, and if NPs are concerned, their supervisors need to be concerned, as we discuss a bit later in this chapter.

So voluntary reasons that can lead to employee separation include professional issues, personal issues, and retirement issues. While it would be nice to think that all reasons for separation are voluntary, this is clearly not the case. It is equally important to address the involuntary reasons behind employee departure.

INVOLUNTARY REASONS FOR SEPARATION

The two involuntary reasons we have elected to address in this chapter include illness/death and job termination. Both are issues that might cause a NP to leave an institution and both merit attention.

Illness and/or Death

Although illness and death are not topics any NP, or supervisor for that matter, likes to ponder, they are issues that lead to employee separation. NPs are not immune to illness and death, despite that fact that so many are young and in the prime of life. Departure due to illness may not be abrupt—often employees who are diagnosed with a debilitating or terminal disease or condition elect to continue to work as long as possible. Certainly the health insurance benefits typically associated with professional employment are a consideration when NPs are dealing with serious medical problems. But eventually, most people suffering from a serious illness will need to leave their jobs, and the nature of that sort of employee departure deserves some attention.

Employee separation as a result of death, however, is typically much more precipitous. NPs who are terminally ill are likely to separate from the institution prior to dying, so deaths of employees are more likely due to accidents. There is no doubt that the sudden death of an employee creates an emotional issue in a unit or department, but it also poses challenges for supervisors who must address the loss both personally and from the professional perspective, as we discuss later in this chapter.

The other category of reasons for involuntary separation is probably more common: termination. Neither group of reasons is particularly palatable, but both need to be addressed.

Employee Termination

There are all sorts of causes for terminating employees, and those interested in the legal definitions of these causes are urged to consult with experts in human resources or any of the texts written on this topic, including Ambrose (1996), Ensman (1998), and Sweet (1989). For pragmatic reasons, we choose to talk about two types of terminations: those that are driven by organizational problems, and those that are driven by employee problems.

Organizational Problems.　There are a number of organizational scenarios that might lead to termination of staff members. For example, in times of financial exigency many units elect, or are required, to eliminate staff positions. Personnel costs consume the greatest portion of most college and university budgets. So when budgets are cut, terminating employees is the only avenue some units can take to lower their costs.

Programmatic changes can also result in staff reductions. In some instances, larger units of the campus (the division of student affairs) may elect to develop a new program or service by drawing on resources from existing units. In other cases, an individual unit may elect to build a new program or strengthen certain elements of the unit. This may be accomplished by internally reallocating resources. Either scenario might require the unit to terminate one or more employees to garner the resources needed for the new or renewed program.

Because most professionals "serve at the pleasure of" the institution, terminations that are caused by organizational issues are usually legal. But supervisors can play a role in diminishing the personal and organizational impact of such forms of separation, as we discuss later. The second form of involuntary termination, separation due to employee problems, requires action on the part of the supervisor.

Employee Problems.　Although most supervisors would like to think that the time and effort they take in recruiting and selecting staff members coupled with the time and effort they spend orienting and supervising NPs would routinely lead to the success of those employees, that is not always the case. Despite the best efforts of all involved, sometimes employee termination is required.

There is any number of problems that can lead to termination of an employee. Some staff members may engage in behaviors that are unethical or even criminal. Consider the NP who drops in on a party being sponsored by a student organization he or she advises and finds that alcohol is being consumed by minors, that the group is serving intoxicated individuals, or that some other violation of campus conduct or legal code is occurring. If the NP fails to take any action, he or she may in fact be found in violation of the law and be held civilly and/or criminally liable for his or her actions.

Other cases involving criminal behavior might be personal as opposed to job related. Along the same vein as the last example, think about the widespread abuse of drugs and alcohol among college students. It is not inconceivable that some of those students are going to pursue careers in higher education or student affairs. It is possible that NPs might be cited for driving under the influence, or for possession of illegal drugs. If this occurs, depending on the circumstances, it might lead to the termination of the staff member.

Other actions on the part of the employee that lead to separation may not be criminal per se but might relate to violations of institutional policy. Many NPs, for example, manage fiscal resources for student organizations. There have been cases where staff members have authorized inappropriate expenditures or requested unauthorized reimbursements for themselves. Such violations of campus policy can lead to termination if sufficiently severe or if they occur on more than one occasion.

Beyond these criminal or policy problems, however, there are performance-related problems that can lead to termination. Some employees just do not seem to grasp certain of their responsibilities, regardless of how many times they receive training. In other cases, a NP may have an attitude that prohibits him or her from successfully negotiating job tasks with others in the unit. Perhaps the staff member does a great job in some areas, but is consistently late with respect to reports and projects. Others may simply not be able to support the direction of the unit over time despite attempts to inculcate staff to the stated purpose and mission of the organization. Our point is not to try to identify every performance deficiency that can lead to termination but simply to point out that staff performance is a frequent cause of separation and one that supervisors need to be prepared to address.

THE ROLE OF SUPERVISORS IN SEPARATION

Supervisors play a role in each of the types of separation described in this chapter. The nature of that role, however, may vary depending on the circumstances that lead up to the termination and whether the termination is voluntary or involuntary.

Supervisors and Voluntary Termination

We have described three groups of reasons that might result in voluntary separation from an organization: professional issues, personal issues, and retirement. The role of the supervisor in each case is different. In the area of professional issues, for example, the supervisor may at times play an active role in assisting the NP to make a job change.

Professional Issues.   One of the professional reasons behind staff departure is upward mobility. Most strong staff members will aspire to higher levels of responsibility and most supervisors will encourage them to pursue those aspirations. In these cases, it may be incumbent on the supervisor to assist the NP in identifying the skills that will be needed to succeed in more responsible jobs and providing staff development opportunities for the NP to learn those skills. Introducing the NP to colleagues, promoting networking, and serving as a reference are other responsibilities that supervisors need to assume if they are to assist NPs meet their professional aspirations.

A second professional issue behind employee separation is an NP's desire to move to a new functional area—for example, from residence life to orientation or student activities. In these kinds of situations, the supervisor faces a related set of responsibilities. Supervisors assisting staff who wish to move up within a functional area are likely to know the types of skills and experiences NPs will need to accomplish that goal. When NPs want to move to another functional area, however, supervisors may need to familiarize themselves with the nature of those other areas before they can assist staff members to identify skills that need to be developed and mechanisms to accomplish that development.

Supervisors are in a similar but even more complex situation when employees plan to leave a unit for a position outside of higher education, a third professional reason for separation. Many who work in higher education and student affairs administration have never worked outside of education or outside the public sector. Assisting NPs in acquiring the skills and experiences that will help them succeed outside the profession or in the corporate world may be challenging. But supervisors have a duty to help NPs achieve their aspirations. And there are some fairly simple steps that supervisors can take to meet that duty. Consider the expertise that those who work in career services might have to offer. Consulting with career experts about the skills sought by employers can provide a basis on which to build a staff development plan. And many of those skills can be honed within the higher education setting. For example, many employers seek professionals who have teamwork skills, leadership experience, and technological know-how. The institutional setting is rife with opportunities to practice such skills or gain experience in these areas.

Assisting the NP who elects to leave a position to pursue further education or training may be a task with which the supervisor is more familiar; after all, supervisors are in the business of higher education. But there are still tasks supervisors in such circumstances ought to assume. In some cases, for example, NPs will be talking about pursuing doctoral study with a supervisor who has not earned that degree. NPs may be interested in graduate study in a field outside of education and that may pose different challenges for the supervisor. We also suspect that the future will bring a spate of departures of NPs who will enroll in job training programs or proprietary schools to pursue technology-related careers. Supervisors may need to educate themselves about the opportunities offered in different types of programs, the admission requirements for such programs, and the costs associated with such study. All these factors can assist the supervisor in helping the NP make a decision about programs to which to apply, how to finance the training, and how to move forward with those plans. Such support for NPs may also mean that the supervisor needs to deal with his or her own feelings about helping subordinates achieve educational levels that exceed his or her own degree attainment.

The final two professional reasons for employee separation we discussed earlier related to earning potential and working environment. In the case of salary, supervisors may have only limited influence. Most supervisors are not empowered to set salary ranges, so they may be limited in terms of actions they can undertake when employees depart due to salary issues. But there are some responsibilities supervisors can assume in these circumstances. First, if the institution is paying salaries that are considerably lower than other schools are paying for the same jobs, it is incumbent on the supervisor to work with the appropriate campus staff to address this issue. Units that routinely lose staff members to other campuses simply because of low salaries may be wasting resources. Supervisors can point out the costs required to recruit and train NPs and suggest that those costs outweigh the costs of increasing salaries for those positions if turnover is high. Providing data on the salary ranges peer institutions are offering to NPs in similar jobs is another way to try to influence policy, as is submitting the paperwork necessary for jobs to be reclassified or upgraded. Supervisors also need to let NPs know that they are taking these steps so that staff members are aware of the efforts the supervisor is making to address salary concerns.

In cases where staff members leave due to a poor working environment, supervisors may play an even more instrumental role. Assuming the supervisor is not part of the problem—that is, is not perpetuating the hostile environment—then steps need to be taken to identify the sources of the problem. Once those sources are known, the supervisor needs to determine the degree to which he or she can effect change directly and to what extent change needs to be implemented from other sources in the unit. NPs who know that supervisors are working to improve a problematic environment may be more tolerant and may try to work with the supervisor to solve the problems.

Supervisors, then, can assume roles in all types of scenarios associated with NPs who leave organizations for professional reasons. But what if the reasons for departure are more personal?

Personal Issues. The personal arena may be more awkward for supervisors who have been trained to believe that there are clear demarcations between the professional and the personal lives of employees. We argue, however, that supervisors can play a role in voluntary separations that are the result of personal issues. The first issue we discussed was that of marriage or commitment to a partner. As noted earlier, many NPs are in the prime age bracket to be dealing with finding a life partner. As human development experts, supervisors should understand this need. So when staff members announce engagements or commitments, supervisors should be understanding and supportive. Moreover, if the NP is leaving to relocate to be with the spouse or partner, supervisors can actively support that departure. If the NP plans to stay in the profession, the supervisor can assist in identifying campuses in the area to which the NP will be moving. Indeed, providing introductions to colleagues at those campuses can go a long way in promoting a NP's career interests.

A second personal reason for employee separation is related to child rearing or caring for ill or aging parents. These are issues with which many supervisors might have experience, in fact, so providing support might be relatively easy. But even supervisors who have not had to deal with child or parental issues can help NPs who need to separate from institutions for such reasons. Connecting NPs with support groups, experts, and publications or other resources that address child rearing and/or parental care concerns demonstrates to staff members that the supervisor cares. Such concern goes a long way toward easing what might otherwise be a difficult transition for the NP.

Mobility issues were the third personal reason we cited for employee separation. Again, mobility may be related to marriage, child rearing, or eldercare issues. In any scenario, however, supervisors can assist NPs. Supervisors should encourage NPs to consult with human resource personnel at the institution to ensure that issues like retirement funds and leave accounts are settled in ways most favorable for the employee. Locating resources about the geographic region to which the employee is moving can also be helpful. This may include locating websites that list housing opportunities or identifying other tasks associated with relocation like registering vehicles, arranging for utilities, registering to vote, or calculating new tax structures. The kind of support supervisors provide to departing employees leaves a lasting impression on those NPs, and that impression will color the way they talk about the institution after their departure.

Retirement. The third reason for voluntary departure is retirement. Although most NPs will not be of an age where retirement is imminent, some will. And even for those who are not contemplating retirement, there are steps supervisors can take to ensure the long-term success of staff members. As we discussed previously, retirement has become a personal rather than an organizational responsibility. The supervisor has an obligation to ensure that employees understand this subtle shift that has occurred in recent years. Supervisors may also include discussions of retirement plans and employee options with respect to retirement during annual evaluations. The purpose here is not to intrude on the NP's personal finances but rather to encourage NPs to develop the personal ownership of their retirement that will serve them well in the future.

In those cases where a NP is leaving due to retirement, supervisors can assume some additional responsibilities. They may ensure that the staff member has consulted with human resource experts available on campus, has filed all appropriate paperwork, and has arranged for things like insurance and/or health care coverage. Beyond these administrative tasks, supervisors can also work with employees to ensure a smooth transition to retirement. The move from professional to retiree can be a challenging one. Assisting staff members to identify support networks and resources to help them through this transition can go a long way toward making this a smooth passage for the employee.

Supervisors and Involuntary Separation

The roles that supervisors play when staff members leave an organization voluntarily are primarily facilitative. When employees leave involuntarily, however, there are other duties supervisors need to assume. We identified two types of involuntary departure: illness or death, and termination.

Illness or Death. Employees who are diagnosed with a serious or terminal illness offer supervisors opportunities to provide both professional and personal support. In professional terms, supervisors need to ensure that the employee fully understands his or her medical benefits and the implications of those benefits with respect to the illness or condition with which the NP has been diagnosed. Supervisors can assist NPs make arrangements for coverage if they need to leave campus periodically for treatment or medical appointments. Job descriptions may need to be reviewed to ensure that the staff member is physically capable of fulfilling duties and, if not, what measures need to be taken to discharge those responsibilities.

In the personal realm, supervisors can offer emotional support to the

NP and/or ensure that the staff member has access to sources of support. The supervisor may need to educate him- or herself about the illness or condition to provide that support. Likewise, if the employee desires, helping the NP identify sources of information about the disease or condition, be those online resources, publications, or organizations, demonstrates a personal commitment to the staff member that can go a long way in making life a bit easier for the afflicted staff member.

In cases of the death of an employee, supervisory responsibilities may also fall into administrative and personal categories but they will be quite different. Depending on the circumstances, the supervisor may be involved in finalizing paperwork with the institution on behalf of the deceased. This can include documenting the death, providing information to insurance companies, and arranging for final paychecks. Many institutions have procedures in place that are initiated when an employee dies. Among other tasks, these can include condolences from campus leaders and deletion of the employee's name from databases that are used to generate mailings to staff members.

From the personal perspective, supervisors may be involved in notifying relatives of the death, depending on the circumstances. Employees typically list the names of those to be contacted in case of an emergency. In such cases, it is often the staff member's supervisor who is contacted by campus officials before next of kin are notified of the death. Supervisors may feel an obligation to perform this task. If the deceased's family lives at a distance, the supervisor may offer assistance with respect to packing the employee's personal belongings in his or her home or office. Many times students and other staff members will want to conduct a memorial service and the supervisor will be asked to coordinate that ceremony. Again, such duties go beyond the formal responsibilities of supervisors but they meet ethical and moral obligations for many individuals.

Termination.   The role that supervisors play in instances of employee termination is perhaps the most important in terms of organizational implications. When mismanaged, employee terminations can absorb time and resources over long periods of time. There have been volumes written about appropriate ways to terminate employees and measures organizations should take to avoid legal and ethical problems. We do not attempt to summarize those here but encourage readers to refer to the sources we have described that address these issues (Coulson, 1981; Finnie & Sniffin, 1984; Lyncheski, 1997). We can, however, address some of the differences in what supervisors can do when the termination is due to organizational issues rather than employee issues.

In cases where the termination results from some organizational problem or decision (budget reduction or program development, for instance), supervisors need to achieve a delicate balance between representing the organization's interests to NPs while simultaneously facilitating the NPs' search for a new job. When decisions about organizational needs result in employee terminations, supervisors need to represent those decisions to staff members in an informed and professional manner. They also need to assist NPs in completing the necessary personnel paperwork and related administrative tasks.

Beyond handling the bureaucratic details associated with termination, however, it is incumbent on supervisors to take every possible measure to assist the staff members in finding new jobs. This includes identifying their strengths and weaknesses, talking with them about their career aspirations and preferences, contacting colleagues who maybe interested in employing them, and serving as a reference for the displaced workers. Clearly this does not mean supervisors need to give glowing recommendations about employees whose performances do not merit such, but when good staff members are terminated because of organizational decisions, supervisors have an ethical obligation to assist NPs to make a successful move.

In instances where the termination is the result of some employee performance deficiency or problem, supervisors are in a more delicate situation. Typically supervisors play a pivotal role in the termination of those they supervise. This involves documenting problematic behavior and notifying staff members of performance deficiencies. In most cases, it is the supervisor who informs the NP that he or she is being terminated. Under these circumstances, it may not be possible to recommend the staff member to others. In cases of termination due to criminal activity, supervisors' hands may be tied with respect to what they can say to potential employees. In these instances, we suggest that the supervisor still has a duty to the staff member to perform, albeit a different type of duty. When terminating staff members, supervisors need to be sure that NPs understand exactly why they are being terminated, the conditions of the termination (e.g., when they need to vacate office space, when they will receive a final paycheck), and the documentation the supervisor has to support the termination decision. Beyond these administrative responsibilities, the supervisor has an ethical obligation to candidly let the staff member know if any sort of letter of reference will be forthcoming and if that letter will be favorable or not. There are any number of other details that supervisors may need to address, but at issue here is the supervisor's role in ensuring that the terminated employee is quite clear on what led to the separation, what will happen between the notification of termination and the employee's actual departure, and what if any future support the supervisor will provide to the staff member. When employees are terminated, supervisors are obligated to protect the institution's property (e.g., office equipment and space, departmental records, intellectual property, etc.). Careful thought must be given to accomplishing this task while maintaining the terminated staff member's dignity.

HOW SEPARATION INTERFACES WITH THE OTHER STAGES OF THE MODEL

It is clear, then, that supervisors play a role when NPs separate from an institution, regardless of the circumstances associated with that separation. In this sense, separation is part of synergistic supervision, and it is important to discuss how separation relates to each of the other stages in the model of supervision described in this book.

The first stage in the model, selection, would seem to have direct links to the issue of separation. Selection procedures are initiated when a unit has job vacancies. Job vacancies typically occur under two circumstances: when units create new positions or when employees separate from units. As Conley (2001) noted, it would seem that the separation stage completes the circle of the model of supervision described by Winston and Creamer (1997).

Orientation is the second stage of the model, and this stage can also be related to separation. Supervisors who provide thorough orientation to the position, the unit, the institution, and (if appropriate) the profession accomplish two things. First, they lay the groundwork for success for the staff member. Staff members who are successful are less likely to leave their positions in the short term so supervisors can help to deter separation. Second, supervisors have an opportunity to further assess newly hired staff members during the orientation stage and to identify potential weaknesses that can be addressed through supervisory or professional development activities. The questions NPs ask, the way they handle their initial responsibilities, and the manner in which they conduct themselves early in their tenure can offer supervisors clues as to where developmental efforts can be made. By providing developmental guidance, supervisors can attempt to improve performance so that separation, when it does come, is voluntary rather than involuntary.

Supervision, the third stage in the model, also interfaces with separation. Supervisors who establish good relations with NPs accomplish two objectives. First, they are more likely to be able to see areas in which the NP excels and other arenas in which performance could be improved. This enables supervisors to address weaknesses or deficiencies proactively so that they do not lead to premature departure on the part of the NP. Second, NPs are more likely to be comfortable talking about their professional aspirations and personal plans with supervisors with whom they have a good relationship. Thus, supervisors will know when employees are thinking about looking for a new position or when a significant relationship might suggest relocation for the NP.

The next stage in the model, professional development, is another mechanism supervisors can use to deter separation. By identifying areas for development and enacting activities that address weaknesses and promote professional aspirations of NPs, supervisors may be able to avoid terminations down the road. Moreover, promoting the professional interests of exceptional NPs may serve to retain them for longer tenures.

Finally, performance appraisal seems to be the logical precursor to separation. When supervisors prepare performance appraisals they are provided with a pretty clear picture about the past successes and failures of NPs. Certainly, supervisors know if a staff member's performance has been sufficiently substandard that it will lead to involuntary termination. Supervisors can also use the performance appraisal to anticipate when outstanding staff members may be thinking of leaving their jobs as well. Thus, when conducted properly, performance appraisal can assist the supervisor in projecting future human resource needs and separation issues.

In conclusion, separation can take any number of forms—some more positive than others. Regardless of form, separation is inextricably linked to the other stages in Winston and Creamer's (1997) model of supervision. Hence it merits attention from supervisors, who need to understand the sources of separation and the role they play when staff members leave jobs.

REFERENCES

Ambrose, D. (1996). *Healing the downsized organization.* New York: Harmony Books.

Abrell, R. (1981). Outpatient counseling: A must in higher education. *Journal of the College and University Personnel Association, 32*(4), 29–31.

Abrell, R. (1985). Outpatient counseling in education: An idea whose time has come. *Clearing House, 58*(6), 248–250.

Brammer, L. M., & Humberger, F. E. (1984). *Outplacement and inplacement counseling.* Englewood Cliffs, NJ: Prentice Hall.

Burns, M. A. (1982). Who leaves the student affairs field? *NASPA Journal, 20,* 9–12.

Butterfield, B. S., & Wolfe, S. (1994). *You can get there from here: The road to downsizing in higher education.* Washington, DC: The College and University Personnel Association. (ERIC Reproduction Document No. ED 378 903)

Conley, V. M. (2001). Separation: An integral aspect of the staffing process. *College Student Affairs Journal, 21*(1), 57–63.

Coulson, R. (1981). *The termination handbook.* New York: Free Press.

Cox, D. W., & Ivy, W. A. (1984). Staff development needs of student affairs professionals. *NASPA Journal, 22,* 26–33.

Davies, G. (1996). The employment support network: An intervention to assist displaced workers. *Journal of Employment Counseling, 33*(4), 146–154.

Eby, L. T., & Buch, K. (1992). *Gender differences in coping with involuntary white collar job loss*. Charlotte, NC: University of North Carolina at Charlotte. (ERIC Document Reproduction Service No. ED 344 157)

Ensman, R. G. (1998). Firing line: Anatomy of an employee termination. *Office Systems, 15*(3), 67–68.

Finnie, R. A., & Sniffin, P. B. (1984). *Good endings: Managing employee terminations.* Washington, DC: College and University Personnel Association. (ERIC Document Reproduction Service No. ED 274 230)

Janasiewicz, B. A., & Wright, D. L. (1993). Job market trends in student affairs: Ten years later. *NASPA Journal, 30,* 145–152.

Latack, J. C., & Dozier, J. B. (1986). After the ax falls: Job loss as a career transition. *Academy of Management Review, 11,* 375–392.

Leana, C. R., & Feldman, D. C. (1990). Individual responses to job loss: Empirical findings from two field studies. *Human Relations, 43*(11), 1155–1181.

Lee, R. J., Guthrie, V. A., & Young, D. P. (1995). The lessons of life at work: Continuous personal development. *Career Planning and Adult Development Journal, 11*(3) 31–35.

Logan, T. (1991). Outplacement services: Managing career transitions. *College and University Personnel Association Journal, 42*(2), 17–22.

Lyncheski, J. E. (1996, July/August). Mix fairness with caution in employee terminations. *Outplacement,* pp. 18–20.

Lyncheski, J. E. (1997). Terminate with dignity and stay out of court. *Getting Results for the Hands-On Manager, 42*(2), 7–8.

Morin, W. J. (1996). You're absolutely, positively on your own. *Fortune, 134*(11), 222–223.

Morin, W. J., & Cabrera, J. C. (1991). *Parting company: How to survive the loss of a job and find another successfully.* San Diego: Harcourt Brace Jovanovich.

Morin, W. J., & Yorks, L. (1982). *Outplacement techniques: A positive approach to terminating employees.* New York: Amacom.

Pedersen, P., Goldberg, A. & Papalia, T. (1991). A model for planning career continuation and change through increase awareness, knowledge and skill. *Journal of Employment Counseling, 28*(2), 74–79.

Phelps, S., & Mason, M. (1991). When women lose their jobs. *Personnel Journal, 70*(8), 64–67.

Quittel, F. (1994). *Fire power: Everything you need to know before and after you lose your job.* Berkeley, CA: Ten Speed Press.

Richmond, J., & Sherman, K. (1991). Student development preparation and placement: A longitudinal study of graduate students' and new professionals' experiences. *Journal of College Student Development, 32,* 8–16.

Sweet, D. H. (1989). *A manager's guide to conducting terminations: Minimizing emotional stress and legal risks.* Lexington, MA: Lexington Books.

Winston, R. B., Jr., & Creamer, D. G. (1997). *Improving staffing practices in student affairs.* San Francisco: Jossey-Bass.

Wolfer, K. S., & Wong, R. G. (1988). *The outplacement solution: Getting the right job after mergers, takeovers, layoffs, and other corporate chaos.* New York: John Wiley and Sons.

Wynne, M. P. (1989). A group approach to outplacement. *Management World, 18*(2), 29–30.

Chapter 7
SUPERVISING STUDENT
AFFAIRS INTERNSHIPS
A Special Case

Diane L. Cooper
Sue A. Saunders

The previous chapters in this text have provided a framework for a proactive, thoughtful, and purposeful method for supervising new professionals in higher education. This chapter explores the various challenges and opportunities related to supervising a particular group of new professionals—students in a practice experience such as internship or practicum. These supervised practice experiences are often the first time graduate students in preparation programs have the opportunity to put the theories they learn in the classroom into practice in a real work setting. The supervisor is then, in addition to providing the on-site work supervision, serving as an educator and often working in conjunction with a faculty member to help the student learn and explore various issues from his or her experience.

GRADUATE ASSISTANTS VERSUS INTERNS IN SUPERVISED PRACTICE

This chapter focuses on supervising graduate students who are working in a student affairs functional unit as part of a class or for other forms of academic credit (typically called practicum or internship). Another form of supervised practice graduate students typically encounter as part of their preparation program are assistantships. This work experience usually varies from internships and practica in several ways. First, the assistantship is often awarded to a graduate student as part of the admission process to graduate school and, although it can be an educational experience, is most often an assignment to a particular work unit in the institution rather than an academic program requirement. Next, the student's work assignments are decided on by the supervisor rather than a mutually agreed-on set of learning objectives that are often negotiated for a student intern. Finally, assistant-ships often require more hours of work per week for a longer period of time than does an internship/practicum. In fact, many assistantships last for the 2-year period of time a student is in his or her preparation program whereas internships or practicum experiences are often for one academic term and may involve as little as five hours per week. As such, the graduate assistant's supervision is more like that of a new full-time professional joining the staff than that of a graduate intern, so the earlier chapters in this text would be very applicable to supervising students in graduate assistantships.

Supervisors of students in internships and practica should view their role as educators of future practitioners. This is a critically important role in the profession and requires the same level of preparation as one would take for a new professional's arrival in a work unit. Forethought and planning will add to the overall experience for the designated supervisor, the rest of the staff in functional area, and the graduate student. This chapter highlights issues supervisors should consider as they assume active educator roles in the preparation of future student affairs professionals.

PRACTITIONER ROLES IN EDUCATING FUTURE PRACTITIONERS

Even though some would argue that student affairs has not evolved to the point of being a fully developed profession, most working in the field have a strong sense of generativity toward the field, which includes preparing new practitioners for entry into the field (Carpenter, Miller, & Winston, 1980; Creamer, Winston, & Miller, 2001). Many current practitioners did not have formal academic preparation for entry into practice, but instead gained skill and knowledge through trial and error, observation of others within the employing institution, on-the-job training, and professional development activities offered through the field's professional organizations. This trend is changing as more and more masters and doctoral level trained new practitio-ners enter the work force each year (Winston & Creamer, 1997).

Most student affairs programs operate from a scientist-practitioner model. Preparation programs see a responsibility not only to assist profes-sionals in training to acquire theoretical foundations but also to the primary importance of translating theory to practice. Student affairs work is ideally focused on theory-to-practice models, intentional actions aimed toward facilitating student growth, and doing its part in the academy to assist in the learning process (Schroeder & Pike, 2001). Special skills and competencies can be taught in the classroom, but the opportunity to apply the information to practice is crucial to serving in a scientist-practitioner role. The scientist-practitioner or scholar-practitioner model also requires that practitioners be thoughtful critical users of theory and creators and investigators of theory and practice models.

Hoberman and Mailick (1994) asserted, "Professional education is directed toward helping students acquire special competencies for diagnosing specific needs and for determining, recommending, and taking appropriate action. Professional education is also expected to socialize students in the 'thought processes' of the profession and to inculcate them with its customs, ethics, working relationships, and the behaviors expected from members of the profession" (pp. 3–4). As Creamer and Winston (2002) point out, "student affairs clearly is part of the applied sector of professional education rather than research-oriented sectors" (p. 11) and, as such, relies heavily on the training graduate students receive as part of their graduate education in supervised practice experiences. But the distinction between training and education is important here. Creamer and Winston go on to say:

> The difference between education and training can be illustrated with the example of learning to drive an automobile. First, one must learn the mechanics of how to operate the vehicle and to coordinate manual activities, awareness of one's surroundings, and awareness of applicable traffic laws and regulations. After having been trained to operate a car, one can then use that information combined with goals to actually make a trip. Making a trip is much more complicated than just learning to operate a car. In the course of reaching one's destination, the driver must be aware of operating his or her vehicle, but must also be aware of other drivers, pedestrians, road conditions, weather, traffic signals and signs, and perhaps one's passenger. Successful professional practitioners need both training and education to fulfill their responsibilities within an institution. (p. 11)

It is clear that the role practitioners take on as educators in the supervised practice experience is critical to the continued development of the field of student affairs.

ESTABLISHING THE INTERNSHIP SITE

A purposeful approach to preparing a site for an intern is the first step in this process. The preparation begins with a discussion among student, faculty internship supervisor, and the internship site supervisor. Ideally, this discussion takes place with enough lead time to plan for the intern's arrival, prepare other staff for the experience, and consider tasks and opportunities for the intern's involvement while he or she is on site.

A five-component model of supervised practice in graduate preparation shown in Figure 7.1 (Creamer & Winston, 2002) shows the areas of concern for site supervisors as they begin to conceptualize the internship experience. From this figure one can see that supervision of interns is conceptualized as the integrating feature of direct experience, translation, applying ethics, and reflection. Each of these components should be considered when establishing the internship site.

There may be differences in expectations related to direct experience in the supervised practice experience based on the preparation program requirements. Some graduate programs require students to spend a percentage of their on-site time performing various tasks. For example, a program may stipulate that 50% of the intern's time must be spent providing direct service to the clients of the functional area. If one's office provides admissions information to students and parents, for example, then an intern will be expected to spend half of the time in the site assisting those two groups. Of course, at the beginning of the internship the student may need to shadow an employee who is providing the service, rather than independently providing the service. It is hoped, however, that after sufficient training, the intern can provide some of the client services independently. This expectation is

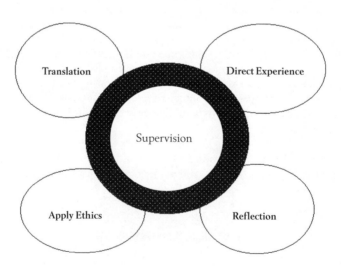

FIGURE 7.1. Model of supervised practice in student affairs graduate preparation programs. (From Creamer and Winston, 2002.)

sometimes related to external credentialing agencies (e.g., Council for Accreditation of Counseling and Related Educational Programs, CACREP) but is more often in place to ensure that interns do not spend the bulk of their time performing clerical tasks. The involvement in direct experience also assists students in translating often-amorphous material they discussed in the classroom to a hands-on integrated learning opportunity.

The appropriate amount of intern involvement in various tasks on site is often an area of concern for supervisors. Creamer and Winston (2002) recommend that for this level of experience, at a minimum the supervisor should create "(a) explicit learning goals that govern the form and content of the experience; (b) activities, assignments, and projects that are related to classroom learning; and (c) numerous opportunities for students to ask questions and explore the subtleties of what is happening around them and receive frequent, candid feedback about their performance" (p. 22).

Another component of Figure 7.1 that needs consideration in establishing the site is the manner in which the intern will be exposed to ethical concerns and considerations and possible legal restrictions and personal liability. As the experience is planned and implemented, it is important for interns to know from the very beginning the ethical codes and guidelines or values that are held in high regard in the work site. Likewise, they need to be familiar with relevant laws, regulations, and institutional policies that play a significant role in the setting's day-to-day operations. In fact, students should know this information as they go about investigating potential internship sites. That way if there is a difference in values or beliefs, a student can self-select out of the internship site early in the selection process rather than beginning the internship and discovering that they are inappropriately placed. For example, suppose that a good bit of the programming a office provides to students takes place on a particular day of the week. If for religious reasons a student cannot work on that day, then she or he will immediately have a problem with attendance. These concerns are less likely to arise from ethical issues, particularly those that are outlined in various professional organization ethical codes.

Internships sites do assume some level of legal liability for the students in supervised practice working in their site. Although most preparation programs require interns to acquire professional liability insurance prior to beginning their internship, site supervisors should make sure such insurance is in place prior to the first day at the site. In the event that the preparation program has not made such a requirement, the site supervisor should discuss the need for the insurance with the intern and, if necessary, assist the intern in getting such a policy. (Several of the professional associations, such as ACPA and NASPA, offer low-cost professional liability insurance for students while involved in activities associated with their academic programs.)

Finally, reflection is crucial to any educationally successful internship experience. "The learning cycle is complete when the learner reflects on knowledge and uses it in practice. Providing an opportunity to complete this learning cycle is one of the more obvious reasons for including supervised practice in academic preparation programs" (Creamer & Winston, 2002, p. 28). Reflective exercises such as journals are often part of the academic requirements of supervised practice; in addition, site supervisors need to consider ways to encourage reflection as a part of the site activities. This may be in written form or part of the regularly scheduled time the supervisor and intern spend together.

At the core of Figure 7.1 is the process of supervision. Winston and Creamer (1997) state that supervision of professional and support staff is in fact the lynchpin to all staffing practices. This applies in supervision of interns as well as new and seasoned professionals. (Chapters 1 and 3 provide detailed discussions of the roles of supervision for new professionals.)

UNDERSTANDING INTERNSHIP EXPERIENCE REQUIREMENTS

Depending on the preparation program expectations, students may be required to complete one, two, or more supervised practice experiences. It also is not uncommon for students to use internships as academic electives in their programs. Interns in the first supervised practice experience may require additional assistance with various program requirements (for example, papers, journals, or various forms) than students who have been through the process previously. It is important that the site supervisor clearly understands the requirements for the academic program related to each internship experience. If a copy of the syllabus is not provided, supervisors should ask for one and any other guidelines or requirements used by the faculty supervisor. If the faculty supervisor does not initiate a conversation with the supervisor, she or he should make an appointment to meet with him or her (or to communicate by telephone or e-mail) so she or he is clear about the program expectations of the site supervisor. Supervisors should keep in mind that the internship is intended to be an academic learning experience; consequently, they should support the academic program's goals and operating procedures. If for some reason supervisors cannot support or agree with program goals or expectations, then they should reframe for accepting interns.

One way to minimize misunderstandings about expectations is through a faculty supervisor/site supervisor agreement form (Gross, 1993; Hellweg, 1985). Figure 7.2 shows an example of an unstructured type of agreement a faculty supervisor and site supervisor could develop to ensure that both individuals have the same understanding of the requirements of the supervised

Internship Agreement Form

Name of Student: _____

Address: _____

Telephone: _____

Academic Term: _____

Placement Site: _____

Address: _____

Site Supervisor: _____

Title: _____

Telephone: _____

Hours of Work per Week: _____

Specific Work Schedule

Is this a paid internship? _____ If yes, rate of pay: $ _____ per _____

Units of academic credit to be earned: _____

Nature of work to be performed by student: _____

Specific products to be completed by the student as a part of the internship:

Specific Conditions (if applicable): _____

_____

Role of the Faculty Supervisor: _____

_____

Signature of Student: _____ Date: _____

Signature of Site Supervisor: _____ Date: _____

Signature of Faculty Supervisor: _____ Date: _____

FIGURE 7.2. Unstructured site supervisor agreement form.

practice experience. In part, the student can use the site supervisor–faculty supervisor agreement form as a type of a job description. It should outline expectations for job tasks as well as designate responsibilities for various activities. (This form differs from the learning objectives for internships that are discussed later in this chapter.)

On the other hand, it may be advisable to have a written agreement that is more defined and prescribed. Figure 7.3 provides an example of such an agreement form. No matter which one prefers as the site supervisor, should the faculty supervisor not provide one with an agreement form prior to the student intern's arrival, the site supervisor may want to construct a form that covers basic responsibilities and expectations of the intern and the site supervisor.

SELECTING AND ORIENTING INTERNS

As with NPs, interns begin their orientation to a new position from the moment they see the position announcement or participate in their first selection interview for the position (Patterson, 1997). Interns form often-indelible first impressions about the site, tasks required, organizational culture, and supervisory style from what is said, or not said, in the position announcement. Because of the short-term nature of internships, it is tempting to forego a detailed position announcement and instead to keep the parameters and requirements of an intern's work open and flexible. In our opinion, interns need to know what is expected of them in detailed terms. A detailed position announcement that reflects a comprehensive position description serves several purposes:

1. The intern can screen out positions that are not congruent with desired learning goals, thus saving everyone a great deal of time and frustration.
2. The supervisor and unit avoid miscommunication with the intern about the nature of the work and the expectations in terms of time on task, skills required.
3. The intern gets the full internship experience performing a service for a unit that is as close as possible to the entry-level professional jobs for which they will apply at the completion of their academic program.
4. Conducting position advertising and selection based on a comprehensive position description (see chapter 2 of this volume) should lead to better productivity and professionalism on the part of the intern as well as to increased dedication on the part of the supervisor.

Although selecting interns is very similar to selecting and orienting new professionals, readers should carefully read chapter 2 of this volume to

**Student Affairs Practicum Site Supervisor Agreement to Provide
Supervision and Consultation with the Student Intern**

As a Student Affairs Practicum Site Supervisor, I will provide the following supervisory, consultation, and tutorial services to the student affairs student under my supervision:

1. Facilitate development of a set of learning goals and outcome objectives that the student will accomplish during the designated 165 practicum clock hours [3 hours credit] over the practicum period.

2. Make available opportunities designed to expose the student to the various characteristics and functional aspects of my administrative unit.

3. Provide opportunities for the student to meet and interact with staff members who work in the unit and others with whom unit members have professional associations.

4. Assign the student responsibilities and otherwise establish avenues designed to actively involve the student in the work of the unit appropriate to the student's level of knowledge and skills.

5. Meet with the student on an individual supervisory interview basis for no less than 30 minutes per week, used to discuss and examine general issues and information to increase the student's knowledge base.

6. Provide opportunity for the student to participate in staff group activities of no less than 60 minutes per week, used to focus upon skill and competence development essential to gaining functional area expertise. This may include discussion of assigned readings and projects.

7. Observe the student's daily work activities and provide formative feedback designed to strengthen the student's ability to function as a professional student service/development practitioner.

8. Provide additional challenges and opportunities designed to increase the student's professional competence in and understanding of the field of student affairs/student development.

9. Evaluate the student's progress on learning goals, outcome objectives, and projects accomplished during the practicum, and provide summative ratings to be used for practicum grading purposes.

10. Write a formal letter of evaluation to be added to the student's permanent academic record.

Practicum Student's Name : _____

Date Practicum Will Be Completed:_____ for 3 hours of practicum credit.

Site Supervisor's Signature: _____

Supervisor's Printed Name: _____ Title _____

Institution & Office: _____

Mailing Address: _____

Phone #: (   ) _____; Fax #: (   ) _____; E-mail:_____

FIGURE 7.3. Prescribed site supervisor agreement form.

identify practical guidelines for selecting new employees. There are, however, several special considerations that should be addressed when selecting interns that may be at variance with hiring and orienting new professionals.

STRUCTURING THE POSITION

Because many units do not have interns every term, it is sometimes difficult to create an internship position that carries the same general responsibilities every term. For example, many units would be reluctant to entrust residence hall paraprofessional (residential assistant, RA) selection to an intern if they could not get another intern for the next RA selection season. It would be simpler to give this task to a graduate assistant or professional staff member rather than shifting these important responsibilities back and forth between a variety of interns and full-time staff. If a unit cannot create one or more fixed internship positions for which the responsibilities are constant from year to year, it is still important to create comprehensive position descriptions for those interns who may be creating a new project for the unit.

Consider the new student orientation unit that has an established parent program and wants to enhance it by creating a parent handbook. Conducting the background research and creating a detailed draft of such a handbook could be one of those self-contained projects that might be handled by an intern during a single term. Once the draft was completed, the professional staff could take over editing, arranging for production, and distribution without assuming an extra major responsibility. Before selecting an intern to take on this responsibility, however, a position description should be developed that contains the title of the supervisor, goals of the position, work activities and procedures of the position, skills and prior experiences desired, and conditions of employment (e.g., how many hours on-site are expected, duration of the internship, remuneration) (Winston & Creamer, 1997; Winston & Miller, 1991). For interns it is also especially important to follow the advice of Stimpson (1993) and include clear statements of the mission of the institution and unit and to articulate the ways in which the internship position is expected to make a contribution to that mission. Because it is often impossible for interns to be "on the job" when their projects are fully implemented and to see the effects of their work, it is often difficult for interns to understand how what they are doing is more than "busy work" and actually contributes to the accomplishment of the unit's mission. Site supervisors need to help interns see the big picture and to understand how activities and functions fit together.

When constructing a position advertisement for an intern, it is helpful to include not only the basic information from the position description but also to identify the non-monetary benefits of working in a particular site. An internship position advertisement might include a description of the skills and competencies that will be learned, the professional development opportunities that are available, the qualifications and special expertise of the supervisory staff, and elements of the organizational culture that may be particularly appealing to interns. Because graduate interns are rare commodities on many campuses, it is important to market the internship position, while not exaggerating the benefits. Failing to deliver what is promised to the intern can easily lead to lowered morale and difficulty recruiting interns in subsequent years.

INTERVIEWING AND SELECTING INTERNS

In an ideal situation, several potential interns would apply for a particular position. However, even if only one person is likely to apply, it is important to have an application process that includes submission of a resumé, a cover letter, and names of references. In this way, interns demonstrate that they have reflected on the ways in which their skills and learning goals are congruent with the position requirements. For each intern who submits application materials, the supervisor should share with that candidate a position description, expectations of interns, information about the service, appropriate planning documents, promotional brochures, and so on. In this way the candidate will begin to gain an idea of the purpose of the internship and the connection of the internship to the larger purposes of the unit.

It is often helpful to establish a small selection committee to review application materials and to interview candidates. A committee that represents both professional and support staff will help the unit staff understand the need for an intern and feel empowered to select the best person. In addition, the internship applicants will gain valuable experience in marketing themselves in a quasi-employment situation. Even though running a formal selection process will take more time than simply having the supervisor pick someone, the benefits in terms of intern productivity and clarity of expectations will generally outweigh the time spent. Supervisors need to use their own judgment in designing an interview process that gives the candidate and unit ample opportunity to evaluate the match without squandering valuable employee time. Time spent in interviewing potential interns can give candidates information about the culture of the unit, opportunities available, and contributions offered to the institution. Even if the candidates are not selected, they gain valuable and hopefully positive information about the work of the unit that can be transmitted to potential future interns. Conducting a well-organized, professionally managed search process not only leads to the selection of the best candidate, but also is excellent public relations. Graduate interns are often well connected with a variety of campus offices and many times freely communicate their opinions of a particular service.

PREPARING THE OTHER STAFF MEMBERS

Site supervisors can have the best of intentions for the arrival of the new intern and still have a difficult situation arise if they do not pay adequate attention to the needs of the other staff at the site. Some employees may be threatened by interns who tend to enthusiastically come in with plans to change the status quo in some way or who want to explain to others how their undergraduate institution did a particular task better. Handling this potential problem is really a two-sided activity. Current staff need to be part of planning for the intern's arrival and may need to be reminded of what it is like to be new to a work setting. The issues for the intern can be handled by appropriate orientation activities.

Holton and Naquin (2001) explain that new employees need to be told that admitting what they do not know is more important than showing what they do know. Because internships are often of a limited duration anyway, the student needs to be instructed that site supervisors, and the rest of the staff, do not expect them to know how to do everything—they are in fact there to learn, not to show current staff how to do their jobs better. Often this discussion relieves the intern of the mistaken belief that staff members have expectations of them that they do not have the experience base to fulfill.

Another issue to discuss with current staff members includes the space requirements and equipment assignment for the intern. It is important to avoid having the current staff feeling as if the intern is somehow interfering with their ability to work or is displacing them from their work space. Current staff need to have a discussion about where the intern will have a work space, what equipment they will be able to access to complete the tasks assigned, and coordinate schedules so that no one feels put on.

Finally, current staff members need to understand that the student intern is spending time in the office as part of an academic endeavor. The intern is not there to take on tasks the current staff members dislike, provide strictly clerical support, or handle tasks more appropriately assigned to an undergraduate student worker. Gross (1993) makes the point that "whether the internship is paid or unpaid, both the supervisor and the intern should realize that the primary aim is learning" (p. 27). If interns spend most of their time making photocopies, even if the wage is $15 an hour, they should not be getting internship credit. On the other hand, no institution should look on the internship as a source of free or cheap labor.

Current staff members should get a copy of the supervised practice syllabus so that they understand the role and purpose of the internship in the student's overall academic program. Having current staff be part of preparing for the intern's arrival, helping to establish goals and selecting work tasks, and deciding on a work schedule will likely have them more committed to ensuring a successful experience for the student intern.

ORIENTING THE INTERN

During the selection process, all candidates should have received documents articulating the mission of the unit, future plans, and promotional descriptions. These documents provide a foundation for the orientation process and if not distributed during the recruitment process should be given to the successful candidate as soon as he or she is identified. Once this foundation is established, it is time to begin orienting the intern to the unit and position. The job- and institution-specific orientation curriculum developed for new professionals (see chapter 2) provides a good model for orienting interns, with a few commonsense modifications. For example, if the intern is doing the internship on his or her home campus, providing information about such topics as housing accommodations or local services is not necessary. If one is selecting an intern who is far away from the home campus (such as a summer intern through programs offered by professional associations such as ACPA, NODA, or ACUHO-I), it is critical to provide help with housing and other living arrangements, especially because interns are often making a minimal salary and will need special assistance if housing is not provided as part of the internship. Another difficulty for many new interns is the lack of office space or appropriate work tools, such as a computer or permanent desk. Even though some units may not have an individual office set aside for interns, it is important that they have a space of their own with a place to store materials and their work in progress.

Because for many the first internship is their first professional-type position, it is important that the norms of the work environment are clear to interns. For example, the type of dress worn to work should not be left for the intern to infer, but clearly articulated. Staff rituals, such as sharing cake on birthdays or providing holiday cards, should be made clear as well. Often interns can be easily embarrassed by their lack of knowledge of professional customs, not recognizing that most professionals take a fair amount of time to develop the savvy to assess a particular culture to ascertain subtle expectations.

Interns are also likely to need some help getting to know others in the office and the expectations of the relationship between interns and various staff. Sometimes interns may not be aware of the fact that a particular secretary is not assigned to help with the intern's tasks, which leads to frustration on both sides. Another somewhat common scenario is when a staff member assumes that if the intern does not "look busy" at a particular time, it is appropriate to assign duties to the intern that may be "less than professional," such as changing a bulletin-board display or taking mail around to other campus offices. Seasoned professionals recognize that there are times when all must "chip in" to help stuff envelopes for a mailing or to clean up the office in preparation for an important visitor. Interns, because of their status as "not quite professional," may tend to see these assignments as more insulting than resulting from simple expediency. Clarifying the role of the intern to other staff members is an important orientation function often overlooked. By the same token, supervisors should be sure to mention to interns the norms of the office that govern who contributes to the more clerical office tasks and under what circumstances professional staff are expected to help out.

It is absolutely crucial that interns learn early on the limits of their authority and the ethics of the particular unit. If there is a particular set of ethical standards endorsed by the unit, the intern should be informed of that fact. If the intern is not authorized to allocate funds, this should be made clear up front, before the intern might inadvertently promise funds to a student organization or vendor. If decisions about office decor, for example, require approval of the department director, it is important that the intern know this fact, before deciding to post political cartoons or holiday decorations on an office door. An important lesson for interns is that all organizations, no matter how large or small, have their own cultures and political dynamics, some of which defy logic and rational analysis. It is much better to explain these dynamics than to allow an intern to be the victim of a faux pas. For supervisors who have been in an environment for several years, what is strange to the newcomer seems quite familiar and normal. Therefore, it might be advisable to have a newer staff member identified to provide information to the intern about "how things really work around here."

ESTABLISHING GOALS AND LEARNING PLANS

Once the intern is selected, the process of establishing learning goals and plans should begin. Because of the requirements of a particular graduate program, an intern may begin to develop internship learning goals before the internship begins or might wait to develop these until after an orientation period has been completed. No matter what the timing of creating goals, two points deserve attention: (a) that the site supervisor be closely involved with the process so that the goals will address real concerns or needs of the site, and (b) that the student, site supervisor, and faculty supervisor agree on these goals.

Before goals are identified, it is important to revisit the overall purposes of any internship so that all understand that in fundamental ways, internships are different from employment experiences. Several scholars (Carter, Cooke, & Neal, 1996; Harcharik, 1993; Ryan & Cassidy, 1996; Toohey, Ryan, & Hughes, 1996) have researched the purposes of internships in higher education. These authors agree that these experiences should offer students an understanding of the world of work, an opportunity to develop their professional skills, an environment in which to link theory with practice, and a chance to enhance future employment prospects. The focus of any internship is fundamentally on what the intern learns. Another, albeit secondary, outcome anticipated from an internship is that the student will contribute positively to the operation of the site. In contrast, the primary purpose of employment is to enhance the work of the institution. Continuous learning by the employee is a necessary element of effective functioning as a professional; but learning, by itself, is not sufficient to make needed professional contributions within a unit. Typically, both professionals and interns will contribute and will learn through their experiences. The difference between the fundamental purposes of the two roles is a matter of degree and emphasis. The emphasis on learning that is being advocated for interns requires that the goal-setting process typically used for employees will need modification. It is not adequate to have an intern complete the goal-setting process done by other professional staff, because in most settings the focus of annual goals is on improvement of the unit. Furthermore, most interns do not have enough time to gain the requisite understanding of the environment that leads to accomplishment of meaningful unit goals. Finally, if one assumes that an intern is only on-site for a semester or two, it is important that the supervisor take more direction than would be typical with NPs to help the intern develop particular projects or activities that can be completed during the course of the internship.

For interns, the goal-setting scheme of innovative and maintenance goals that is articulated in chapter 3 of this volume for NPs may be problematic because interns are not on-site long enough to learn much from the maintenance-type goals. Instead, we advocate that, for interns, the goal-setting approach developed by Hirt and Janosik (2002) be used. To gain a full understanding of this approach, readers are advised to consult *Learning Through the Supervised Practice Experience in Student Affairs* (Cooper et al., 2002, chapter 2). To use this approach, supervisors need to begin by helping interns assess their current level of competence and the skills that they desire to refine through the internship experience. Supervisors should be aware of a common flaw of this type of learning-focused goal setting. Because they are delighted at the opportunity to attend to their own learning, students may believe that a wide variety of skills can be enhanced through a 10 hour per week, semester-long internship. In reality, both the faculty and site supervisors can perform a valuable service by making sure that the learning goals are realistic and achievable.

Hirt and Janosik (2002) advocate a learning contract that consists of eight elements:

- Student information.
- Site supervisor information.
- Internship faculty coordinator information.
- A purpose statement.
- Objectives, activities, and skills and competencies.
- Site location information.
- Proposed work schedule.
- Appropriate signatures.

An example contract created by Hirt and Janosik is included in Appendix E.

The purpose statement is a critical component of the contract. It should be an overview of what the intern hopes to accomplish and should reflect the projects and activities identified by the supervisor in the position description and announcement. The objectives and activities sections outline more specifically what will be accomplished and the tasks that will be undertaken. The site supervisor who assists in creation of the objectives and activities sections should challenge the intern to be clear, but to avoid so much detail that every possible activity is documented. For example, rather than, as Jane did, stating that she would research conflict resolution models, another intern who was too focused on details could have specified the number of conflict resolution models to be researched, the methodology to be used for such research, the criteria that would be used to ascertain the efficacy of particular models, and the specifications of the research report that would result from these efforts. That much detail would overwhelm almost any intern, and furthermore, could close off possible new directions for research that would likely emerge during the course of the project.

One of the most important features of the Hirt and Janosik (2002) learning contract is the section on skills and competencies. Again, this section outlines clearly, but simply, what the intern aspires to learn and develop through the particular activities. Supervisors should encourage students to review their entire list of skills and competencies to be sure what is identified for this particular internship is congruent with the set of skills the students sees as most important for future professional development. If the internship skills do not match with what the student sees as most important, the supervisor may decide to help the student rearrange work activities or to assist the student in finding ways outside the placement site to develop the desired skills. According to Hirt and Janosik, the most challenging part of the contract is the estimation of time that will be spent on each activity. Even though the nature of these activities may cause the time amounts to change slightly, an initial time estimate will prevent a student from being "sidetracked," spending too much time on one element of the internship while ignoring others.

Even though the learning contract is an excellent tool, its usefulness is limited if it is completed and then forgotten until the end of the term. During regular supervision sessions, the supervisor should pull out the learning contract and discuss the following questions:

- Describe your progress in each of the activities.
- What has been especially challenging?
- Are there strategies you might employ to meet these challenges?
- Are there strategies that the supervisor or others in the environment might employ to address the challenges?
- What are your successes in making progress with the learning contract?
- In what areas are you seeing positive skill development?
- In what areas is your skill development stalled or particularly problematic?
- How might we work together to make sure that you are developing the skills most important to you?

Supervising Interns: Special Considerations

One primary task of supervisors and interns alike is to set realistic expectations for the experience. Because internships are important to future career success, interns typically desire to make contributions to the site that enhance current skills and build new competencies that are marketable and can be documented on a resumé or in a portfolio. For some graduate students an internship is the first taste of applying their skills to the real world with the accompanying excitement and intense motivation. It can be tempting for a supervisor to mistake enthusiasm for more mature skill development and to treat interns in the same fashion as NPs. The needs and skill development of most interns require, however, a slightly different supervision approach than is depicted in chapter 3.

Needs of Supervisees

To function as an effective supervisor of interns, one should know what the intern needs to contribute to the organization's functions and to develop more fully as a student affairs practitioner. The needs of interns may be different from desires. The task of the supervisor is to use his or her greater professional and life experience to separate what elements of the internship experience will be of actual benefit to the office and the intern rather than succumbing to the immediate desires of the intern. Occasionally an intern desires, for example, to have total autonomy in a project or to be given direction about minute details, which would be counterproductive to the intern's development (and to the functioning of one's office). Including elements in the supervisory relationship that will achieve the needs of the intern requires reflection and careful thought. The following list of supervisor attributes articulated by Winston and Hirt (in chapter 3) would be appropriate for interns and new professionals alike.

- Interpreting the institutional and office culture in ways that the intern finds meaningful.
- Willingness to engage in one-on-one interaction to help resolve problems, understand the background of a situation, or clarify expectations.
- Desire to support the intern so that he or she can learn from mistakes rather than to become debilitated or demoralized by them.
- Expertise in articulating expectations and organizing tasks so that it is possible to complete the work in the time available.
- Facility in giving frequent feedback that focuses on strengths and deficits, rather than solely on deficits.
- Allowing a degree of autonomy that allows for minor, predictable mistakes, but does not jeopardize the particular project or office operations.
- Functioning in an open, consistent fashion.
- Being a positive role model as an ethical, productive professional.

Special Needs of Interns

As supervisees, interns bring several special considerations to the experience. Because interns are typically immersed in learning student development and organizational theories, legal principles, innovative interventions, and assessment and evaluation strategies, they often need opportunities to see how their classroom experience is in operation at the internship site. They may also desire, either formally or informally, to evaluate how well the internship site matches up to what is advocated in class as excellent professional practice. How, then, might a supervisor accommodate an intern's need to understand and evaluate the site in terms of classroom content?

POWER RELATIONSHIPS

In chapter 3, Hirt and Winston discuss ways in which the power differential affects supervision with new professionals. As with supervising new professionals, the supervisor's ability to use power wisely is a critical component in working with interns. There are, however, some characteristics of the internship site supervisor relationship that affect the constructive use of power. Because interns may receive no paycheck (or a very small stipend), are not eligible for promotions, and may not be in the site long enough to benefit from the supervisor's sponsorship, reliance on coercive or reward power is less feasible. Yet interns do tend to rely intently on their supervisor's greater experience, thus giving them expert power. In addition, because interns are new to higher education and aspire to upper level positions, they often have great respect for the administrative title, education, and prior experience of the supervisor, and give them considerable legitimate power in the supervisory relationship. The use of referent power, which "depends on feelings of friendship and loyalty that are usually developed slowly over a long period of time" (Yukl, 1998, p. 186), will be different than with NPs because of the short-term nature of the internship experience.

Even though the intern is usually on-site for one term or at most a year, it is still important to maximize referent and expert power by establishing a synergistic type of relationship based on clear and mutually defined expectations for performance, mutual trust and respect, open communication, and sharing of insights and understandings on the part of both the supervisor and supervisee. Although supervisors of interns typically use power appropriately in their work with interns, there are definite ways that power could be abused. Angrily threatening to lower an intern's grade, for example, would be a misuse of coercive power. Treating the intern's short-term status as preventing meaningful accomplishment would be a misuse of referent power. Promising a full-time job before the search process was completed would be a clear misuse of reward power. Failing to listen to the intern's perception of events because of his or her limited experience would be a misuse of expert power. Frequent misuse of power could lead to lack of motivation from the intern, numerous end-runs, limited productivity, and a higher likelihood that the intern would use what influence he or she possessed to damage the reputation of the site and supervisor.

AVOIDING THE TEMPTATION TO MICROMANAGE INTERNS

In chapter 3, Winston and Hirt argue that micromanagement can, over time, diminish productivity, creativity, and the employee's self-esteem. Because of interns' lack of prior experience it is tempting for some supervisors to either give assignments that are peripheral to the organization or to micromanage. If the supervisor and intern along with the consultation of the faculty supervisor develop that type of learning contract based on an adequate assessment of skills described earlier, the supervisor may be more inclined to give important, but developmentally appropriate, work to the intern. Also, matching assignments with skill level can help supervisors avoid the time-consuming and frustrating task of managing unnecessary details.

Because of limited experience, interns may need more supervision about how to handle the details of a project than would a new or experienced professional. For example, if an intern were assigned the task of developing an orientation program for older adult students, that intern would likely need more details about the characteristics of the target population and the purpose and intended goals of the intervention, and would need more frequent checks on progress than would a more experienced staff member. Because the time devoted by interns is relatively short, they need to be encouraged to seek prior approval if they deviate from the original plan. In the example of the orientation program, an experienced staff member might have learned through experience that student leaders were given significant responsibility for implementing orientation programs, but an intern may not know this. Even though the supervisor should tell the intern about this organizational norm, the supervisor should also check to be sure how student leaders are being integrated into the planning process, so that the student leaders are involved in a way commensurate with typical practice. If a supervisor fails to check on progress in some detail, an intern can inadvertently cause political problems for the office that could be difficult to overcome.

PRACTICAL SUGGESTIONS FOR SUPERVISING INTERNS

According to Winston and Creamer (2002), good internship supervision is "based on (a) a trusting and supportive relationship between supervisor and intern, (b) an internship structure that permits interns to observe widely and to assume some responsibilities normally associated with professionals in the site, (c) theory-based practice, (d) open communication and candor, (e) mutual respect, (f) practice that emphasizes observance of professional ethical standards, and (g) accountability" (pp. 69–70). The following practical suggestions can help the supervisor achieve a relationship that incorporates these attributes.

Explain Dynamics of the Site

Because interns rarely have extensive prior experience, they can easily miss the subtle organizational dynamics at work. They may be puzzled as to why, for example, a secretary who has been with the institution for many years is able to delegate tasks "up" much more readily than the new professional can transfer tasks to the secretary. Certain staff members being included on important decisions when others at the same level are not may seem inexplicable. Furthermore, the decision-making process or the ways certain staff members communicate with their supervisors may be obscure or confusing to a newcomer. It is often difficult to explain these subtleties to an intern for a variety of reasons, such as (a) to fully understand the dynamic one might need to know information which is private or thought to be so by the supervisor's supervisor, (b) what might be "strange" to a new intern has become "familiar" to the site supervisor and thus the supervisor may not explain it, and (c) the supervisor may be unaware of certain dynamics whereas the intern, because of a perceived lack of power, is in a position to observe how staff members interact in unguarded moments.

Gaining an understanding about organizational dynamics, although challenging for the supervisor to share, is a crucial part of the learning that occurs in an internship. An internship is often one of the first places an intern sees organizational culture played out large. The job of the supervisor is to interpret those dynamics by (a) making sure that the intern is oriented to the formal organizational structure through strategic plans, organizational values statements, departmental missions, organizational charts, and the like; (b) scheduling time for each staff member to meet the intern and to talk about how things work at that particular site; (c) including within the one-on-one time an opportunity to explain organizational dynamics from the supervisor's perspective and to solicit the impressions of the intern; and (d) establishing ground rules for conversations about organizational dynamics that will foster a rational conversation rather than character assassination.

Open and Productive Communication

The importance of private meeting time of the supervisor and intern cannot be overstated. Weekly or biweekly supervision meetings are *essential*. For these meetings to be productive, agendas should be established in a manner such that both the supervisor and intern can contribute items. Use of e-mail may be helpful in this regard. At the regular supervision meeting, the intern should give an informal progress report about the tasks that have been assigned. The supervisor should also be asking what the intern feels she or he is learning through the experience and see if there is a need to expand or redirect the learning contract.

The supervisor also needs to establish an open environment in supervision sessions so that the intern can ask for help, admit errors, or look for explanations. The best way to do this is by being a role model who admits lack of complete knowledge or understanding, who acknowledges that some conclusions are tentative, and who talks openly about professional values and ethics and personal integrity.

Communication can also be enhanced if the supervisor and intern discuss role expectations openly. They should, as part of early supervision sessions, determine the answers to the following questions: (a) What do the supervisor and intern want most from each other in terms of the quality of relationship; (b) what types of behaviors, if exhibited by the supervisor or intern, could be impediments to learning; (c) what do both agree to do if they have a disagreement or conflict; and (d) how much time is to be devoted to supervisory sessions and how will they be conducted?

Dealing with Interns Who Are Not Meeting Expectations

Even with the most careful planning and supervision, there may be times when interns do not meet expectations, either about a relatively inconsequential issue or about a major project. Because of the fact that an intern is a short-term staff member, it is often tempting to let the problem ride out its course, avoid too much confrontation, and move on to the next intern and hope for better. Site supervisors, however, are critically important teachers in the internship experience and can serve the student and profession by adopting reasonable standards of accountability. Many times, faculty members in a preparation program do not see, for example, how students may handle interpersonal conflicts in less than an appropriate way or how they might belittle staff perceived to have less power. If interns aspire to an administrative position in student affairs, they need exemplary interpersonal skills to communicate effectively with a variety of constituencies. Well-timed and direct feedback about interpersonal skills, for instance, can be a turning point for an aspiring student affairs professional.

Holding interns accountable for both completion of tasks and relationships with others requires careful thought and planning. Giving regular, frequent feedback is advisable. Commentary about the quality and quantity of progress toward achieving learning goals is often the most productive way to give feedback. There are times, however, when the supervisor needs to comment on the intern's interpersonal style, method of handling conflict, professional demeanor, or general attitude. It is important that these topics not be avoided and there are better ways to have these conversations. The following steps should be followed:

- Criticize in private.
- Focus on positive contributions in addition to negative behaviors.
- Identify negative behaviors forthrightly, but spend most of the conversation focusing on strategies for improvement.
- Create a plan for improvement, write objectives, and check to see that objectives are being addressed.
- Consult with the faculty supervisor to advise him or her about the difficulties and plan to address them.
- Document conversation and keep copies of the plan.
- Follow up implementation of the plan.

There are times when the intern's performance is such that the relationship needs to be terminated. This happens less frequently with interns because of their short-term status, but there may be times when a graduate student, either an intern or graduate assistant, commits such an egregious error (such as sexual harassment, encouraging [condoning] underage students to consume alcohol, fund mismanagement, or other actions that would put the institution at legal risk) that the student must be terminated. In most ways, termination of an intern is similar to involuntary separation of an NP (see chapter 6, in this volume). Specifically, as with employees, documentation of deficiencies must be kept, the intern must understand he or she is being terminated, and the conditions of termination need to be addressed. With interns, however, it is important that the faculty supervisor be involved in all steps of the process from the identification of the problem through the actual termination. The faculty supervisor is ultimately responsible for grades, and failure to complete an internship may lead to the intern's removal from the academic program. The faculty supervisor is the ultimate decision maker in determining whether the intern is placed in another internship for the remainder of the term or whether that person receives a failing grade. In the case of graduate assistants, the faculty coordinator of the graduate program should also be made aware of the decision to terminate, because the loss of financial support (often with tuition remission) may lead the intern to decide to withdraw from the academic program. If the graduate program and supervisor view the assistantship as related to and, in essence, extensions of the academic experience, it is important for the faculty coordinator to understand the graduate assistant's deficiencies so that they can be addressed in the academic arena also

LEGAL AND ETHICAL ISSUES IN INTERNSHIP

As part of any supervised practice experience, students often encounter legal and/or ethical issues at the work site. These encounters are usually not profound in nature. More often, what students experience or hear about becomes more of a discussion issue or cause for some personal reflection.

Site supervisors are under the same legal and ethical standards working with a student intern as they would be with a full-time employee. The institution's policies on such things as sexual harassment or fraternization and federal regulations such as the Americans with Disabilities Act strictures about dealing with persons with handicaps or various discrimination acts must be followed. Several employment issues may, however, be handled in a somewhat different manner.

Site supervisors are under ethical obligations (see Appendices A and B) to provide timely and honest feedback about performance. The time-limited nature of the internship may make it important to handle evaluation and termination issues differently for interns than for full-time staff (this topic has been discussed in full in the previous section). For example, a site supervisor may be under institutional or state guidelines for the time and manner a supervisor can terminate an employee. With an increasingly litigious society, following these guidelines methodically is crucial to minimize risk management concerns. Student interns are in the workplace as part of an educational process. As such, issues arising that may necessitate termination usually are handled with different guidelines. The syllabus for internship or the internship handbook should outline procedures that the site supervisor, faculty supervisor, and student will follow to handle concerns that may point toward termination of the internship. Also, because grades are involved, students maintain whatever rights the credit-granted institution provides to challenge grades. Having clear and complete documentation about student and site expectations about how to handle site termination will usually assist the site supervisor with these types of decisions.

No doubt the more pressing liability concern for site supervisor of interns involves issues of confidentiality. Although this is typically a concern of most student service offices, it becomes magnified when interns, who are also matriculated students at that institution, are in possible contact with the records of other students. "This information and resulting student record is regulated by the Family Educational Rights and Privacy Act of 1974 (20 U.S.C. § 1232g), popularly known as the Buckley Amendment or FERPA.

The Act and its implementing regulations, 34 C. F. R. Part 99, apply to all public and private educational agencies or institutions that receive federal funds from the U. S. Department of Education or whose students receive such funds under federal loan programs" (Janosik & Hirt, 2002). As part of any orientation or introduction to the work site, interns need to be clearly informed about the stipulations and policies of the office related to compliance with the confidentiality of student records.

Ethical Concerns

Laws and federal guidelines do not always cover what is appropriate and inappropriate behavior in the workplace. In fact, it would be more likely that professional ethics will be more often used than legal codes or regulations. Students in supervised practice should have already received and discussed ethical standards and guidelines from professional organizations in student affairs (e.g., ACPA and NASPA).

The NASPA statement provides a good general review of the expectations for ethical behavior primarily from an institutional perspective. It addresses 18 different topic areas. The ACPA statement, on the other hand, is more comprehensive and is more focused on the conduct of individual practitioners. It includes a preamble, a mechanism for enforcement, a section on general ethical principles, and a very detailed section on ethical standards (Janosik & Hirt, 2002). Both are useful to discuss with a student in supervised practice so that they have a reference point to begin thinking about acting in ethical ways.

Dual Relationships

One particular set of issues seems to arise most frequently when discussing supervised work experience with site supervisors. That problem is around the complexities of dual relationships, or those situations where interns have, by virtue of work requirements, multiple roles in dealing with students, staff, or other constituencies. For example, an intern lives in a residence hall and has become friends with a group of students but then in an internship site is supervising some of the same students. Or perhaps more common, a graduate student comes in contact with a student in the internship site and they really enjoy spending together, so they begin to have a more social relationship away from the internship site.

Section 2.2 of the ACPA Ethical Code states, "Avoid dual relationships with students (e.g., counselor/employer, supervisor/best friend, or faculty/

sexual partner) that may involve incompatible roles and conflicting responsibilities." This is particularly difficult to avoid in a small campus setting where many more opportunities exist for these types of relationships to develop. And certainly not all dual relationships are illegal or unethical (Pearson & Piazza, 1997), for instance. However, they are also a challenge for interns who are typically not that much older than some of the students they will be serving or working with in the supervised practice setting.

Supervisors should make sure that new employees (interns included) know the institutional policies regarding sexual harassment, yet few, outside of those in counseling and medical settings, have the difficult discussion about dual relationships (Cobia & Boes, 2000). Most practitioners would not consider "hanging out" on the weekend with a student worker in one's office, yet at times supervisors look the other way when it is obvious that a graduate student intern and an undergraduate student worker are doing just that. At the very least, supervisors need to encourage interns to examine the appropriateness of the relationships they develop with others while they are in the work setting (Rupert & Holmes, 1997). They need to understand that how a relationship looks to or is interpreted by others is as critical as the actual intent. Learning this difficult lesson now will be of great service to them in their later professional life.

EVALUATING THE INTERNSHIP

Providing honest and accurate evaluations of work performance is an ethical obligation for practitioners in student affairs. The American College Personnel Association *Statement of Ethical Principles and Standards* (1992) mandates in Section 3.11 that professionals "evaluate job performance of subordinates regularly and recommend appropriate actions to enhance professional development and improve performance."

Unlike the performance appraisal process outlined previously in this text, evaluating the student intern has some very different goals. Again, the short-term nature of the experience is part of the reason for this difference as is the educational or learning function that accompanies supervised practice. Also, Kruger (2000) commented that the purpose of putting theory to practice through supervised practice should cause supervisors to think about performance evaluation in a different way from the more traditional approach with full-time staff. (See chapter 5 in this volume for a review of performance appraisal issues with new professionals.)

In addition to the differences already mentioned, supervised practice often includes a reflective component or requirement where interns regularly journal or discuss the application of theory to practice, various issues or tasks from the site, as well as their personal appraisal of their actual performance. Cooper and Saunders (2002) note that a well-run supervised practice experience will result in creating more reflective practitioners "who understand their strengths, weaknesses, preferences, and learning styles, as well as the specifics of the theories. Most important, a reflective practitioner uses his or her own appraisal as a central source of data in determining effectiveness. Even though incorporating evaluation feedback from site and faculty supervisors is essential, depending totally on others to appraise the supervised practice performance renders an incomplete picture that misses the rich and detailed information about individual learning that only the student can provide. Interns' personal appraisals of the supervised practice experience should include both formative and summative approaches" (pp. 156–157). Ideally then, evaluation includes feedback from the faculty supervisor and site supervisor but also includes a reflective component where students are encouraged to grade themselves on their performance, accomplishments, and learning during the supervised practice experience (See Appendix 6.3 from Cooper and Saunders [2002] for a structured example supervisors could encourage interns to use.)

Analysis of Work Performance

Supervisors of interns should concentrate on two components of work performance in the evaluation process. First, the actual task performed, programs conducted, written material created, or other specific assignments need to be evaluated. The goals of the site and the learning objective of the internship related to these tasks should be reviewed and some measure of accomplishment assigned (see Appendix C). The overall purpose of this supervisory evaluation is to assess achievement of outcomes and performance quality. The evaluation the intern receives from the site supervisor is designed to look at the experience as a whole, identifying strengths and weaknesses. As supervisors, it is critical to remember that students should receive regular feedback about their day-to-day performance continuously during the term, but the final evaluation allows the supervisor and intern to identify patterns, themes, and issues that emerged during the entire course of the internship.

Evaluating interns is similar to part of the performance appraisal process for new professionals in that supervisors provide observations of the quality of the work performed. Winston and Creamer (1997) urge supervisors to consider both accomplishments and effectiveness with staff and certainly the same would hold for evaluation of interns. The learning objectives become the primary basis for considering accomplishments where effectiveness is based on the supervisor's observation of both attention to the task and also the interactions with others on site.

This evaluation time should be prescheduled close to the end of the supervised practice experience. One concern interns often express is that the evaluation time seemed to be viewed by the supervisor as a nuisance or squeezed in between other meetings or tasks. Typically, most people experience some degree of anxiety about the evaluation process—both those acting as evaluator and those being evaluated. Because this may be one of the first professional evaluation experiences for interns, trying to approach it as an important culminating experience that is designed to teach rather than punish will help ease that anxiety and make the intern feel as if supervisors look forward to that private time together.

One important purpose of assessing skill development and task accomplishment through the supervised practice experience is to assist interns to identify the broad, transferable competencies that have been gained. "Rather than focusing on the specific work tasks or the quality of interpersonal relationships, the assessment of transferable skills requires that one think more globally, synthesizing different elements of the internship experience" (Cooper & Saunders, 2002, p. 164). Lock (2000) points out that "functional/transferable skills are things that [one does], such as teaching, organizing, persuading, assembling, supervising, computing, researching, analyzing, deciding, operating, and designing" (p. 213). It is critically important to help interns identify transferable skills, because they are what they can use as they highlight the skills acquired through internship later on in their professional preparation program as they prepare for a job interview or develop a cover letter.

Evaluating the Site in Terms of Classroom Content

Recognize that part of the intern's learning is to evaluate, sometimes critically, the functioning of the office as well as the actions of the supervisor. This evaluation should occur informally, through the intern's casual conversations or class discussions, even if the supervisor never talks about how the intern is fitting classroom learning with internship experience. It is important for interns to have the opportunity to evaluate the experience they had in the site. Appendix D provides a sample of such an evaluation form. This gives the interns a chance to reflect on how various aspects of the work site enhanced their learning, as well as providing a low-risk opportunity to point out deficiencies or barriers.

Managing this internship dynamic requires preparation. First, it is important for the internship supervisor to understand the fundamental content taught in the preparation program. This does not mean that the supervisor has to read all of the course material or syllabi or become an expert in unfamiliar content. The supervisor does need to understand the curricular emphases of the preparation program, the learning objectives that the program is trying to achieve, and the basic content that is to be covered. A conversation with the faculty liaison to the internship along with a careful review of the preparation program's website should provide an adequate understanding of the program. Once this understanding is achieved, the site supervisor should remember to explain the task assignments or expectations of the internship in terms of what is being taught in class. For example, if the intern is assigned to develop a parent orientation handbook, the supervisor might talk with the intern about what the literature says about the college choice process and characteristics of diverse student populations and their families.

Second, the supervisor should open the door for discussion with the intern about how what is learned in the classroom fits with what is being observed in the site. It is helpful for the intern to complete an assessment of the site at the close of the internship and one element of that assessment should be to comment upon the degree to which the site's organizational structure, resources, and personnel helped or hindered achievement of goals. (For further information about internship evaluation strategies, see Cooper & Saunders, 2002.) Another way for interns to assess their site and to acquire valuable experience in integrating classroom learning with observations from the site is to use the CAS Standards (Miller, 2001) as a template for providing feedback about the operations of the site.

Third, even though it is normal for interns to critique their site in terms of what they learn in class, it is important that the supervisor work with the intern to share criticisms appropriately. An intern who makes unsubstantiated and extreme criticisms of a site to anyone in hearing distance can damage the reputation of the office with upper level administrators, faculty in the preparation program, or other individuals on campus. The preparation program should cover information about how to share criticism in an ethical fashion. Specifically, interns should be told to share criticisms in private with supervisors, in sessions with their faculty supervisor, or in internship classes where the "ground rules" discourage unwarranted gossiping about the weaknesses of a site or unflattering incidents. If the preparation program does not cover this information, the site supervisor should do so.

CONCLUSION

Students involved in supervised practice present some supervisory needs that differ from working with new, full-time professional staff. Students in supervised practice will often have a more prescribed set of tasks and feedback requirements and will often receive joint supervision from a faculty member in the preparation program and a site supervisor. Although internships generally are relatively short-term, it is important to remember that students are learning how to become new professionals through the work they are doing and the activities they observe staff involved with in the site. Supervision in this situation is crucially important to the health of the student affairs profession and the expectations of those who will fill positions in the future.

REFERENCES

American College Personnel Association. (1992). *Statement of ethical principles and standards*. Available online: http ://www.acpa.nche.edu/pubs/prncstan.htm

Carpenter, D. S., Miller, T. K., & Winston, R. B., Jr. (1980). Toward the professionalization of student affairs. *NASPA Journal, 18*(2), 16–22.

Carter, R., Cooke, F., & Neal, B. (1996). Action centered learning in industry. In J. Tait & P. Knight (Eds.), *The management of independent learning* (pp. 65–73). London: Koga Page.

Cobia, D. C., & Boes, S. R. (2000). Professional disclosure statements and formal plans for supervision: Two strategies for minimizing the risk of ethical conflicts in post-master's supervision. *Journal of Counseling & Development, 78*(3), 293–296.

Cooper, D. L., & Saunders, S.A. (2002). Evaluating the internship experience. In D. L. Cooper, S. A. Saunders, R. B. Winston, Jr., J. B. Hirt, D. G. Creamer, & S. M. Janosik (Eds.), *Learning through supervised practice in student affairs* (pp. 153–170). New York: Brunner-Routledge.

Cooper, D. L., Saunders, S. A., Winston, R. B., Jr., Hirt, J. B., Creamer, D. G., & Janosik, S. M. (Eds.). (2002). *Learning through supervised practice in student affairs*. New York: Brunner-Routledge.

Creamer, D. G., & Winston, R. B., Jr. (2002). Foundations of the supervised practice experience: Definitions, context, and philosophy. In D. L. Cooper, S. A. Saunders, R. B. Winston, Jr., J. B. Hirt, D. G. Creamer, & S. M. Janosik (Eds.), *Learning through supervised practice in student affairs* (pp. 1–34). New York: Brunner-Routledge.

Creamer, D. G., Winston, R. B., Jr., & Miller, T. K. (2001). The professional student affairs administrator: Roles and functions. In R. B. Winston, Jr., D. G. Creamer, T. K. Miller, & Associates, *The professional student affairs administrator: Educator, leader, and manger* (pp. 3–38). New York: Brunner-Routledge.

Gross, L. S. (1993). *The internship experience*. Prospect Heights, IL: Waveland Press.

Harcharik, K. (1993). Piaget and the university internship experience. *Journal of Cooperative Education, 29*, 24–32.

Hellweg, S.A. (1985). *Internship in the communication arts and science*. Scottsdale, AZ: Gorsuch Scarisbrick.

Hirt, J. B., & Janosik, S. (2002) Structure and design of the supervised practice experience. In D. L. Cooper, S. A. Saunders, R. B. Winston, Jr., J. B. Hirt, D. G. Creamer, & S. M. Janosik (Eds.), *Learning through supervised practice in student affairs* (pp. 35–64). New York: Brunner-Routledge.

Hoberman, S., & Mailick, S. (1994). Introduction. In S. Hoberman & S. Mailick (Eds.), *Professional education in the United States: Experiential learning, issues, and prospects* (pp. 3–6). Westport, CT: Praeger.

Holton, E. F., & Naquin, S. S. (2001). *Helping your new employee succeed.* San Francisco: Berrett-Koehler.

Janosik, S. M., & Hirt, J. B. (2002). Legal and ethical issues. In D. L. Cooper, S. A. Saunders, R. B. Winston, Jr., J. B. Hirt, D. G. Creamer, & S. M. Janosik (Eds.), *Learning through supervised practice in student affairs* (pp. 133–152). New York: Brunner-Routledge.

Kruger, K. (2000). New alternatives for professional development. In M. J. Barr & M. K. Dessler (Eds.), *The handbook of student affairs administration* (2nd ed., pp. 535–553). San Francisco: Jossey-Bass.

Lock, R. D. (2000). *Taking charge of your career direction: Career planning guide, Book 1* (4th ed.). Belmont, CA: Wadsworth/Thomson Learning.

Miller, T. K. (Ed.). (2001). *The CAS book of professional standards for higher education.* Washington, DC: Council for the Advancement of Standards in Higher Education.

Patterson, V. (1997). The employers' guide: Successful intern/co-op programs. *Journal of Career Planning & Employment, 57*(2), 30–34, 55–56, 59.

Pearson, B., & Piazza, N. (1997). Classification of dual relationships in the helping professions. *Counselor Education and Supervision, 37,* 89–99.

Rupert, P. A., & Holmes, D. L. (1997). Dual relationships in higher education: Professional and institutional guidelines. *Journal of Higher Education, 68,* 660–678.

Ryan, M., & Cassidy, J. R. (1996). Internships and excellence. *Liberal Education, 82*(3), 16–23.

Schroeder, C. C., & Pike, G. R. (2001). The scholarship of application in student affairs. *Journal of College Student Development, 42,* 342–355.

Stimpson, R. F. (1993). Selecting and training competent staff. In M. J. Barr & Associates, *The handbook of student affairs administration* (pp. 135–151). San Francisco: Jossey-Bass.

Toohey, S., Ryan, G., & Hughes, C. (1996). Assessing the practicum. *Assessment and evaluation in higher education, 21,* 215–227.

Winston, R. B., Jr., & Creamer, D. L. (2002). Internship supervision: Relationships that support learning. In D. L. Cooper, S. A. Saunders, R. B. Winston, Jr., J. B. Hirt, D. G. Creamer, & S. M. Janosik (Eds.), *Learning through supervised practice in student affairs.* New York: Brunner-Routledge.

Winston, R. B., Jr., & Creamer, D. G. (1997). *Improving staffing practices in student affairs.* San Francisco: Jossey-Bass.

Winston, R. B., Jr., & Miller, T. K. (1991). Human resource management: Professional preparation and staff selection. In T. K. Miller, R. B. Winston, Jr., & Associates (Eds.), *Administration and leadership in student affairs: Actualizing student development in higher education* (2nd ed., pp. 449–489). Muncie, IN: Accelerated Development.

Yukl, G. (1998). *Leadership in organizations* (4th ed.). Upper Saddle River, NJ: Prentice Hall.

AMERICAN COLLEGE PERSONNEL ASSOCIATION
Statement of Ethical Principles and Standards

As Presented by the ACPA Standing Committee on Ethics
and Approved by the ACPA Executive Council, November 1992

Preamble

The American College Personnel Association (ACPA) is an association whose members are dedicated to enhancing the worth, dignity, potential, and uniqueness of each individual within post-secondary educational institutions and thus to the service of society. ACPA members are committed to contributing to the comprehensive education of the student, protecting human rights, advancing knowledge of student growth and development, and promoting the effectiveness of institutional programs, services, and organizational units. As a means of supporting these commitments, members of ACPA subscribe to the following principles and standards of ethical conduct. Acceptance of membership in ACPA signifies that the member agrees to adhere to the provisions of this statement.

This statement is designed to address issues particularly relevant to college student affairs practice. Persons charged with duties in various functional areas of higher education are also encouraged to consult ethical standards specific to their professional responsibilities.

Use of This Statement

The principal purpose of this statement is to assist student affairs professionals in regulating their own behavior by sensitizing them to potential ethical problems and by providing standards useful in daily practice. Observance of ethical behavior also benefits fellow professionals and students due to the effect of modeling. Self-regulation is the most effective and preferred means of assuring ethical behavior. If, however, a professional observes conduct by a fellow professional that seems contrary to the provisions of this document, several courses of action are available.

- Initiate a private conference. Because unethical conduct often is due to a lack of awareness or understanding ethical standards, a private conference with the professional(s) about the conduct in question is an important initial line of action. This conference, if pursued in a spirit of collegiality and sincerity, often may resolve the ethical concern and promote future ethical conduct.
- Pursue institutional remedies. If private consultation does not produce the desired results, institutional channels for resolving alleged ethical improprieties may be pursued. All student affairs divisions should have a widely-publicized process for addressing allegations of ethical misconduct.
- Contact ACPA Ethics Committee. If the ACPA member is unsure about whether a particular activity or practice falls under the provisions of this statement, the Ethics Committee may be contacted in writing. The member should describe in reasonable detail (omitting data that would identify the person(s) as much as possible) the potentially unethical conduct or practices and the circumstances surrounding the situation. Members of the Committee or others in the Association will provide the member with a summary of opinions regarding the ethical appropriateness of the conduct or practice in question. Because these opinions are based on limited information, no specific situation or action will be judged unethical. The responses rendered by the Committee are advisory only and are not an official statement on behalf of ACPA.
- Request consultation from ACPA Ethics Committee. If the institution wants further assistance in resolving the controversy, an institutional representative may request on-campus consultation. Provided all parties to the controversy agree, a team of consultants selected by the Ethics Committee will visit the campus at the institution's expense to hear the allegations and to review the facts and circumstances. The team will advise institutional leadership on possible actions consistent with both the content and spirit of the ACPA Statement of Ethical Principles and Standards. Compliance with the recommendations is voluntary. No sanctions will be imposed by ACPA. Institutional leaders remain responsible for assuring ethical conduct and practice. The consultation team will maintain confidentiality surrounding the process to the extent possible.
- Submit complaint to ACPA Ethics Committee. If the alleged misconduct may be a violation of the ACPA Statement of Ethical Principles and Standards, the person charged is unavailable or produces unsatisfactory results, then proceedings against the individual(s) may be brought to the ACPA Ethics Committee for review. Details regarding the procedures may be obtained by contacting the Executive Director at ACPA Headquarters.

Ethical Principles

No statement of ethical standards can anticipate all situations that have ethical implications. When student affairs professionals are presented with dilemmas that are not explicitly addressed herein, five ethical principles may be used in conjunction with the four enumerated standards (Professional Responsibility and Competence, Student Learning and Development, Responsibility to the Institution, Responsibility to Society) to assist in making decisions and determining appropriate courses of action. Ethical principles should guide the behaviors of professionals in everyday practice. Principles, however, are not just guidelines for reaction when something goes wrong or when a complaint is raised. Adhering to ethical principles also calls for action. These principles include the following:

- Act to benefit others. Service to humanity is the basic tenet underlying student affairs practice. Hence, student affairs professionals exist to: [a] promote healthy social, physical, academic, moral, cognitive, career, and personality development of students; [b] bring a developmental perspective to the institution's total educational process and learning environment; [c] contribute to the effective functioning of the institution; and [d] provide programs and services consistent with this principle.
- Promote justice. Student affairs professionals are committed to assuring fundamental fairness for all individuals within the academic community. In pursuit of this goal, the principles of impartiality, equity, and reciprocity (treating others as one would desire to be treated) are basic. When there are greater needs than resources available or when the interests of constituencies conflict, justice requires honest consideration of all claims and requests and equitable (not necessarily equal) distribution of goods and services. A crucial aspect of promoting justice is demonstrating an appreciation for human differences and opposing intolerance and bigotry concerning these differences. Important human differences include, but are not limited to, characteristics such as age, culture, ethnicity, gender, disabling condition, race, religion, or sexual/affectional orientation.
- Respect autonomy. Student affairs professionals respect and promote individual autonomy and privacy. Students' freedom of choice and action are not restricted unless their actions significantly interfere with the welfare of others or the accomplishment of the institution's mission.
- Be faithful. Student affairs professionals are truthful, honor agreements, and are trustworthy in the performance of their duties.
- Do no harm. Student affairs professionals do not engage in activities that cause either physical or psychological damage to others. In addition to their personal actions, student affairs professionals are especially vigilant to assure that the institutional policies do not: [a] hinder students'

opportunities to benefit from the learning experiences available in the environment; [b] threaten individuals' self-worth, dignity, or safety; or [c] discriminate unjustly or illegally.

Ethical Standards

Four ethical standards related to primary constituencies with whom student affairs professionals work—fellow professionals, students, educational institutions, and society—are specified.

1. *Professional Responsibility and Competence.* Student affairs professionals are responsible for promoting students' learning and development, enhancing the understanding of student life, and advancing the profession and its ideals. They possess the knowledge, skills, emotional stability, and maturity to discharge responsibilities as administrators, advisors, consultants, counselors, programmers, researchers, and teachers. High levels of professional competence are expected in the performance of their duties and responsibilities. They ultimately are responsible for the consequences of their actions or inaction.

As ACPA members, student affairs professionals will:

1.1 Adopt a professional lifestyle characterized by use of sound theoretical principles and a personal value system congruent with the basic tenets of the profession.

1.2 Contribute to the development of the profession (e.g., recruiting students to the profession, serving professional organizations, educating new professionals, improving professional practices, and conducting and reporting research).

1.3 Maintain and enhance professional effectiveness by improving skills and acquiring new knowledge.

1.4 Monitor their personal and professional functioning and effectiveness and seek assistance from appropriate professionals as needed.

1.5 Represent their professional credentials, competencies, and limitations accurately and correct any misrepresentations of these qualifications by others.

1.6 Establish fees for professional services after consideration of the ability of the recipient to pay. They will provide some services, including professional development activities for colleagues, for little or no remuneration.

1.7 Refrain from attitudes or actions that impinge on colleagues' dignity, moral code, privacy, worth, professional functioning, and/or personal growth.

1.8 Abstain from sexual harassment.

1.9 Abstain from sexual intimacies with colleagues or with staff for whom they have supervisory, evaluative, or instructional responsibility.

1.10 Refrain from using their positions to seek unjustified personal gains, sexual favors, unfair advantages, or unearned goods and services not normally accorded those in such positions.

1.11 Inform students of the nature and/or limits of confidentiality. They will share information about the students only in accordance with institutional policies and applicable laws, when given their permission, or when required to prevent personal harm to themselves or others.

1.12 Use records and electronically stored information only to accomplish legitimate, institutional purposes and to benefit students.

1.13 Define job responsibilities, decision-making procedures, mutual expectations, accountability procedures, and evaluation criteria with subordinates and supervisors.

1.14 Acknowledge contributions by others to program development, program implementation, evaluations, and reports.

1.15 Assure that participation by staff in planned activities that emphasize self-disclosure or other relatively intimate or personal involvement is voluntary and that the leader(s) of such activities do not have administrative, supervisory, or evaluative authority over participants.

1.16 Adhere to professional practices in securing positions: [a] represent education and experiences accurately; [b] respond to offers promptly; [c] accept only those positions they intend to assume; [d] advise current employer and all institutions at which applications are pending immediately when they sign a contract; and [e] inform their employers at least thirty days before leaving a position.

1.17 Gain approval of research plans involving human subjects from the institutional committee with oversight responsibility prior to initiation of the study. In the absence of such a committee, they will seek to create procedures to protect the rights and assure the safety of research participants.

1.18 Conduct and report research studies accurately. They will not engage in fraudulent research nor will they distort or misrepresent their data or deliberately bias their results.

1.19 Cite previous works on a topic when writing or when speaking to professional audiences.

1.20 Acknowledge major contributions to research projects and professional writings through joint authorships with the principal contributor listed first. They will acknowledge minor technical or professional contributions in notes or introductory statements.

1.21 Not demand co-authorship of publications when their involvement was ancillary or unduly pressure others for joint authorship.

1.22 Share original research data with qualified others upon request.

1.23 Communicate the results of any research judged to be of value to other professionals and not withhold results reflecting unfavorably on specific institutions, programs, services, or prevailing opinion.

1.24 Submit manuscripts for consideration to only one journal at a time. They will not seek to publish previously published or accepted-for-publication materials in other media or publications without first informing all editors and/or publishers concerned. They will make appropriate references in the text and receive permission to use if copyrights are involved.

1.25 Support professional preparation program efforts by providing assistantships, practica, field placements, and consultation to students and faculty.

As ACPA members, preparation program faculty will:

1.26 Inform prospective graduate students of program expectations, predominant theoretical orientations, skills needed for successful completion, and employment of recent graduates.

1.27 Assure that required experiences involving self-disclosure are communicated to prospective graduate students. When the program offers experiences that emphasize self-disclosure or other relatively intimate or personal involvement (e.g., group or individual counseling or growth groups), professionals must not have current or anticipated administrative, supervisory, or evaluative authority over participants.

1.28 Provide graduate students with a broad knowledge base consisting of theory, research, and practice.

1.29 Inform graduate students of the ethical responsibilities and standards of the profession.

1.30 Assess all relevant competencies and interpersonal functioning of students throughout the program, communicate these assessments to students, and take appropriate corrective actions including dismissal when warranted.

1.31 Assure that field supervisors are qualified to provide supervision to graduate students and are informed of their ethical responsibilities in this role.

2. *Student Learning and Development.* Student development is an essential purpose of higher education, and the pursuit of this aim is a major responsibility of student affairs. Development is complex and includes cognitive, physical, moral, social, career, spiritual, personality, and educational dimensions. Professionals must be sensitive to the variety of backgrounds, cultures, and personal characteristics evident in the student population and use ap-

propriate theoretical perspectives to identify learning opportunities and to reduce barriers that inhibit development.

As ACPA members, student affairs professionals will:

2.1 Treat students as individuals who possess dignity, worth, and the ability to be self-directed.
2.2 Avoid dual relationships with students (e.g., counselor/employer, supervisor/best friend, or faculty/sexual partner) that may involve incompatible roles and conflicting responsibilities.
2.3 Abstain from sexual harassment.
2.4 Abstain from sexual intimacies with clients or with students for whom they have supervisory, evaluative, or instructional responsibility.
2.5 Inform students of the conditions under which they may receive assistance and the limits of confidentiality when the counseling relationship is initiated.
2.6 Avoid entering or continuing helping relationships if benefits to students are unlikely. They will refer students to appropriate specialists and recognize that if the referral is declined, they are not obligated to continue the relationship.
2.7 Inform students about the purpose of assessment and make explicit the planned use of results prior to assessment.
2.8 Provide appropriate information to students prior to and following the use of any assessment procedure to place results in proper perspective with other relevant factors (e.g., socioeconomic, ethnic, cultural, and gender related experiences).
2.9 Confront students regarding issues, attitudes, and behaviors that have ethical implications.

3. *Responsibility to the Institution.* Institutions of higher education provide the context for student affairs practice. Institutional mission, policies, organizational structure, and culture, combined with individual judgment and professional standards, define and delimit the nature and extent of practice. Student affairs professionals share responsibility with other members of the academic community for fulfilling the institutional mission. Responsibility to promote the development of individual students and to support the institution's policies and interests require that professionals balance competing demands.

As ACPA members, student affairs professionals will:

3.1 Contribute to their institution by supporting its mission, goals, and policies.

3.2 Seek resolution when they and their institution encounter substantial disagreements concerning professional or personal values. Resolution may require sustained efforts to modify institutional policies and practices or result in voluntary termination of employment.

3.3 Recognize that conflicts among students, colleagues, or the institution should be resolved without diminishing appropriate obligations to any party involved.

3.4 Assure that information provided about the institution is factual and accurate.

3.5 Inform appropriate officials of conditions that may be disruptive or damaging to their institution.

3.6 Inform supervisors of conditions or practices that may restrict institutional or professional effectiveness.

3.7 Recognize their fiduciary responsibility to the institution. They will assure that funds for which they have oversight are expended following established procedures and in ways that optimize value, are accounted for properly, and contribute to the accomplishment of the institution's mission. They also will assure equipment, facilities, personnel, and other resources are used to promote the welfare of the institution and students.

3.8 Restrict their private interests, obligations, and transactions in ways to minimize conflicts of interest or the appearance of conflicts of interest. They will identify their personal views and actions as private citizens from those expressed or undertaken as institutional representatives.

3.9 Collaborate and share professional expertise with members of the academic community.

3.10 Evaluate programs, services, and organizational structure regularly and systematically to assure conformity to published standards and guidelines. Evaluations should be conducted using rigorous evaluation methods and principles, and the results should be made available to appropriate institutional personnel.

3.11 Evaluate job performance of subordinates regularly and recommend appropriate actions to enhance professional development and improve performance.

3.12 Provide fair and honest assessments of colleagues' job performance.

3.13 Seek evaluations of their job performance and/or services they provide.

3.14 Provide training to student affairs search and screening committee members who are unfamiliar with the profession.

3.15 Disseminate information that accurately describes the responsibilities of position vacancies, required qualifications, and the institution.

3.16 Follow a published interview and selection process that periodically notifies applicants of their status.

4. *Responsibility to Society.* Student affairs professionals, both as citizens and practitioners, have a responsibility to contribute to the improvement of the communities in which they live and work. They respect individuality and recognize that worth is not diminished by characteristics such as age, culture, ethnicity, gender, disabling condition, race, religion, or sexual/affectional orientation. Student affairs professionals work to protect human rights and promote an appreciation of human diversity in higher education.

As ACPA members, student affairs professionals will:

4.1 Assist students in becoming productive and responsible citizens.
4.2 Demonstrate concern for the welfare of all students and work for constructive change on behalf of students.
4.3 Not discriminate on the basis of age, culture, ethnicity, gender, disabling condition, race, religion, or sexual/affectional orientation. They will work to modify discriminatory practices.
4.4 Demonstrate regard for social codes and moral expectations of the communities in which they live and work. They will recognize that violations of accepted moral and legal standards may involve their clients, students, or colleagues in damaging personal conflicts and may impugn the integrity of the profession, their own reputations, and that of the employing institution.
4.5 Report to the appropriate authority any condition that is likely to harm their clients and/or others.

NASPA STANDARDS OF PROFESSIONAL PRACTICE

NASPA: Student Affairs Administrators in Higher Education is an organization of colleges, universities, agencies, and professional educators whose members are committed to providing services and education that enhance student growth and development. The association seeks to promote student personnel work as a profession which requires personal integrity, belief in the dignity and worth of individuals, respect for individual differences and diversity, a commitment to service, and dedication to the development of individuals and the college community through education. NASPA supports student personnel work by providing opportunities for its members to expand knowledge and skills through professional education and experience. The following standards were endorsed by NASPA at the December 1990 board of directors meeting in Washington, DC.

1. Professional Services. Members of NASPA fulfill the responsibilities of their position by supporting the educational interests, rights, and welfare of students in accordance with the mission of the employing institution.

2. Agreement with Institutional Mission and Goals. Members who accept employment with an educational institution subscribe to the general mission and goals of the institution.

3. Management of Institutional Resources. Members seek to advance the welfare of the employing institution through accountability for the proper use of institutional funds, personnel, equipment, and other resources. Members inform appropriate officials of conditions which may be potentially disruptive or damaging to the institution's mission, personnel, and property.

4. Employment Relationship. Members honor employment relationships. Members do not commence new duties or obligations at another institution under a new contractual agreement until termination of an

existing contract, unless otherwise agreed to by the member and the member's current and new supervisors. Members adhere to professional practices in securing positions and employment relationships.

5. Conflict of Interest. Members recognize their obligation to the employing institution and seek to avoid private interests, obligations, and transactions which are in conflict of interest or give the appearance of impropriety. Members clearly distinguish between statements and actions which represent their own personal views and those which represent their employing institution when important to do so.

6. Legal Authority. Members respect and acknowledge all lawful authority. Members refrain from conduct involving dishonesty, fraud, deceit, and misrepresentation or unlawful discrimination. NASPA recognizes that legal issues are often ambiguous, and members should seek the advice of counsel as appropriate. Members demonstrate concern for the legal, social codes and moral expectations of the communities in which they live and work even when the dictates of one's conscience may require behavior as a private citizen which is not in keeping with these codes/expectations.

7. Equal Consideration and Treatment of Others. Members execute professional responsibilities with fairness and impartiality and show equal consideration to individuals regardless of status or position. Members respect individuality and promote an appreciation of human diversity in higher education. In keeping with the mission of their respective institution and remaining cognizant of federal, state, and local laws, they do not discriminate on the basis of race, religion, creed, gender, age, national origin, sexual orientation, or physical disability. Members do not engage in or tolerate harassment in any form and should exercise professional judgment in entering into intimate relationships with those for whom they have any supervisory, evaluative, or instructional responsibility.

8. Student Behavior. Members demonstrate and promote responsible behavior and support actions that enhance personal growth and development of students. Members foster conditions designed to ensure a student's acceptance of responsibility for his/her own behavior. Members inform and educate students as to sanctions or constraints on student behavior which may result from violations of law or institutional policies.

9. Integrity of Information and Research. Members ensure that all information conveyed to others is accurate and in appropriate context. In their research and publications, members conduct and report research

studies to ensure accurate interpretation of findings, and they adhere to accepted professional standards of academic integrity.

10. Confidentiality. Members ensure that confidentiality is maintained with respect to all privileged communications and to educational and professional records considered confidential. They inform all parties of the nature and/or limits of confidentiality. Members share information only in accordance with institutional policies and relevant statutes when given the informed consent or when required to prevent personal harm to themselves or others.

11. Research Involving Human Subjects. Members are aware of and take responsibility for all pertinent ethical principles and institutional requirements when planning any research activity dealing with human subjects. (See *Ethical Principles in the Conduct of Research with Human Participants*, Washington, DC: American Psychological Association, 1982.)

12. Representation of Professional Competence. Members at all times represent accurately their professional credentials, competencies, and limitations and act to correct any misrepresentations of these qualifications by others. Members make proper referrals to appropriate professionals when the member's professional competence does not meet the task or issue in question.

13. Selection and Promotion Practices. Members support nondiscriminatory, fair employment practices by appropriately publicizing staff vacancies, selection criteria, deadlines, and promotion criteria in accordance with the spirit and intent of equal opportunity policies and established legal guidelines and institutional policies.

14. References. Members, when serving as a reference, provide accurate and complete information about candidates, including both relevant strengths and limitations of a professional and personal nature.

15. Job Definitions and Performance Evaluation. Members clearly define with subordinates and supervisors job responsibilities and decision-making procedures, mutual expectations, accountability procedures, and evaluation criteria.

16. Campus Community. Members promote a sense of community among all areas of the campus by working cooperatively with students, faculty, staff, and others outside the institution to address the common goals of student learning and development. Members foster a climate of collegiality and mutual respect in their work relationships.

17. Professional Development. Members have an obligation to continue personal professional growth and to contribute to the development of the profession by enhancing personal knowledge and skills, sharing ideas and information, improving professional practices, conducting and reporting research, and participating in association activities. Members promote and facilitate the professional growth of staff and they emphasize ethical standards in professional preparation and development programs.

18. Assessment. embers regularly and systematically assess organizational structures, programs, and services to determine whether the developmental goals and needs of students are being met and to ensure conformity to published standards and guidelines such as those of the Council for the Advancement of Standards for Student Services/Development Programs (CAS). Members collect data which include responses from students and other significant constituencies and make assessment results available to appropriate institutional officials for the purpose of revising and improving program goals and implementation.

ENDING THE INTERNSHIP EXPERIENCE QUESTIONNAIRE

When preparing to complete the supervised practice experience, take a few minutes to reflect on this experience and to answer the following questions.

1. Thinking back to the beginning of your internship experience, what goals did you set for yourself? Now that you are almost finished with the experience, how have you met those goals?

   Goals I set   Ways that I went about meeting each goal

2. What were some ways the staff at your internship site helped you become integrated into your new environment? Please consider the ways in which you were integrated into the social structure as well as how you learned about policies and procedures of the site.

3. How have staff members at your site helped you prepare for leaving the site? Please consider not only ways in which you will terminate with clients but also ways that you will finish up work site tasks, say goodbye to colleagues, and leave the location.

4. What feelings are you experiencing now that you are preparing to terminate this internship experience?

STUDENT LEARNING AND SKILLS EVALUATION
OF PRACTICUM/INTERNSHIP EXPERIENCE

I. Practicum / Internship Assignment Information:

Name:_____

Field Work Assignment: _____ Institution: _____

Site Supervisor: _____

Faculty Supervisor: _____

Total hours spent: On task _____; In direct student contact _____;

With supervisor _____

II. Assessment of Learning Opportunity: Using the scale below, indicate the level of opportunity provided by the practicum/internship for personal and professional development in the following areas:

> 1 = No Opportunity   2 = Minimal Opportunity
> 3 = Reasonable Opportunity   4 = Substantial Opportunity

INTELLECTUAL DOMAIN (Circle one for each area)

1. Generating (conceptualizing) new ideas and issues	1	2	3	4
2. Solving problems based on critical issues and/or ideas	1	2	3	4
3. Analyzing problems and issues from multiple perspectives	1	2	3	4
4. Critically analyzing situations for patterns and themes	1	2	3	4
5. Evaluating issues based on personal judgments	1	2	3	4

Describe your personal intellectual development as a result of this practicum/internship experience:

CAREER DOMAIN (Circle one response for each area)

> 1 = No Opportunity   2 = Minimal Opportunity
> 3 = Reasonable Opportunity   4 = Substantial Opportunity

1. Setting challenging goals	1 2 3 4
2. Taking appropriate risks	1 2 3 4
3. Taking initiative (perceiving what needs to be done and doing it)	1 2 3 4
4. Getting things done (focusing on results/improvement)	1 2 3 4
5. Working toward more effectiveness/efficiency)	1 2 3 4
6. Showing persistence (staying with tasks)	1 2 3 4
7. Using available resources to solve problems	1 2 3 4

Describe the career development you accomplished as a result of this practicum/internship:

III. Specific Practicum/Internship Site Evaluation Issues (Use this scale to respond to items below)

> 1 = Strongly Disagree   2 = Disagree   3 = Agree   4 = Strongly Agree

1. The preparation program orientation information gave me a clear overview of what to expect.	1 2 3 4
2. The site orientation to this particular practicum/internship setting was adequate.	1 2 3 4
3. The time available to me in this practicum/internship experience was adequate for accomplishing the learning goals I set at the beginning of the term.	1 2 3 4
4. There was adequate time available for getting to know my site supervisor well and discussing important issues.	1 2 3 4
5. I was *not* adequately prepared for the level of responsibility placed on me in this practicum/internship experience.	1 2 3 4

6. I received adequate and appropriate feedback from my site supervisor about my overall performance and my strengths and weaknesses. 1 2 3 4
7. Overall, my relations with site staff members were positive and colleagial. 1 2 3 4
8. This experience was well structured and designed to facilitate my learning. 1 2 3 4
9. I was provided an adequate balance of supervision (direction) and independence. 1 2 3 4
10. I was provided adequate freedom to exercise my own style and judgment. 1 2 3 4
11. Overall, I am personally satisfied with this practicum/ internship experience. 1 2 3 4
12. I would encourage other students to do practicum/ internship at this site. 1 2 3 4

SAMPLE PRACTICUM CONTRACT

The following is a sample practicum contract. Although you should think creatively when creating this document, make sure that you address each item that appears in bold.

SAMPLE

Student Information
Jane Doe
jdoe@su.edu
00 Rose Lane, Blacksburg, Virginia 24060
(H) 951-0000
(W) 231-0000

Practicum Site Supervisor Information:
Jemal Smith
jsmith@su.edu
Assistant Dean of Students
107 Brodie Hall, State University, Collegetown, VA 24061
(W) 231-0001

Faculty Practicum Coordinator Information:
Dale Jones
djones@su.edu
Associate Professor
123 Abner Hall, State University, Collegetown, VA 24061
(W) 231-0002

Statement of Purpose: The purpose of this practicum is to gain a better understanding of the role and function of the Dean of Students office in mediating and student disputes by assisting in the research and development of a new conflict resolution model. This practicum will also provide an opportunity to become familiar with the various programs and positions within the Dean of Students office at State University.

Objectives and Activities:

Objective 1: To assist with the development of a peer conflict resolution model proposal.

Activities:

a. Research conflict resolution models of other universities and suggestions from the National Association of Mediation in Education. [20 hours]
b. Meet regularly with the site supervisor to discuss progress. [15 hours]
c. Consult with other Dean of Students staff members on model components. [5 hours]

Skills and Competencies: These activities will hone research skills, will contribute valuable information needed to tailor this model to State University, and will provide an opportunity for collaboration with many student affairs professionals.

Time Required: 40 Hours

Objective 2: To conceptualize the logistics of the conflict resolution model.

Activities:

a. Draft curriculum and training outline for staff and students. [30 hours]
b. Determining parameters of the model (size of peer educator population, target organization for recruiting, etc.) [10 hours]
c. Develop a marketing plan for recruiting students for participation. [20 hours]

Skills and Competencies: In using the research of the first objective to determine the logistics of the conflict resolution model, the link from theory to practice that is so crucial in student affairs will be provided in this objective. It will be necessary to weigh available resources, human and financial, in creating the model components and in planning for the implementation of the model. Strategies for creative marketing will also be learned through this objective.

Time Required: 60 Hours

Objective 3: To gain an understanding of the roles and functions of the various positions within the Office of the Dean of Students and the issues that confront each professional staff member.

Activities:

a. Review available policy manuals and other office literature. [5 hours]
b. Attend weekly staff meetings. [30 hours]
c. Interview office staff on their respective roles. [5 hours]
d. Field telephone calls from students and parents and assist in problem solving. [10 hours]

Skills and Competencies: This objective will provide insight into the problems and issues of State University students and the various protocols for handling such issues within the Office of the Dean of Students. This objective will provide opportunities for developing professional relationships within the student affairs field. Completion of this objective will also allow for professional development through the "hands-on" experience of dealing with students and parental concerns.

Time Required: 50 Hours

TOTAL HOURS: 150 Hours

Site Location: The Office of the Dean of Students will provide office space for the internship student in room 111 Brodie Hall.

Proposed Work Schedule: The student and supervisor have agreed that the student will be in the office on Monday and Wednesday from 9:00AM to 12:00 noon and Fridays from 1:00PM to 5:00PM. Over the course of the 15 week semester, the 150 hour contract will be satisfied. Changes in the schedule will be made as needed.

Signatures

Student Signature: _____ Date: _____

Site Supervisor: _____ Date: _____

Faculty Internship Coordinator: _____ Date: _____

APPENDIX

PROFESSIONAL ASSOCIATIONS IN HIGHER EDUCATION AND STUDENT AFFAIRS

American Association of Collegiate Registrars and Admissions Officers
One Dupont Circle, NW, Suite 520,
Washington, DC 20036-1135
(202) 293-9161
E-mail: info@aacrao.com
Fax: (202) 872-8857

American Association of Community Colleges
One Dupont Circle, NW, Suite 410
Washington, DC 20036
(202) 728-0200
Fax: (202) 833-2467
http://www.aacc.nche.edu/

American College Personnel Association
One Dupont Circle Suite 300
Washington, DC 20036
(202) 835-2272
Fax: (202) 296-3286
E-mail: info@acpa.nche.edu

American Association of University Women
1111 Sixteenth Street NW
Washington, DC 20036
(800) 326-AAUW
Fax: (202) 872-1425
TDD: (202) 785-7777
E-mail: info@aauw.org
http://www.aauw.org

American College Health Association
PO Box 28937
Baltimore, MD 21240-8937

(410) 859-1500
Fax: (410) 859-1510
http://www.acha.org

American Counseling Association
5999 Stevenson Avenue
Alexandria, VA 22304-3300
http://www.counseling.org

Association of Black Admissions and Financial Aid Officers in the Ivy League and Sister
    Schools, Inc.
PO Box 381402
Cambridge, MA 02238-1402
http://www.sas.cornell.edu/admissions/aba/abafaoilss.htm

Association for Student Judicial Administrators Central Office
PO Box 2237
College Station, TX 77841-2237
(409) 845-5262
Fax: (409) 458-1714
E-mail: asja@tamu.edu
http://www. asja.tamu.edu/

Association of College Unions International
One City Center, Suite 200
120 W. Seventh St.
Bloomington, IN 47404-3925
(812) 855-8550
Fax: (812) 855-0162
E-mail: acui@indiana.edu
http://www.indiana.edu/~acui

Canadian Association of College & University Student Services
c/o Office of Student Affairs
214 College Street, Room 307
University of Toronto
Toronto, ON M5T 2Z9, Canada
(416) 978-4027
Fax: (416) 971-2037
E-mail: webmaster@cacuss.ca
CACUSS General Delivery E-mail: cacuss@cacuss.ca

Collegiate Information and Visitor Services Association
CIVSA National Headquarters
Campus Information Services
Rutgers–The State University of New Jersey
542 George Street
New Brunswick, NJ 08901-1167

(732) 932-9342 x675
E-mail: civsa_HQ@cis.rutgers.edu

National Association of Foreign Student Administrators: Association of International
    Educators
1307 New York Avenue, NW, Eighth Floor,
Washington, DC 20005-4701
(202) 737-3699
Fax: (202) 737-3657
E-mail: inbox@nafsa.org

National Career Development Association Headquarters
Juliet Miller, Executive Director
4700 Reed Road - Suite M
Columbus, OH 43220
(614) 326-1750; (888) 326-1750 (toll free)
Fax: (614) 326-1760
E-mail: millerncda@aol.com

Council of Higher Education Management Associations
Barbara Smith
c/o NACUBO
2501 M Street, NW, Suite 400
Washington, DC 20037
(202) 861-2577
Fax: (202) 296-1592
E-mail: bsmith@nacubo.org
http://chema-www.colorado.edu/

US Students Council
205 East 42nd Street
New York, NY 10017
(212) 822-2600 and (888) COUNCIL
Fax: (212) 822-2699
E-mail: info@ciee.org
http://www.ciee.org/index.htm

Institute of International Education
809 United Nations Plaza
New York, NY 10017-3580
http://www.iie.org/

Jesuit Association of Student Personnel Administrators
http://jaspa.creighton.edu/welcome.htm

National Academic Advising Association
Executive Office
Kansas State University

2323 Anderson Ave, Suite 225
Manhattan, KS 66502-2912
(785) 532-5717
Fax: (785) 532-7732
E-mail: nacada@ksu.edu
http://www.ksu.edu/nacada/index.html

National Association of Advisors for the Health Professions
PO Box 1518
Champaign, IL 61824-1518
(217) 355-0063
Fax: (217) 355-1284
E-mail: staff@naahp.org
http://www.naahp.org/

National Association for Campus Activities
Alan Davis, Executive Director
13 Harbison Way
Columbia, SC 29212-3401
(803) 732-6222
Fax: (803) 749-1047
E-mail: aland@naca.org
http://www.naca.org

National Association for College Admission Counseling
Joyce E. Smith, Executive Director
1631 Prince Street
Alexandria, VA 22314-2818
(703) 836-2222 and (800) 822-6285
Fax: (703) 836-8015
E-mail: jsmith@nacac.com
http://www.nacac.com

National Association of College and University Food Services
1405 S. Harrison Road
Manly Miles Building, Suite 305
Michigan State University
East Lansing, MI 48824-5242
(517) 332-2494
Fax: (517) 332-8144
http://www.nacufs.org/

National Association of College and University Residence Halls
Bob Tattershall, National Advisor
c/o Housing Services
PO Box 641726

Pullman, WA 99164-1726
(509) 335-7789; (509) 332-4486
Fax: (509) 335-3415
E-mail: tattersh@wsu.edu
http://www.nacurh.okstate.edu/

National Association of College Auxiliary Services
PO Box 870
Staunton, VA 24402
(540) 885-8826
Fax: (540) 885-8355
E-mail: nacas@cfw.com
http://www.nacas.org/

National Association of College Stores
500 East Lorain Street
Oberlin, OH 44074
(800) 622-7498
Fax: (440) 775-4769
E-mail: webteam@nacs.org
http://www.nacs.org/

National Association of Colleges and Employers
http://career.marshall.edu/nace.html

National Association of Graduate Admissions Professionals
Jeffrey Johnson
School of Public Health and Tropical Medicine
Tulane University
1500 Canal Street, Suite 700
New Orleans, LA 70112
(504) 588-5387
Fax: (504) 584-1667
E-mail: jjohnso1@mailhost.tcs.tulane.edu
http://www.nagap.org

National Association for Managers of Student Services in Colleges (UK)
http://www.namss.org.uk

National Association of Student Affairs Professionals
c/o Edna L. Hickman
Financial Secretary
Southern University–Baton Rouge
PO Box 13405
Baton Rouge, LA 70813
http://www.angelfire.com/ga/nasap

National Association of Student Financial Aid Administrators
1129 20th Street NW, Suite 400
Washington, DC 20036-3489
E-mail: ask@nasfaa.org
http://www.nasfaa.org

National Association of Student Personnel Administrators
1875 Connecticut Avenue, NW, Suite 418
Washington, DC 20009
(202) 265-7500
Fax: (202) 797-1157
E-mail: office@naspa.org
http://www.naspa.org

National Intramural-Recreational Sports Association
4185 SW Research Way
Corvallis, OR 97333-1067
(541) 766-8211
Fax: (541) 766-8284
E-mail: nirsa@nirsa.org
http://www.nirsa.org/

National Organization of Men's Outreach for Rape Education (NO MORE)
John D. Foubert, Founder
Assistant Dean of Students
University of Virginia
Dabney House, Station #1
Charlottesville, VA 22904
(804) 924-3736
Fax: (804) 924-8956
E-mail: nomore@umail.umd.edu
http://www.glue.umd.edu/~spmurphy/mainbody.html

National Orientation Directors Association—Home Office
Indiana University
Office of Orientation Programs
Maxwell Hall 122
Bloomington, IN 47405-4601
(812) 855-3907
Fax: (812) 855-1319
E-mail: noda1@indiana.edu
http://www.indiana.edu/noda1

INDEX